The Culture Of Cynicism

To
Jacques Ellul

The Culture of Cynicism

American Morality in Decline

Richard Stivers

BLACKWELL
Oxford UK & Cambridge USA

First published 1994

Blackwell Publishers
238 Main Street
Cambridge, Massachusetts 02142
USA

108 Cowley Road
Oxford OX4 1JF
UK

Library of Congress Cataloging-in-Publication Data

Stivers, Richard.
   The Culture of Cynicism : American Morality in Decline / Richard
Stivers.
      p.   cm.
   Includes bibliographical references and index.
   ISBN 1-55786-532-9 (alk. paper). – ISBN 1-55786-533-7 (paperback; alk.
paper)
   1. United States–Moral conditions.   2. Cynicism.   I. Title.
HN90.M6S75   1994
306′ .0973–dc20
                                                                              93-39085
                                                                                    CIP

British Library Cataloguing in Publication Data

A CIP catalogue record for this book is available from the British Library.

Typeset in 11 on 12 pt Palatino by TecSet Ltd, Wallington, Surrey.
Printed in America.

This book is printed on acid-free paper.

Table of Contents

Preface

Morality is character, character is that which is engraved; but the sand and the sea have no character and neither has abstract intelligence, for character is really inwardness. Immorality, as energy, is also character; but to be neither moral nor immoral is merely ambiguous, and ambiguity enters into life when the qualitative distinctions are weakened by a gnawing reflection. The revolt of the passions is elemental, the dissolution brought about by ambiguity is a silent sorites that goes on night and day. The distinction between good and evil is enervated by a superficial, superior and theoretical knowledge of evil, and by a supercilious cleverness which is aware that goodness is neither appreciated nor worth while in this world, that it is tantamount to stupidity.

Søren Kierkegaard, *The Present Age*

American society is experiencing a moral decline, the critics say. Conservative critics point to the high volume of street crime, the erosion of civility, and the loss of respect for authority; liberal critics look at the lack of compassion for the poor, increased greed and selfishness, and the extinction of a concern for the common good. I find myself agreeing with both sides of the debate. As serious as the above problems are, most critics seem to think they can be solved by a greater exercise of moral authority or by political reform. But the decline runs much deeper than this. For it is not signaled by a series of discrete moral problems that the conventional morality can no longer control, but by the *very morality itself*, a morality that encourages, even promotes, cynical and self-serving behavior.

Although this book is about American morality as it is currently practiced, it is about the future morality of all modern societies as well. As some have observed, at a certain threshold technology begins to destroy culture (each of which is unique) and works to create a universal civilization. In this sense, as the most technologically advanced society, America is the future of all modern societies.

Every culture possesses aesthetical and ethical dimensions. Since the nineteenth century, the tendency has been to regard the aesthetical dimension as the dominant if not exclusive dimension of culture. Friedrich Nietzsche, some of whose ideas represent the logical conclusion of the Romantic movement, absolutizes great works of art, finding the meaning of history in the moment of artistic creation. At the same time, he relativizes morality, reducing it to a mediocre expression of the will to power. Many intellectuals who write about culture are the stepchildren of Nietzsche.

By contrast, Søren Kierkegaard, without demeaning the aesthetical, regards the ethical as the superior dimension. His interest is not the conservative one of social order but the radical one of individual freedom. The ethical dimension of culture is more directly related to the human search for meaning – the meaning of life, the meaning of history. A sense of ultimate meaning is needed to limit individual and collective power and as a prophylactic to despair. Moreover, it is essential for the potential development of the freedom of the individual.

Many contemporary studies of culture – whether of high or popular culture – center on art and entertainment. Somehow morality is not culture. Following Kierkegaard rather than Nietzsche here, I consider the study of morality to be the surest guide to the understanding of culture.

In the course of the book I describe the new American morality. It possesses two characteristics, unprecedented as far as I can determine: (1) its various forms and complexity rule out genuine ethical choice and thus make its discovery difficult; (2) its content is exclusively that of power and is without meaning.

Perhaps no one has better understood the reasons why we so often secretly desire to gloss over reality with our concepts than Kierkegaard. When reality becomes too painful or devoid of meaning, we seek intellectual distraction from it. He observed that when the ideas we espouse are cut off from self-knowledge and a decision to act, they become fantastic. Our ideas under these circumstances conceal rather than reveal reality. His great insight is that part of our knowledge comes from ethical action.[1] This contradicts, of course, the spirit of modern science – detached observation.

Ethical action can increase one's understanding of reality in two ways. First, in action the concept undergoes the test of reality. Ethical action makes the context to which the concept is applied come alive.[2] Genuine knowledge of cultural context is self-knowledge, which, in turn, demands personal involvement. Aesthetical action requires less of us in our involvement with others. Moreover, because social life is itself morally constituted, it is only through ethical action that we can fully experience social life. Second, ethical action can provide the wherewithal to resist cynicism and idealism, both of which conceal reality. Cynicism makes it worse than it is; idealism, better than it is. Ethical action has a source other than reality itself, whereas cynicism and idealism both draw their inspiration from reality in the very act of deceiving us about it. They are thus ideological.

A technological civilization, however, greatly diminishes the opportunity for ethical action. As I argue in the chapters to follow, morality in the conventional sense of the term has all but disappeared; at the same time a technological and bureaucratic morality has arisen to fill the void. But this latter morality leaves no room for individual ethical decision. The other major forms of this new morality – public opinion and visual images in the media – are oriented to aesthetical concerns. In the modern world freedom is closely identified with consumer choice. As a consequence the individual can make genuine ethical decisions at a heavy price – *nonconformity*. We are ensnared in a vicious circle: If ethical action is needed to understand social reality, then the reduced opportunity to make ethical choices leaves us only dimly aware of the ersatz morality that has us in its embrace.

The new American morality is in a very real sense an anti-morality. That is, every traditional morality has placed some limitations on the exercise of power – political and personal. Because of our fascination with technology, indeed our tacit adoration of it, we do not perceive the need to limit its growth and expansion into every sphere of human existence. Technology is at bottom nothing more than an expression of power: it is the most efficacious and efficient means of acting. My thesis is that technical and bureaucratic rules are the "morality" of technology. Never has any society been hemmed in by so many rules and regulations.

Public opinion and the visual images of the media are the other major forms of this new American morality. Both public opinion and visual images serve the interest of technology. Technology through its promise of more consumer goods and services stimulates our desire, and public opinion forms to demand the realization of our fantasies. In the past, public opinion formed around a Christian morality and was subservient to it. Today public opinion is largely but not exclusively wedded to the growth of technology and its promise. This form of the new morality is an expression of the instinctual power of desire.

The visual images of the media represent technology's possibilities – a more spectacular and consumption-filled future. The visual images of the media both in advertising and its adjunct programs in television are the language of technology. They are the vehicle by which desire is stimulated and around which public opinion is formed. Here again this form of the new American morality is wedded to instinctual power.

Technology can only continue to grow as long as Americans and all like-minded peoples remain its zealots. What technology is objectively – the power of science and organization – is matched subjectively by the instinctual power of desire. The new American morality, then, is exclusively one of power.

But a morality of power is simultaneously a morality without meaning. Technology, at an advanced level, as I argue in chapters 4 and 6, makes shared experiences and traditions irrelevant. Deep symbolic meaning – the meaning of life and the meaning of history – is used to interpret such experiences and traditions. When symbolic meaning loses its practical import, it survives only as nostalgia or as a game.

The new American morality or anti-morality represents the demands of a technological civilization. Rather than serving the interest of freedom it is the principal cause of our enslavement and the demise of our culture.

Acknowledgments

It is paradoxical that the most solitary of acts – writing – should leave one indebted to so many. Illinois State University gave me a sabbatical leave to begin this work. The Earhart Foundation, that *least* bureaucratic of granting agencies, provided me with a fellowship research grant to write the book.

My excellent typist, Sharon Foiles cheerfully endured the many revisions. Laurie Evans typed the index. Deborah Carter and Mark Calvert helped with the proofs and the index. Editor, Jill Landeryou and copy editor, Kirstie Morrison worked to improve the manuscript.

Charles Lemert and John McGuigan offered advice in the early stages of writing. David Anderson helped me understand certain philosophical concepts that were discussed, and Wib Leonard provided me with ideas and references about changes in American sports. Norman Denzin and Andrew Greeley constructively critiqued the manuscript. My former student and friend, Kim Goudreau urged me to rethink the preface. It needed rethinking. Senior Editor, Simon Prosser has been a pleasure to work with. His insights, suggestions, and encouragement made my job that much easier. My largest debt is to my colleague and friend, Moody Simms who gave the manuscript a careful reading and made a number of important recommendations. He never made me feel that my frequent requests of his time and opinion were a burden.

The Absence of Morality, or Morality Assumes New Forms

To suggest that there may be a common morality in America today is to fly in the face of common sense. Most people with whom I converse maintain either that there is no effective morality in America or that there is a plethora of moralities, each of which is a special-interest morality specific to a gender, ethnic, age, or occupational group. And those few who claim there is a common morality are hard pressed to describe it; they never seem to get beyond vague generalities.

Senator Daniel Patrick Moynihan would be sympathetic to the position that there is no common American morality. In a recent article in *The American Scholar,* he argues that definitions of deviancy are constricting because the volume of what used to be considered deviant exceeds what American society can handle.[1] As a variation on a theme by Emile Durkheim (and later Kai Erikson) that the amount of deviancy tends to remain constant over the long run, Moynihan's position is that deviancy operates according to the law of supply and demand. Society "needs" deviancy not just in theory but in practice as a way of maintaining the distinction between good and evil (the normal and the pathological). When the supply diminishes, there is demand to define as deviant what was previously regarded as normal. When the supply is abundant (as with the high rate of crime today) the demand diminishes, meaning that we begin to look the other way or "normalize" some forms of deviancy.

Moynihan is vague about the explanation for this phenomenon – it is simply "a pattern we observe in ourselves." At the same time he is troubled by the normalization of deviancy, for he refers to it (and the high incidence of deviancy itself) as evidence of the "manifest decline of the American civic order." My argument is that this so-called normalization of deviance has less to do with some mechanism by which America constricts or expands its definitions of deviancy than with a radical change in the content and form of American morality.

I maintain that there is an American morality, but it has little in common with traditional morality. Moreover, this morality contains an ephemeral dimension that gives rise to a host of constantly changing subsidiary moralities. This morality, then, has both necessary and ephemeral dimensions. Its necessary side is composed of technical rules that provide the basis for a common morality. The ephemeral side is made up of public opinion, peer group norms, and visual images in the media, which leave us with a sense of infinite variation, perhaps even of anarchy. Yet the two sides are intimately related.

There has been little work in the social sciences on the subject of morality, let alone American morality. Only in France does the sociology of morality continue to be a recognized area of specialization. Polish philosopher Maria Ossowska[2] calls it a "neglected field"; Sociologist Alvin Gouldner[3] points out that while sociologists often employ norms, values, and beliefs in their explanations, they almost never describe the content of these moral phenomena. Hence sociologists usually treat morality in a purely formal way.

The exceptions are worth noting. Robert Jackall's *Moral Mazes: the World of Corporate Managers* is an excellent portrait of the morality of the American corporation;[4] M. P. Baumgartner's *The Moral Order of a Suburb* contains important insights about American suburban life.[5] As evidenced by the titles, however, these works do not attempt to describe and interpret American morality as a whole.

The sociological works[6] that come closest to doing so are perhaps David Riesman's *The Lonely Crowd*,[7] Robert Bellah's *Habits of the Heart*,[8] and James Davison Hunter's *Culture Wars*.[9] None is a study primarily about American morality, but all have much to say about it. Whereas Riesman calls attention to the collectivizing force of the peer group (the other-directed character type), Bellah focuses on the individualism of American culture. Bellah would no doubt agree with French anthropologist Louis Dumont that the individual is the "cardinal modern value."[10] One of my purposes is to demonstrate how extreme individualism and extreme collectivism can co-exist in the same morality. British philosopher Alasdair MacIntyre has already called attention to the paradox,[11] as did Tocqueville in the 1830s.

Some of those, who like Bellah, stress the individualism of American morality readily point out collectivizing influences in American life, such as bureaucracy, but they do not interpret these to be part of the morality itself. One of my purposes here is to make a case that the norms of the new American morality are more *behavioral* than *attitudinal*. A morality whose content is fundamentally behavioral (technical rules and visual images) is a radical departure from traditional morality. All traditional moralities are comprised of moral attitudes that assume the form of practical knowledge.[12] A morality, primarily but not exclusively, of behavior is a consequence of technology's increasing hold over human action. Such a morality can only be effective when accompanied by what some have called the "bureaucratic mind," that is, the attitude that one must obey all rules.

And yet this new morality is more than a morality of technical and bureaucratic rules. Its internal complexity reflects the tension between technology as chief factor in the organization of American society (the necessary) and those forces that are transitory (the ephemeral) and, while collective in form, make a fundamental appeal to the individual (public opinion, peer group norms, and the visual images of the media). The latter, the ephemeral and individualizing forms of this morality, are a kind of compensation for the abstract and impersonal nature of a society dominated by technology. These compensatory forces, however, are not free from the influence of technology, as we shall later see.

Hunter's book calls attention to the basic "moral visions" that erupt in conflict over specific issues such as abortion or school prayer. His subtle argument is that Americans are split along the lines of orthodox versus progressive world views (most Americans do not identify with either position at its extreme). Historically the debate has been set in religious terms, but recently it has been broadened. The unifying theme of cultural orthodoxy is *"the commitment on the part of adherents to an external, definable, and transcendent authority,"* whereas that of cultural progressivism is *"the tendency to resymbolize historic faiths according to the prevailing assumptions of contemporary life."*[13] Conservative secularists side with the culturally orthodox at times, just as secular humanists often join ranks with cultural progressives. For example, there are Jews, Christians, and secularists on both sides of the abortion issue.

My argument is that beneath the conflict between rival ideologies there is mythological consensus. In chapter 3 the fundamental American myth is identified and discussed. The paradox of ideological diversity and mythological unity is an international phenomenon as well, as witnessed by the fact that capitalism, socialism, and communism (in their various nationalistic forms) are opposed on the level of ideology but united on that of myth – the common belief in technological progress and increased consumption. Therefore, it is still possible to talk about a common American morality that is a reflection of a unifying myth. This common morality, however, contains contradictory features – both in terms of its content and its forms – that give rise to innumerable conflicts between special interest groups. Such conflicts are complicated by the ideological residue of a Judaic – Christian morality that has been reduced to the status of moral custom.

The level at which this book is written is somewhere between "grand theory" and "abstracted empiricism."[14] Both grand theory and abstracted empiricism take phenomena out of context but in different ways. The former tries to create a logical system that denies differences in meaning that are bound to context. Moral philosophy by and large is written at this level. For example, John Rawls[15] treats justice as though it were potentially a universal with a fixed meaning. The lived concept of justice, however, necessarily varies from culture to culture and historical period to historical period. Its meaning is dependent upon context. To treat justice as a logical concept rather than a dialectical concept (a concept whose meaning depends in large part upon the context of its use) is simultaneously to reify the concept and to make it overly abstract.

If moral philosophers often fall prey to the temptation of grand theory, social scientists who write about morality and values often succumb to the methodological precision of abstracted empiricism. This process involves the fragmentation of reality into isolated facts (of opinion and behavior) in order to measure them and then arbitrarily reconstruct them according to some hypotheses (usually stated at a low level of theory). Such studies depend upon surveys of moral opinion.[16] It is not that surveys provide us with no useful information, but rather that the information has to be reinterpreted carefully. No individual accurately and fully represents the larger culture in her attitudes. Much of what any of us knows remains tacit. The methodological individualism of survey research allows one to obtain at best a collection of *individual* attitudes and behavior, not a *societal* morality. Moreover, it does not permit one to get at tacit knowledge.

Those outside academic life who write about morality often do so at the level of current events, political or otherwise. For example, Dr. Jack Kevorkian, the euthanasiast from Michigan, has set off a nation-wide interest in the ethical issue of suicide through the use of his "suicide machine" to assist those who desire to take their own lives. Books and a made-for-television movie will certainly follow in the wake of the publicity. Each news item creates a short-lived moral controversy; moral discussion follows current events. The experience of current events is similar to that of statistical facts: both appear to be almost random in composition. If there is an American morality, as I so argue, it is not situated at the level of events.

Only qualitative research that involves a reading of the larger culture can provide us with a sense of American morality. This reading needs to be partly historical, for we only apprehend the qualitative side of life in temporal change. It should involve an interpretation of American culture through an analysis of its foundation – the *sacred*.[17]

Whatever is most important to the continued existence of a society is spontaneously regarded as sacred.[18] We apprehend the sacred through an analysis of mythical belief and ritual practices (or their religious substitutes). The sacred is a more general phenomenon than organized religion, which is one form the experience of the sacred may assume. In traditional societies, for instance, nature (or more precisely, those parts of nature that were most necessary for the group's survival) was regarded as sacred. Mythical beliefs included a narrative about the creation of the world and the traditional society's place in nature. Ritual practices involved actions that supplicated the forces of nature for assistance and sought its renewal. Myth is the theory of the sacred; ritual, the practice of the sacred.

Lived or social morality is an indirect expression of what is experienced as sacred. It frequently becomes a way of harnessing the power of the sacred or of protecting it. Lived morality is not primarily a matter of individual ethical choice or even the practice of virtue, but rather an expression of collective belief and allegiance. Ethical choice and the practice of virtue take place only within the context of religious sentiments (in the broadest sense of this phrase).

In chapters 2 and 3 of this book I will describe the myth of technological utopianism in American culture and its symbolic values of success, survival, happiness, and health by placing it into historical perspective. Having identified technology as the chief sacred in American society, I then turn in chapters 4 through 6 to an exploration of how technology affects the various forms this morality assumes: organizational and psychological rules, public opinion, peer group norms, and visual images.

Categories of the Moral

Eschewing those approaches to the study of morality that take it out of its true context – history and collective experience – and thus simplify it, we find that morality is much more complex in practice. It reflects the tensions and contradictions that people in all societies experience. There are three main moral categories: *lived morality*, *moral custom*, and *theoretical morality*.[19]

Lived or social morality is the morality that a group of people actually live out. This does not suggest that lived morality means simply "behavior," but rather that lived morality is in one way or another reflected in individual and collective attitudes, and that it exercises some control over action. Morality as people live it out collectively is an amalgam of paradigms of experience, initially expressed in metaphor and analogy, that are interrelated through common belief and a common sense of the sacred but without the individual's consciousness of how it all fits together. Deeply held collective beliefs remain in part tacit. They constitute a kind of collective practical knowledge.[20] Our consciousness of these beliefs and moral norms is about the parts not the whole (the system of relationships among the parts). Lived morality, then, is not a free creation, the result of a contract, as some moral philosophers and social scientists would have us believe; rather it is a spontaneous, unconscious creation, reflecting the perception of necessity.

Moral custom is simply the lived morality of the past that survives in the present. It is tolerated so long as it does not come into direct conflict with the lived morality of the present. Each period of history is both continuous and discontinuous with the preceding one. Moral custom represents that which is continuous with the past. It is an effective morality only with respect to actions not fully controlled by the lived morality.

Theoretical morality is a system of descriptive or normative ethics.[21] The former involves an attempt to account for a particular morality or the diversity of morality in the form of a systematic explanation. Descriptive ethics does not prescribe and proscribe action; instead it describes and explains. Normative ethics sets forth a theory of the good and a system of ethical obligation thought to be universally binding. Most theories of normative ethics have been created by religious leaders and philosophers, such as Confucius, Aristotle, Thomas Aquinas. Both descriptive ethics and normative ethics are a relatively late development in human evolution. Theoretical morality is an outcropping of civilization itself, that is, it is a reflection of an increasing tendency to subject life to rational control.[22]

It is extremely rare, however, for a theory of normative ethics to become the lived morality of a society. What is its main purpose then? Normative ethics functions either as an ideology or a utopia.[23] As an ideology, a system of normative ethics would directly or indirectly justify the extant system of authority. The Calvinist work ethic was a direct reflection of "good" capitalist practices – efficiency in the interest of unlimited profit. Existentialist ethics in the twentieth century has sometimes acted as an indirect support for a technological civilization. By becoming a compensation for an existence so heavily under the sway of bureaucratic and state power, existentialist ethics generally provided an ethic that could only be put into practice in a small group of independent, like-minded people. For example, the ethic of freedom to do whatever one wishes as long as it does not interfere with someone else's freedom is only manageable in a context of a small group of people, each one of whom knows all the others in a honest, intimate way. Such an ethic is unrealistic, not because it could never become the operative morality of a society, but because no individual could have the knowledge to implement it.[24] Those few cases in which a system of normative ethics became a lived morality are indicative of a utopia that was realized. The ethics of Confucius and of Moses became for a time lived moralities.

Theories of extant moralities – descriptive ethics – have a chance of shedding some light on the subject of their inquiry to the extent that they do not become grand theories and do not attempt to create a singular theory of morality. Grand and universal theories of lived morality distract us from a critical understanding of it. As such they too function as ideology.

Moral Custom

Which moralities in American society have been reduced to moral custom? Christian and middle-class or bourgeois morality.

Christian morality, as it developed in the Middle Ages, is exceedingly complex. Although it starts out as a normative ethics, it is an anti-theory in the sense that it is expressed through parable and metaphor rather than as a code of rules. This morality places a great emphasis on individual virtue; the paramount virtue is self-sacrificial love. Consistent with and dependent upon love is an emphasis on humility and poverty (both material and spiritual). The dilemma of Christian morality centers about the value of freedom.[25] Properly understood Christian love is necessarily tied to freedom: love of the other forms the boundary to the freedom of the self, just as love without freedom becomes mere conformity. Contemporary Protestant theologians, such as Jurgen Moltman,[26] have even gone so far as to suggest that Christian love *is* Christian freedom.

This understanding of love and freedom, as lived by Francis of Assisi and a few others, was perpetually challenged by an emphasis on the value of order. The idea of Christendom, a Christian civilization controlled by Christian institutions, contradicts the idea that Christ wants believers who have freely chosen to accept the challenge of faith. French theologian and historian Jacques Ellul[27] suggests that Christianity has foundered on an ambivalence toward freedom and order. Does God want everyone to be a Christian, or does he want

everyone free to choose whether to be a Christian or not? The answer, of
course, is both.

As Christian morality finally became reconciled to Christendom, a
Christian social order, it was increasingly used to justify the exercise of
political and economic power. The earlier emphasis on a fair price and
economic justice gave way to the Protestant work ethic. In the aftermath
of the Protestant Reformation, one's moral worth and even one's
predestined state could be demonstrated by hard work and, especially,
economic success. The burgeoning capitalist order found a champion in
Christianity. Furthermore, the increase and centralization of power in
the state (necessary for the development of capitalism) was accompanied
by a strong Christian emphasis on the obedience to secular authority.

At this point Christian morality was well on its way to becoming a
middle class morality (see chapter 3). By the eighteenth century this
morality was in place. A synthesis of Christian and capitalist,
technological moralities, middle-class morality retains a number of
Christian virtues and values – thrift, sobriety, industry, prudence – but
places them in the service of profit-making, efficiency, respectability,
and material well-being. The Christian ideal of self-sacrificial love gives
way to that of respectable well-being, a comfortable and secure life,
basking in the light of respectability. To be considered respectable, the
rising middle classes needed the moral and religious practices of
Christianity; to obtain material well-being, they had to rely on capitalism
and technology.

Lived Morality

By the late twentieth century a new lived morality has become
dominant; it is the one I am describing in this book. Jacques Ellul has
termed it "technological morality," a morality geared entirely toward
efficiency.[28] The crucial point is that first money and then technology
became objects of awe and reverence – became sacred – and as such
destroyed the efficacy of Christian and finally even middle–class
morality. Søren Kierkegaard, Karl Marx, and Samuel Butler, among
others, recognized that money had become sacred in the nineteenth
century.

Samuel Butler's *Erewhon*, sometimes regarded as the first science
fiction novel, satirizes the worship of money. In this society of the
future, there are two banking systems. The first is the conventional one,
the only one that people admit to. These banks resemble cathedrals both
inside and outside; the bankers dress like ministers and there is even
organ music. Women and children frequent these banks, more than men

but everyone retains an account in them and carries some of their currency. The real currency, the currency effective in economic transactions, has to operate as an underground currency. No one will admit to its existence, despite its great power. In nineteenth-century England, Butler suggests, Christianity appears to be the dominant religion, but the real, unconscious religion is money. Christian religion and morality can co-exist with the sacred of money as long as they do not get in its way.

By the twentieth century technology was beginning to supersede money as the chief sacred of western civilization.[29] The new lived morality and its mythological justification flow from this fundamental experience – that technology as ultimate power is the solution to all problems.

Before describing how this new lived morality works, I want to emphasize that Christian and middle-class moralities have not disappeared, but have been reduced to the status of moral custom. This means two things: (1) they are moralities subordinate to the dominant morality; (2) they are only potentially effective in regard to those attitudes and actions not subject to technical regulation. Like theoretical morality, the existence of moral custom distracts us from recognizing the dominant lived morality of today.

It is also important to note that the American morality I am describing exists to a lesser extent in all modern societies insofar as they are becoming full members of a technological civilization. For reasons I mention in chapter 2, the United States has more than any other country defined itself in terms of technology. And when the United States became the pre-eminent technological society after the Second World War, its fate was sealed. American lived morality is the future morality of *all* modern societies.

My argument is that the *content* of American lived morality (chapters 2 and 3) includes four values: success, survival, happiness, and health. I refer to these values as mythological symbols and demonstrate how they are interrelated in the myth of technological utopianism. Technology promises both collective success and survival (as the solution to material and social problems) and individual happiness and health (the well-being of consumption). All other values are derivative from or a combination of these fundamental symbols. Next I demonstrate that technology, statistical normality, and the material visual image are the *forms* this morality has assumed (chapters 4–6). Technology (in the largest sense of the term) is the single most important factor in the survival and success of modern societies. As such it forms the *necessary* side of American morality. It gives rise to a host of techniques for the control and manipulation of humans. These human techniques tend to supplant traditional moral forms.

Statistical morality, whether as peer group norms or public opinion, makes up part of the *ephemeral* side of modern morality. Modern technology demands constant experimentation in both production and consumption. The consumer must be provided then with a constantly shifting set of aesthetical norms centering on happiness and health: enter public opinion. At the same time, in the cracks of a technological civilization, in those areas of life from the inner city to the corporation not fully covered by technical rules, emerge peer group norms to assure the survival or success of the group and the individual.

The universe of visual images in the mass media (especially television) forms part of the ephemeral side of modern morality, specifically that which is most *compensatory*. The abstract images of the computer provide information that allows technology to form a kind of system; the concrete images of advertising and television, on the other hand, offer us reverse images of a technological society. A technological society is an eminently abstract society in its reliance on bureaucracy, technical rules, and expert systems. The compensatory images of the mass media provide an exciting, emotionally-satisfying world that is experienced as spectacle. Under certain circumstances these images act as norms.

In chapter 7, I argue that modern American morality is organized around a series of dialectics or struggles, between manipulation and adjustment (within the necessary), the necessary and the ephemeral, the necessary and the compensatory. These interrelated dialectics are a way of conceptualizing the major tensions and contradictions of a technological civilization.

Theoretical Morality

The confusion between lived morality and theoretical morality parallels that between lived morality and moral custom. Theoretical morality, whether descriptive or normative in intent, tends to have an individualistic bias. It assumes that morality is a consequence of individual preference or choice. The demise of a belief in natural law in the nineteenth century created a moral lacuna. The dazzling success of modern science, most evident in technology, led eventually to the creation of a scientific worldview. In this view, objectivity was equated with scientific knowledge. Truth became scientific truth. Because science necessarily limits itself to the empirical world, the existence of transcendental, religious values is outside its purview. Consequently, values and belief come to be seen as subjective.

Alasdair MacIntyre maintains that moral philosophy in the twentieth century typically assumes one of two forms: emotivism or proceduralism.[30] Both share in common, however, a belief that morality is individualistic at its origin. That is, individuals first exist outside of society and later create the rules of society. Emotivism reduces linguistic meaning to emotional predilection and in so doing transforms moral judgment into aesthetical preference. Everyone has feelings of approval or disapproval about certain actions without there being a rational basis for settling moral disagreements, for moral approval is grounded not just in preference but in self-interest. Emotivism destroys the idea that there can be a widely accepted normative theory of ethics. As MacIntyre notes, emotivism's position is that "*all* moral disagreement is rationally interminable."[31] Therefore moral consensus is achieved by extra-rational methods, such as manipulation. (Nietzsche's theory that morality is an expression of the will to power is of course a close relative of emotivism.)

Modern proceduralism is sometimes a response to emotivism and other subjectivist theories of ethics. In this view there are no transcendent metaphysical moral principles; it is enough that they come to possess an intersubjective reality. The aim of proceduralist ethics is to derive a set of moral principles or procedural rules (including rules for deciding between conflicting moral principles) from certain premises. Such theories establish a methodology by which individuals can settle moral disputes within the same cultural framework. In perhaps the most famous, recent, proceduralist account, *A Theory of Justice*, John Rawls attempts to articulate the two basic principles of justice.

As MacIntyre observes, proceduralist theorists have trouble convincing their colleagues, let alone the public, about the validity of their moral arguments.[32] This is often because the premises upon which the moral principles are built appear to be arbitrary. It would seem, then, that proceduralism offers little promise of overcoming the subjectivistic trap of emotivism. Both emotivism and proceduralism share an individualistic bias and deny the existence of universal moral principles.

Existentialist ethics, which flourished between the two World Wars and for a brief time after the Second World War in Europe, attempted to ground ethics in the freedom of the individual. The existentialist theorists often articulated their views as a critique of mass society. In the United States existentialist ethics took the form of situation ethics. The freedom of the individual and a respect for the freedom of the other are the only limitations on what one should do in a moral situation.

All of these theoretical moralities to a greater or lesser extent make the mistake of abstracting the individual from the sociological reality of a technological society. The individuals of emotivism are as confined to irrational preference as those of rational principle theory are to a logical rationality. Of the three, only existentialist ethics has provided a critique of the contemporary society. But what has been gained in the critique is lost in the idealism of the normative proposal that freedom is the only absolute value: my freedom as long as it does not interfere with your freedom. But how can I be sure of what you regard as your freedom? Does my understanding of your freedom take precedence over yours? And what if the exercise of my freedom always interferes with someone else's freedom? What then becomes of my freedom?

Theoretical moralities, either descriptive or normative, tend to be comprehensive. Alongside these general statements about ethics there are a host of specialized ethical statements of various occupational and professional groups. Every major occupational group possesses a code of ethics. These various ethical codes suffer from the same defect as the previously discussed theoretical moralities: the abstraction of the individual from his sociological reality in a technological civilization. This problem is further complicated by the fact that each occupation understands technology in a specialized way consistent with its function. Moreover, the typical view is that technology is neutral so that only the ends to which it is put are of ethical concern. This unrealistic understanding of technology prevents the occupational group from coming up with ethical pronouncements that can be effectively put into practice.

Dutch psychiatrist J. H. van den Berg has demonstrated how unrealistic modern medical ethics has been.[33] Medical technology has upset the traditional relationship between doctor and patient, one in which the doctor attempts to keep the patient alive as long as possible. This has resulted in medical practices that are cruel – keeping someone alive in a state of extreme pain, physical or emotional, by extraordinary technological means. Van den Berg, who is himself a physician, argues that the true dilemma of medical ethics today is the unwillingness to place limits on the creation and use of medical technology. Without the imposition of limits we will continue to prolong life without regard to the quality of life. The inability to accept death is part of the myth of technological utopianism.

Finally we need to consider educational techniques that appear to be theoretical moralities: values clarification and cognitive moral develop-ment (based on the work of Lawrence Kohlberg).[34] Both are techniques that allow students to create their own morality. As techniques, however, they are contentless; moreover, they stand in opposition to traditional morality. Their sentimental assumption is that if you allow students (and anyone else for that matter) the opportunity to discuss various ethical ideas and apply them to hypothetical situations, the students' own moral position will emerge. This is a variation of the "good things happen in groups" theme.

Christina Sommers points out the profound contradiction of these two influential approaches to teaching ethics in school.[35] They make morality a completely subjective phenomenon. By asserting that everyone's view is equally correct, they make "radical tolerance" the exclusive virtue of their group techniques. At the same time, by providing students with hypothetical cases that involve the actions of organizations, such as corporations and governmental bodies, they imply that effective moral responsibility resides in bureaucratic structures. The individual's moral decision is reduced to consumer choice, approving or disapproving of what these more or less autonomous organizations do. The values clarification movement and the cognitive moral development program accurately reflect a technological civilization in turning morality into technique and consumer choice simultaneously.

In chapter 8, I make several suggestions about ethical action in a technological society. Although I too talk about the individual and freedom, I do so in a way that does not abstract the individual from her sociological reality. Moreover, I attempt to explain why realistic ethical action today has to begin with the individual. Finally, I discuss the necessary limitation on freedom that gives it significance and orientation.

A Pessimistic or a Realistic Assessment

No doubt the reader will be tempted to call this work pessimistic, if not apocalyptic. The social portrait to follow is bleak indeed. There are always three positions one can take toward life: cynicism, idealism, and realism. Cynicism makes things worse than they are in that it makes permanent the current condition, leaving us with no hope of transcending it. Idealism refuses to confront reality as it is but overlays it with sentimentality. What cynicism and idealism share in common is an acceptance of reality as it is but with a bad conscience. The cynic masquerades as a realist; the idealist pretends to be hopeful.

To take a realistic view one must have a reason to do so – one must discover a source of hope to *impose* upon reality in order to make it yield meaning. I intend this work to be realistic. This will become apparent in chapter 8.

2

Success Morality: From Economic to Political Ideology

The cultural value of success has been transformed from an individual and economic phenomenon to a collective, technical, and political one. This change is part of the larger collectivization of modern society. The irony in this is that everywhere individualism appears to be rampant.[1]

Actually, modern individualism is but one of the many faces of collectivism. For modern individualism, as Reinhold Niebuhr sagely observed,[2] is a celebration of the autonomous individual who desires freedom without limits, and therefore quickly becomes prey to all sorts of collective pressures. Success, originally a matter of entrepreneurship, evolves into efficiency, which is by definition not a matter of individual choice; rather it involves the rational coordination and control of the collective efforts of individuals. If economic success eventually becomes technological efficiency, this efficiency is set within the context of the nation-state. The modern nation-state in turn has coupled its destiny to the engine of technological progress.

The following is a brief history of the success ethic. The history begins in the Middle Ages in Europe and culminates in the modern period in United States. Much of what will be said about success in nineteenth- and twentieth-century America, however, applies to other modern societies as well. In this sense the United States should be regarded as the epitome of the technological society.

The European Origins of the Success Ethic

The Middle Ages, like any period, is best defined by its contradictions.[3] There was, for instance, a contradiction between Christian freedom and an all encompassing social morality that typified Christendom. The Christian figural view of reality,[4] the idea that certain events and persons not connected in a linear way – historical or causal – are nevertheless related to other events and persons through God's Providence, acted as a contradiction to scholasticism, a static, metaphysical system that unwittingly reduced God's involvement in human affairs to a minimum.

During much of the Middle Ages there were strong limits placed upon economic success. Theologians and moral philosophers condemned usury as a sin and developed the idea of a "just" price. Moreover, numerous sermons were delivered about avarice and the difficulty of the wealthy to attain heaven. Concurrently there were other forces at work: monasteries that became respositories for the wealth of the noblemen, the need to finance the Crusades and other military adventures, and an increase in trade in the late twelfth century.[5] The reality of money, its political, military and economic usefulness, was intruding upon the ethical admonitions against its accumulation. Contradictory views about money and success did not come into full flower until the fourteenth century, however.[6]

Christendom, as was previously noted, was based on a social morality rather than faith.[7] Recognizing that few individuals had a strong and abiding faith, yet sensing the obligation to place everything under the lordship of Christ, church leaders opted to construct a Christian social order, a set of Christian institutions held together by a total morality. Moreover, the faith of the few worked to construct a reservoir of grace that would overflow on command upon those who at best held to the minimum requirements of this social morality. Still, Christian morality was a morality of nonpower – love, service, humility – best exemplified in the person of Francis of Assisi; it stood opposed to the quest for economic, political, and military power. Economic success was severely criticized.

A morality without faith, however, was efficacious only as long as the larger worldview or ideology sustained it. But as scholasticism began to be challenged during the Renaissance, Christian social morality became less vital. It was soon syncretized with competing moralities such as that of chivalry. Chivalrous morality promoted the "values of conquest, the joy of fighting, the joy of hunting and frolicking in the freedom of the natural life, and, finally, the joy of courtship."[8] The morality of well-being, the joy of possession, especially of luxuries,[9] and the happiness one enjoyed today as a hedge against one's future death, even though it originated with the business classes, slowly worked its way into aristocratic sentiments with the admission of some of the newly rich into aristocratic circles. Unlike the calculating, prudential approach the later bourgeoisie brought to the pursuit of happiness or well-being, fourteenth-century aristocrats provided a heroic dimension to the joy of possession.

The ideological counterparts to these secular moralities were the political and economic theories of Machiavelli, Mandeville, Locke, Hobbes, and Smith, which attempted to understand human nature as it was, not as it should be. Human nature was naturally hedonistic and rational. But in each theory there was some concept or mechanism that allowed for things as they are to have a morally beneficial outcome. Even for Hobbes the brutality of human nature in its original state of nature results in a political contract whereby the sovereign institutes Articles of Peace that insure harmonious social relationships.

Albert Hirschman argues persuasively that by the seventeenth century many thinkers had come to believe that ethics and religion could not by themselves control the passions of men.[10] Distinguishing between passions like avarice which could be rationally controlled and those which could not, such as sexual lust, many theorists saw the pursuit of rational interests as a palliative to the wild passions. The interests would balance the passions. Eventually these rational interests were narrowed to mean the economic interests. In the work of Adam Smith we find avarice relegated to the role of a selfish passion that has the unintended consequence of being socially useful.

Hence these secular ideologies accomplished more than a redefinition of human nature; they divided social institutions into autonomous spheres. The economy became separate from politics and morality, morality from religion and law.[11] The economy could be made an independent category more or less free from political control on the assumption that it was comprised of a natural harmony or balance of interests and was thus self-regulating. Likewise the economy could be separated from morality on the assumption that economic self-regulation is morally good, that is, benefits the great majority.[12] The recognition that morality could be distinguished from religion represents an attempt to establish morality on immanentistic (the belief that the world is self-contained and thus can be understood without reference to anything transcendent) and rational grounds alone, whereas the splitting off of morality from law tends to make morality a private affair. Morality now referred to one's relationship with friends and family.

By the time of Adam Smith the economy was established in thought as the paramount social institution and human nature was defined in economic terms: humans acted according to economically rational principles. As Dumont points out, the common denominator in these secular ideologies is that "relations between men are subordinated to relations between men and things."[13] Politics and morality are of less import than the economy and technology. In Smith's theory the private sphere shrinks in both quantity and importance before the public sphere of economic relations. So much activity is directly or indirectly defined as economic in nature that the purely private realm of morality and religion dwindles.

At the base of this new economic ideology lay a belief in the value of private property and economic freedom. As R. H. Tawney notes,[14] there is little difference whether one defends private property as a natural right (French version) or as a right useful to the commonwealth (British version); for in both cases, that of the *philosophes* and the utilitarians, private property was thought to be the bedrock underlying the organization of society. Although the British utilitarians often scorned the French *philosophes* for their naive view of human nature – man as naturally good, easily educated – their view of a self-regulating economy that sanctifies human egoism was equally naive.

The secular ideologies emanating from Machiavelli and culminating in Smith succeeded in establishing several ideas: that humans act out of self-interest, especially economic self-interest, and that private property and economic freedom are the cornerstone of a rational society. The pursuit of economic success, in this view, is as socially beneficial as any altruistic act praised by Christian ethics, and is, moreover, more natural.

Although the Protestant Reformation was mainly directed against the medieval church and scholasticism, it was, at least in the beginning, radically opposed to this secular economic ideology. The political and economic ideologies developed from Machiavelli to Smith are based on an immanentism, a view that we live in a self-contained material world. The belief that God is active in human history is absent from these theories. If God has a part to play in these theories, especially those that emerged concomitant with the rise of modern science, it is that of an architect or engineer. If the universe is a machine, God is its orginator. But once created, this machine is autonomous.[15] A sense of God's presence and continued participation in the world is lost. Political and economic mechanisms of order, substitutes for God, abound: self-regulating economy, progress, invisible hand of God, social contract.

The Protestant Reformation by contrast voiced a belief in a transcendent, wholly-other God whose providence continued to guide the world through the freedom of believers. The Protestant reformers had nothing in common with the immanentistic theorists of the time. Luther and Calvin would have emphatically opposed the economic virtues that some Lutherans, Calvinists, and Puritans advocated much later.[16] Protestant leaders in the sixteenth century still turned to the Bible for answers to perplexing moral questions about economic relationships and transactions. If anything, Tawney notes, the reformers tended to be stricter in their economic admonitions as a corrective for perceived abuses in Renaissance Italy and Holland and in the Roman Church. Luther, for instance, retaining an ostensibly Medieval conception of economic ethics, denounced as pagan the commercial developments of the preceding two centuries and condemned usury. Yet at the same time he rejected the Medieval attitude that work with few exceptions (religion, education) is a curse, substituting the view that one's specific occupation is a calling from God.[17] This, of course, does not mean that one can revel in the success or fruits of one's labor, for they belong to God alone.

Although some reformers such as Zwingli actually repudiated the ownership of private property as sinful, their criticism was deflected by their position of the need to obey civil authorities who had now permitted the charging of interest.[18] Calvin too condemned wealth, more precisely, the misuse of wealth, as in acts of self-indulgence or ostentatious display. Early Calvinism attempted to moralize about a civilization already becoming commercial; in this sense it can be said that Calvinism provided moral restraints for economic transactions. Calvin, for instance, provided rules for usury: no interest was to be charged to the poor and no interest beyond the lawful maximum to the wealthy. Tawney puts it well:

> [Early Calvinism] no longer suspects the whole world of economic motives as alien to the life of the spirit, or distrusts the capitalist as one who has necessarily grown rich on the misfortunes of his neighbor, or regards poverty as in itself meritorious, and it is perhaps the first systematic body of religious teaching which can be said to recognize and applaud the economic virtues.[19]

Frugality, diligence, prudence, moderation, sobriety, honesty, and success comprise the economic virtues. Among the religious progeny of Calvinism, Puritanism is most closely associated with the economic virtues. The triumph of Puritanism in the seventeenth century represents the rationalization of Christianity into a method. Not satisfied with a minimalist morality, the Puritan searched for a rigorous moral discipline for his inner religious life and its outward manifestations. Above all the Puritan wanted to be thought of as a man of character. The concept of character is the key to understanding the dramatic change from a social morality enforced by the church to an emphasis on individualistic ethics.[21] In practice, however, the local church exercised as much moral control over the individual as had the centralized Roman church. Still, the theoretical emphasis on individualistic ethics would eventually permit an even greater accommodation to the demands of a commercial civilization. (It is important to keep in mind that the rationalists and empiricists also championed the individual's ability to make moral decisions.)

Character is everything: riches are the blessings God heaps upon those who have steadfastly followed his will through a life of strenuous work and prayer; poverty is a sign of moral failure. The lesson of the Book of Job had been forgotten. As Tawney observes, "success in business is in itself almost a sign of spiritual grace, for it is proof that a man labored faithfully in his vocation, and that 'God has blessed his trade.' "[22] Max Weber argued that the doctrine of individual predestination played a critical part in permitting the association between economic success and grace.[23] The Calvinist was literally driven to find external and verifiable signs of election, and what better sign than success in one's calling.

David Zaret has recently called attention to the Puritan interpretation of the Biblical idea of covenant in seventeenth-century England.[24] The covenant of grace that God makes with his people, more specifically the covenant about election to heaven, was defined by lay Puritans as a kind of economic contract. Those lay Puritans engaged in capitalistic transactions perceived God's covenant as having the same qualities of "accumulation, exchange, and ownership" that secular contracts possessed.[25] Faith and God's grace became a kind of possession, a property that one owned and could add to. Election to heaven is, of course, the principal part of this contract. Now the circle is complete. Not merely is economic success itself a sign of election, but the form of God's covenant is that of an economic contract.

The relationships among moral character, election (grace), and success are worth exploring. Moral character is a sign of grace but it is also something one acquires through discipline and effort; moreover, it leads to success, which in itself is a sign of election. Moral character is achieved through aseticism, largely in the practice of the economic virtues. Hence moral character is a consequence of the successful practice of the economic virtues, while economic success becomes the chief sign of moral character. Finally, both moral character and economic success, which have become almost interchangeable, are signs of election. But the turning of Christianity into a method, the practice of the ascetic virtues, and the equation of moral character with economic success, meant that religion had become a barrier against God and a source of human pride. When faith becomes a method which can be successfully acquired and practiced by humans, then the work of the Holy Spirit becomes superfluous. Faith has been reduced to morality.

By the late eighteenth century, Christianity had lost much of its hold over western civilization. Certainly there were devout Protestants and Catholics, but in addition there were many among the middle classes (or bourgeoisie) for whom religion was merely a sign of respectability. The middle classes of the eighteenth century represent diverse groups. There were differences between Catholic and Protestant middle classes, between the newer and older middle classes, and between those of great wealth and those of modest income. The Protestant middle classes tended to be more anxious about their salvation and thus about success than their Catholic counterparts, although this difference diminished in time. The new middle classes, financiers and industrialists, tended to emulate the opulent life styles of the nobility more than did the old middle classes, the professionals and small merchants.[26] Differences notwithstanding, the various middle classes shared a common morality.

This middle class (bourgeois) morality was one of success and of well-being (health and happiness), frequently justified through a Christian rhetoric. The actual definition of success, however, was not made in religious – rather in strictly economic – terms.[27] We have already seen that economic success was a sign of divine election for some Christians, and for utilitarians and the *philosophes* a sign of natural virtue and reason. For both Christian and humanist, private property was a prerequisite for the various freedoms of the eighteenth century.

Success for the middle classes was at once an individual accomplishment and something done for one's family. In the aristocratic classes the family was important as lineage and property; the marriage partners were capable of leading independent lives. In the middle-class family there was a great emphasis on affectionate relationships among family members.[28] H. Richard Niebuhr suggests that the emphasis on family life was due to the middle classes' social standing, status being limited to the nuclear family, and was a compensation for the "suppressed social character" of religion.[29] The physical and spiritual well-being of family members was a consequence of the father's success. Success, which earlier had been linked to God's play and one's election, was now tied to the health and happiness of one's family. The bourgeois father attempted to provide for the future success of his children.[30] But beyond the rational goals of family enhancement, the making of money had become, as Weber observed,[31] an irrational force; it was now an end in itself.

The American Success Ethic

The seventeenth-century Puritans in America shared much in common with their counterparts in England. America was to be the locus of a great religious experiment, an attempt to live out collectively God's kingdom on earth. Puritans, thwarted by the state religion of England, desired a situation in which the local religious community could work out the practical implications of being a Christian. Genuine freedom of the individual was nonexistent, however, as local churches exercised enormous controls over the individual expression of faith.[32]

The American Puritans eventually regarded economic success as one of the chief indicators of election to heaven.[33] As Tawney notes, even though American Puritanism was the most totalitarian form of Calvinism, it too featured a theology that championed individualism. Nor did American Puritans immediately succumb to the seduction of an autonomous success ethic, for early on they were highly critical of the taking of unwarranted profits.[34] Eventually the Puritan experimental community was transformed into a secular community in which individualism, especially economic individualism, flourished. By the late eighteenth century, Puritanism had lost most of its motivating force. "The victory of the bourgeoisie over Calvinism," Niebuhr proclaims, "was more total in America than it was in England."[35] With the triumph of a secular middle–class morality, economic success became a paramount cultural goal.

Benjamin Franklin was the first major proponent of a success ethic unencumbered by a Christian rationale. A deist in theory, he punctuated the first success manual with aphorisms: "*Time* is money . . .;" "*credit* is money . . .;" "The good paymaster is lord of another man's purse;" "Remember, that money is of the prolific, generating nature."[36] His most important essays on the topic include: "Advice to a Young Tradesman;" "The Way to Wealth;" and "Necessary Hints to those that would be Rich." Weber regarded Franklin as the perfect embodiment of the spirit of capitalism. Yet even with Franklin the success ethic is not justified in hedonistic terms; instead it is seen as the culmination of practicing natural virtues. Moreover, one's individual success is to benefit the community. As with other Enlightenment thinkers, Franklin never equated self-interest with selfishness.[37] During much of the eighteenth century the yeoman farmer and independent property owner of middling income were the chief models of success.[38] It was not until the mid nineteenth century that Americans openly defined success in economic, individualistic, and competitive terms.[39]

Books on achieving success are more numerous than those on any other subject in the nineteenth and early twentieth century.[40] This popular literature constitutes a wealth of information about American attitudes toward success. The novels, how-to books, pamphlets, and articles are not solely about success, however; happiness and health are also frequent themes. These materials form the heart of American popular culture during this period. They reveal how Americans who first associated success with moral character later linked it to the power of mind to motivate the self into a successful attitude (self-manipulation), and the power of personality to control both subordinates and superiors (manipulation of others). Success was eventually seen to be a consequence of a psychological technique.

Even after success had been shorn of its peculiarly religious motivation, as with Benjamin Franklin, it still retained a strong aura of traditional morality well into the nineteenth century: success and failure were viewed as a result of the presence or absence of character. By the 1830s the idea of success had been translated into a moral program. To achieve success one must possess the following qualities: industry, frugality, perservance, initiative, sobriety, punctuality, courage, self-reliance, and honesty.[41] Success readily follows in the train of moral character; moreover, moral character can be inferred from success. So close was the identification of economic success with moral virtue that the two became as one. Moral virtue had become less important as an end in itself and more important as a means to economic success.

American ambivalence about success was expressed in the distinction between material success and true success. The former was represented as money, whereas the latter was defined in terms of individual happiness, the love and respect of others, doing one's best whatever the outcome, and peace of mind.[42] Most interesting for our purposes is the tendency to define true success as a psychological phenomenon even prior to the "mind-cure" movement. Somehow the pursuit of true success was less offensive than the single-minded devotion to material success. And yet the turning of happiness or peace of mind into an end in itself was just as antithetical to the spirit of Christianity.

The association of success with moral character is most exemplified in the myth of the self-made man, who through sheer force of will and strength of character manages to rise from poverty to become rich and famous.[43] This basic plot line dominated both Christian and secular novels throughout most of the nineteenth century. There are many variations of the theme of upward social mobility. Rarely was the mobile individual truly poor to begin with; often he was of rural origin, confronting a hostile urban environment for the first time. The stories, while extolling success, were nevertheless directed against the perceived excesses of an industrial civilization. Hence the protagonist is never devoted exclusively to the pursuit of wealth but rather is an upholder of rural virtue. The hero never becomes a speculator (a form of gambling), rarely an industrial giant, but usually an entrepreneur.[44]

The myth of the self-made man or "from rags to riches" is often associated with Horatio Alger, author of nearly 100 novels for juvenile readers. He was without question the most widely read novelist of the self-made man. Writing in the late nineteenth century, Alger achieved his greatest sales in the Progressive period. Perhaps his writings, some have argued, were compensatory for the brutal competition of the Gilded Age. Alger's heroes are virtuous, gentle young people, not the acquisitive "fittest" of social Darwinism. Alger's writing provides idealized images of pre-industrialized America, a time when the striving to get ahead was under control.[45]

Competing with the literature on success that stressed moral character was a serious literature that exposes the invidiously competitive side of the success ethic. The authors who wrote about success in a realistic way included, among others, Theodore Dreiser, Jack London, David Graham Phillips, Frank Norris, and Robert Herrick. They portrayed heroic, virtuous failures and unhappy, anxiety-ridden successes; they suggested that the children of the successful were often spoiled brats; and they implied that success was a specter that would not vanish even with reform. Criticisms notwithstanding, these realistic novelists had been socialized into the success ethic and finally came to see it as the foundation of American society.[46] Because they could propose no alternative, these writers embraced the very myth they criticized, something William James had observed when he stated that Americans exclusively worshipped the bitch-goddess *SUCCESS*.

Not all realistic descriptions of competition and success were critical, however. In the late nineteenth century proponents of social Darwinism advocated unbridled competition and the "survival of the fittest." Applying Darwinian theory in ways Darwin himself would never have done, social Darwinists saw the successful businessman as the most fit member of the human race, as the one who had best adapted to the struggle for existence in the business world. Here there were no moral qualms about acquisition, for the belief in progress implied that morality went hand in hand with power. The fittest members of society (the strongest, the most successful) are the bearers of evolutionary progress, which extends even to the domain of morality. Hofstadter maintains that the British social Darwinist Herbert Spencer had a sizeable impact upon the thinking of middle-and working-class Americans.[47] His theories were widely disseminated in popular magazines.

The main difference between the success-as-a-consequence-of moral-character pamphleteers and the social Darwinists was not over middle-class morality. Herbert Spencer and William Graham Sumner were staunch advocates of the economic virtues. Rather, the difference lay in the ultimate justification for success: social Darwinists found the rationale for success in science and evolutionary progress, whereas the success manuals still turned to religion for an ideological defense. In the late nineteenth century, the uneasy truce between science and religion and the ascendent scientific worldview made it easier to pursue wealth, great wealth at that, without scruple. With evolutionary progress perceived as a deterministic process, power and goodness became identical. Success is not the result of moral character, nor even the proof that one possesses such character; rather it is moral character itself.

In the second half of the nineteenth century, a rival to the character success ethic emerged: psychological techniques of self-manipulation, which went by the names of "mind cure," "mind power," and "new thought." The mind power ethic of success seemed to hold sway from the 1880s through the 1920s (although it continued long after that).[48] It claimed that the key to success was not one's character but one's state of mind.

Advocating the use of mind to help cure physical illness, mind cure enthusiasts were concerned about the nervous American, whose loss of energy and general anxiety had become debilitating. Mind cure advocates anticipated the theory of the placebo in their recognition that the patient's belief that she was going to get well was part of the cure, if not the cure itself.[49]

From mind cure came religious movements such as Christian Science and New Thought. The quasi-mystical religious philosophies directed their followers to put their minds in communication with the "Universal," "the Divine Mind," "All-Power," "All Supply," "the great Fountain Head," and "Mother-Father."[50] This modern day pantheism sought to tap the rich resources for healing and success that Nature could provide.

Most important for our purposes are the popular psychologies, often referred to as mind-power or positive thinking, that promised personal success in life. Some of these psychologies were thoroughly secular; some were in adjunct to New Thought; still others were articulated within a Christian context. Not all of these popular psychologies are directed toward the power of mind; a few stress will power. Frank Haddock, for example, author of *Power for Success*, *Business Power*, and *Practical Psychology*, published *Power of Will* in 1907. Claiming that will is more important than mind, Haddock rejected those religious inspirational writers, Christian and New Thought alike, who wanted their readers to subordinate their minds to the mind of a higher power. Instead Haddock outlined a set of exercises for the will, a psychological discipline by which success could be achieved:

> *Exercise No. 10.* Stand erect. Summon a sense of resolution. Absorbed in self, think calmly but with power these words: "I am standing erect. All is well! I am conscious of nothing but good!" Attaining the Mood indicated, walk slowly and deliberately about the room. Do not strut. Be natural, yet encourage a sense of forcefulness. Rest in a chair. Repeat, with rests, fifteen minutes.[51]

As Donald Meyer observes in *The Positive Thinkers*,[52] Haddock's goal was to turn his reader into a spiritual automaton, the embodiment of psychological efficiency so that success is certain.

Will power never actually supplanted mind power as a psychological tool. Not that it matters, for in the end both are minor variations of a single theme – psychological efficiency through self-manipulation. Modern-day magic replaced moral character.

The next step in the evolution of the success ethic was the emphasis on developing one's personality for the manipulation of others. Implicit in the personality ethic is the recognition that success had become an organizational phenomenon, wherein the individual's ability to relate to and control others is crucial to his mobility. Dale Carnegie, especially in his *How to Win Friends and Influence People*, was the most popular proponent of the personality ethic. The book was published in 1936, in the midst of the Great Depression. By 1971 the book had sold 8,000,000 copies in English and had been translated into thirty languages and dialects.[53]

The book contains a host of rules – rules to get people to like you, to win people to your way of thinking, to change people without their being resentful – and plenty of homely illustrations. The six rules to get people to like you are:

Rule 1: "Become genuinely interested in other people."
Rule 2: "Smile."
Rule 3: "Remember that a man's name is to him the sweetest and most important sound in the English language."
Rule 4: "Be a good listener. Encourage others to talk about themselves."
Rule 5: "Talk in terms of the other man's interests."
Rule 6: "Make the other person feel important – and do it sincerely."[54]

Later on Carnegie lays down rules for manipulating others:

Rule 5: "Let the other man save his face."
Rule 6: "Praise the slightest improvement and praise every improvement. Be 'hearty in your approbation and lavish in your praise.'"

Rule 7: "Give a man a fine reputation to live up to."
Rule 8: "Use encouragement. Make the fault you want to correct seem
        easy to correct; make the thing you want the other person to do
        seem easy to do."
Rule 9: "Make the other person happy about doing the thing you
        suggest."[55]

We see here shades of "positive reinforcement" as promulgated by the
behaviorists later in twentieth century.

The question of sincerity for Carnegie and other personality
engineers was nettlesome. Sincerity for those who stressed character
as a means to success is essentially moral. To be sincere means to act
toward one's self and toward others according to one's belief. One's
feelings toward others are of little consequence; duty is everything. For
the followers of the personality ethic, sincerity is aesthetical, or, more
precisely, technical. Sincerity here involves the disintegration of the
unitary, moral self in favor of multiple selves,[56] each of which becomes a
role player. If one doesn't *feel* positive toward the other, the only choice
is to role-play sincerity. As Meyer observes, to role play is "to engage in
the disintegration of one's own awareness of reality, one's own ego-
consciousness, one's own integration as a self."[57] The personality ethic
simply extends the self-manipulation of the mind-power ethic to the
other: I manipulate myself so that I can manipulate everyone else. If
character places some moral limitations on achieving success, mind
power and personality releases them; for the manipulation of self and
other is nothing but power whose only limitation is efficiency.

Changes in the Meaning of Success

"Everyone knows that success with the great masses spells money,"
wrote John Van Dyke in his 1908 book *The Money God*.[58] By the
1970s success was most often defined as great wealth.[59] As we have
previously seen, the Puritans defined success in less baldly materialistic
terms; moreover, the idea of true success was often used to critique
material success. These qualifications notwithstanding, the dominant
idea of success from the seventeenth through the early twentieth century
was that of individual economic success. In the late nineteenth century,
however, two remarkable phenomena, seemingly contradictory, began to
change the definition of success. Moreover, together they offered
increasingly attractive alternatives to individual economic success. On
the one hand, there is the rationalization and objectification of society in
the forms of technology and bureaucracy; on the other hand, there is the

extreme interiorization of human life so that everything not capable of being measured, of becoming a fact, becomes the merely subjective.[60] Objective success became less individual and more collective, less economic and more technological; subjective success became a state of mind – happiness and health – and less a matter of production than of consumption.

Two new movements, scientific management (begun in the 1880s and popularized in the 1910s) and human relations (from the late 1920s) helped to initiate the cultural redefinition of success. Concomitantly the growth of bureaucratic organizations and the increasing importance of technique in human relationships led to a greater collectivization of the economy and of politics. The new meaning of success reflected these changes. Scientific management, the brainchild of Frederick Taylor, was a plan to increase industrial efficiency. The genius of Taylor was to visualize productivity as a system. The work of both management and labor is to be organized according to scientific principles. Each person's work is to be broken down into its basic elements and reconstituted scientifically resulting in the single most efficient method. Training of workers is to follow scientific guidelines. Specialization according to expertise is required. But at the center of this vision is the notion that the *relationships* within the management team, within the labor team, and between the teams must be scientifically cordinated so as to form a system.[61]

Success writers, many of whom did not fully understand Taylor's ideas, popularized scientific management as personal efficiency. They told their readers to imagine themselves as machines living according to ratios between "input and output, effort and results, expenditure and income."[62] Finding in scientific management a similar concern with natural harmony, New Thought devotees supported the growing cult of efficiency. Harkening back to the character ethic, New Thoughters equated efficiency with morality.[63] Yet the mind-power ethic and the personality ethic of success were only psychological techniques. Hence both form and content of success had become technique (efficiency).

In analyzing popular magazines, Theodore Greene discovered that by 1914 the new definition of success was "results" (efficacy), especially efficiency in the acquisition of results.[64] This, of course, reflects the growing importance of technique in the economy. The entrepreneurial function – the ability to revolutionize production "by exploiting an invention or an untried technological possibility for producing a new commodity" – was losing significance in the face of the routinization of technological progress, that is, the objectified work of teams of experts able to provide technical advice on every phase of the business operation.[65] Joseph Schumpeter summarizes this idea, "Rationalized and specialized office work will eventually blot out personality, the calculable result, the 'vision'."[66]

The idea of technical efficiency quickly leads to the idea of organizational efficiency as evidenced by Taylorism. During the Progressive period just about everyone turned to organizational efficiency as the basis for reform or even for upholding the traditional order. Labor and management, socialist and liberal, religious believer and secularist saw better organization as the key to economic and political order.[67] The success manuals, too, reflected this change.

Self-help entrepreneur Dale Carnegie, for example, offered administrator Charles Schwab as a hero to his readers because Schwab was a man who knew how to organize and relate to his inferiors in an efficient way. Meyer calls him the first "hero-bureaucrat,"[68] but it seems that even earlier, about the time of the First World War, popular magazines had begun to proffer the organization man, the administrator, as a hero. The new hero was a high salaried manager rather than an entrepreneur; he was someone who had a "positive" effect upon his subordinates and who knew how to adjust his own ambitions to the needs of the organization. In short, his success and that of the organization were one and the same.[69]

The decline of the individual as hero did not go unrecognized. John Rockefeller wistfully noted: "The day of combination is here to stay. Individualism has gone, never to return."[70] He was right, of course. For bureaucracy had not just become the organizational form of government; it also had invaded the economy. Moreover, the increasing support of business by government in terms of planning, tax loop-holes, and incentives demanded that the bureaucracies of each sector, polity and economy, become interrelated.[71]

"If at the center of nineteenth-century social imagination there had stood a man, in the twentieth he was replaced by the vision of a system," wrote Donald Meyer,[72] expressing this thought perfectly. And yet it was difficult to represent the system as a hero despite the literary attempts to do so in the mid twentieth century.[73] Not only was the post First World War bureaucratic hero unexciting, but efficiency, whether of the system or individual, was not "the ingredients for a new vision to capture the American imagination."[74] But when the system became the nation-state, the American democratic system, a new hero and a new definition of success would enthrall Americans.

At the same time that individual success was being transformed into technological and bureaucratic success, it was being translated into psychological success, that is, happiness and health (well-being). Psychological well-being assumed two related forms: the consumption of goods and services to achieve the good life and the use of psychological techniques to allay the anxiety modern societies produced. Psychological well-being, health and happiness, is the subject of the next chapter, but a few words are appropriate here.

First, the devotees of mind power, as early as the late nineteenth century, had advocated "ease, relaxation, and comfort" over against the ascetic virtues associated with the character ethic.[75] Second, by the twentieth century, beginning in the Progressive period, the criticism of the striving for success in business as the rat race signaled an emphasis on a different set of values – health, leisure, fun.[76] The advocates of positive thinking, such as Dale Carnegie and Norman Vincent Peale, seemed more intent on providing the means for achieving inner peace and serenity than for achieving material success. Summarizing the literature of positive thinking, John Cawelti[77] notes:

> On the whole, positive thinking is less a new expression of the traditional ideal of rising in the world than a revelation of the failure of the dream. Without the social and religious sanctions of the eighteenth and nineteenth centuries, the dream of success is no longer a magical idea for Americans. Once success had been the road to religious salvation and middle class respectability. When these goals lost their force, success, too, lost much of its savor. There is no particular satisfaction in being able to purchase more of the same goods which an ever-more-efficient technology produces in ever-increasing amounts, and it is not easy to see what else success, without its social and religious sanctions, can offer. Sensing this vacuum, the exponents of positive thinking try to fill it by establishing a relation between material success and an inner serenity, showing that happiness is the true way to success. Where its nineteenth-century proponents had proclaimed that the quest for success would lead to those moral and religious ends which alone create true happiness, the positive thinkers seem to be affirming the contrary, that success itself is contingent upon the individual achieving a happy and serene mental outlook. But such a reversal suggests that mid-twentieth-century prophets of success are no longer sure of the value of what they preach. If, in order to become successful, one must first become confident, serene, and happy, what then is the point of going on to become successful?

One recent study of the success theme concludes that success in the twentieth century has become individual self-fulfilment.[78] A survey of American businessmen by the American Management Association in 1972 found that the largest number of respondents defined success as the achievement of goals. Upon closer inspection, however, the achievement of goals meant something entirely subjective. Achievement was defined variously as: satisfaction with one's outward performance; satisfaction with one's life; and satisfaction with a goal achieved, a task accomplished, or a job well done. Note that success has become psychological satisfaction. When other definitions of success such as self-actualization, happiness, peace of mind, and enjoyment in doing or in being are added to that of satisfaction, it becomes evident that close to 70 percent of the respondents defined success in predominantly psychological terms.[79]

In the 1940s Leo Lowenthal's content analysis of popular magazines concluded that American heroes, "idols of success," were more often than not entertainers. The earlier hero had been someone whose work was integral to industrial productivity; the new hero was one whose work was a leisure-time pursuit for everyone else – in short, an entertainer.[80] Individual success moved from the arena of production to that of consumption, argued David Riesman, when the product most in demand became the personality and when morality as defined by the peer group became largely a matter of taste. The peer group, a "tutor in consumption," set fleeting standards about how and what to consume – music, clothes, automobiles, sex, and other people. Riesman observed that "people and friendships are viewed as the greatest of all consumables; the peer-group is itself a main object of consumption, its own main competition in taste."[81] Success, then, became popularity that could be attained through the psychological manipulation of others or through one's pattern of consumption. The role advertising has played in this is, of course, enormous, for it presents all of life as an enormous spectacle of goods and services to be consumed. Once again, individual success appears to be merging with happiness, a psychological state.

The foregoing discussion was not intended to suggest that individual economic success had *disappeared* as an American value, but rather that the intensity of its motivation was weakening. Success was becoming, on the one hand, more collective – technological, bureaucratic, and political – and less entrepreneurial, and on the other hand, more psychological as it became, for all intents and purposes, health and happiness.

The Nationalization of Success

Nationalism, wherever it exists, eventually ends up supporting the unlimited power or success of the nation-state. Some have dated the emergence of a self-conscious American nationalism to the eighteenth century.[82] The United States was from its inception a self-conscious experiment.[83]

The Puritans wanted to create a "new Jerusalem," a living community of saints. They set out to perfect the religious expression and forms of their faith that had been restricted in England. This was a self-conscious religious experiment in community building, in this sense similar to that of Christendom in the Middle Ages. The basis of organization was to be the local congregation. If the principle of freedom was used by Puritans to criticize the centralization of power in the Anglican Church, it, in turn, could be directed against their efforts, for the local congregations stifled the expression of individual freedom. One does not need to look beyond the infamous case of Anne Hutchinson. The Puritans, in their attempt to establish legal "theocracy," defined many of their criminal laws almost word for word from the Old Testament. In their strict asceticism and insatiable desire for assurance about faith and salvation, the Puritans were marked in their dealings with evil-doers less by the severity of their punishments than by their cold righteousness.[84] Despite their protestations of humble finitude over against a transcedent God who is wholly other, the Puritans exuded a pride in their ability to know God's will and carry it out. The local congregation was the locus of this pride.

Nationalism and Democracy

From the local community to the nation as a source of identity and pride is a rather long leap, as events surrounding the founding of the United States and the writing of the Constitution indicate. Political nationalism was not an especially strong force until the age of Andrew Jackson, a time when democratic sentiments became more pronounced. From the time of the Revolution, however, there persisted a belief that the Old World (Europe) was ensnared in vice, injustice, and ignorance, whereas the New World (America) was enlightened and free of impurity. Slowly but surely the eschatological hopes of Christians were transformed into a belief in the millenarian utopian possibilities of the United States. This view in itself did not lead Americans to believe they had a mission to the rest of the world. It took in addition the idea of a redeemer nation:

> Chosen race, chosen nation; millennial-utopian destiny for mankind; a continuing war between good (progress) and evil (reaction) in which the United States is to play a starring role as world redeemer.[85]

Once again, Ernest Turveson in his masterful account of American nationalistic and utopian sentiments summarizes this idea: "Providence, or history, has put a special responsibility on the American people to spread the blessings of liberty, democracy, and equality to others throughout the earth, and to defeat, if necessary by force, the sinister power of darkness."[86]

Although patriots everywhere applaud their country's military victories, Americans of the nineteenth century appeared to do so in a most conspicuous and emphatic way.[87] But America's mission was actually less military than it was religious, economic, and political. The idea of manifest destiny expressed the aspirations of many Americans. Manifest Destiny, in addition to advocating westward expansion, the exploitation of the continent's natural resources and the exportation of the American political system, articulated the utopian hopes of Americans. These hopes were either secular, that America would come to rival and even surpass the cultural accomplishments of Europe, or religious, that Christian progress would culminate in the United States.[88]

In 1858 an editor of *Harper's New Monthly Magazine* asserted that "the American Constitution has a moral meaning, as sacredness, over and above what political science and civil combats can ever give to the organic law of a commonwealth."[89] He went on to say that the principles of American democracy emerged from the Christian idea of Christ's second coming, the new creation. And, anticipating the discussion of civil religion in the twentieth century, he maintained that although there was a separation of church and state, there still remained a national religion. No better statement linking Christianity to American democracy exists.

Although he later appeared to have misgivings about his nationalistic religiosity, Herman Melville in *White Jacket* referred to America as the "political Messiah." Expecting America to carry the torch of liberty and democracy to the rest of the world, he compared it (America) to Israel as a chosen people. Melville, taking a page from Adam Smith and giving it a political twist, asserted that "national selfishness is unbounded philanthropy; for we cannot do a good to America, but we give alms to the world."[90]

Perhaps the most popular catechism of American nationalism in the late nineteenth century was Josiah Strong's *Our Country: Its Possible Future and Its Present Crisis*. Originally published in 1885, by 1916 it had sold 175,000 copies. Strong spent much of his life promulgating the good news of America's mission to the world. His book assimilated most of the dominant ideologies of the time – social Darwinism, laissez-faire capitalism, Anglo-Saxonism, and liberal Protestant Christianity. Although Strong believed in material progress and even imperialism, he was worried about America's spiritual state. His faith in America and in the Anglo-Saxon race was only equaled by his disdain for immigrants,

Catholics, large cities, saloons, tobacco, socialists, and business monopolies. The United States was to be home for a new and finer physical type of Anglo Saxon, a race that "will move down upon Mexico, down upon Central and South America, out upon the islands of the sea, over upon Africa and beyond. And can anyone doubt that the result of this competition of races will be the 'survival of the fittest?' "[91]

Crass expressions of social Darwinism were nowhere apparent in Herbert Croly's *The Promise of American Life*. Published in 1909 it sold a scant 7,500 copies; still, its influence on intellectuals prior to the First World War was enormous. His "new nationalism," undoubtedly influenced by Theodore Roosevelt and Alexander Hamilton, was an expression of eastern, urban progressive thought. Roosevelt thought that an increase in national power sustained by a strong mass emotion of nationalism might be enough to overt the civilizational decline some pessimists like Henry Adams were predicting. Croly's genius was to define nationalism in terms of organizational and technological efficiency. As Arthur Schlesinger Jr. observes, Croly's nationalism "meant in particular the acceptance of the basic elements of the great society, especially the corporation and the trade union – an acceptance designed to preserve the efficiency of the large organizations and at the same time to make them socially responsible. And it meant a readiness to deal with technical problems in technical terms."[92]

The beginning of Croly's book aptly describes early twentieth-century nationalism:

> The average American is nothing if not patriotic. "The Americans are filled," says Mr. Emil Reich in his "Success among the Nations," "with such an implicit and absolute confidence in their Union and in their future success that any remark other than laudatory is unacceptable to the majority of them. We have had many opportunities of hearing public speakers in American cast doubts upon the very existence of God and of Providence, question the historic nature or veracity of the whole fabric of Christianity; but never has it been our fortune to catch the slightest whisper of doubt, the slightest want of faith, in the chief God of America – unlimited belief in the future of America."[93]

Croly agreed with the content of Reich's statement. Reich's insight is remarkable indeed for the beginning of the twentieth century. The nation has conquered the god of American Christianity and become one itself in the process. The success or power of the nation became a moral virtue.

It was Woodrow Wilson, however, who finally moved America beyond isolationism. For a while it was possible to have it both ways – to

talk about a mission to the world and to advocate military isolationism –
as long as technology was limited and imperialism was muted. By the
First World War, however, this was no longer possible. Wilson claimed
that the American mission was the "redemption of the world."[94] The
League of Nations was the short-lived embodiment of that dream.

In 1955 President Dwight Eisenhower, speaking on behalf of the
American Legion's "back to God" campaign declared that "Recognition
of the Supreme Being is the first, the most basic, expression of
Americanism. Without God, there could be no American form of
government, nor an American way of life."[95] As Will Herberg pointed
out, God, in Eisenhower's scheme, had become simply the *means* to
acquire the ultimate goal and value – the American way of life.

At the center of American nationalism stand two themes: democracy
and technology. These are the essential components of American
identity. America and democracy are synonymous in world opinion
because of the American Revolution, Declaration of Independence,
Constitution, and continuous democratic form of government.
Tocqueville's *Democracy in America* provides superb insights into this
relationship. He refers to public opinion as a quasi-religion with the
majority as its prophet. In an age of equality, individuals have little
confidence in the thoughts of their peers, whom they know personally,
but enormous faith in the opinions of an unknown and thus impersonal
majority. Moreover, because the origin of power in a democracy is in the
people, once that power is established, Americans do not think it needs
to be limited. Tocqueville further argues that although Americans often
hate those in power they love state power itself, for they see it as a means
to control their competitors and to enhance their own interests. In short,
Tocqueville demonstrates that democracy increases nationalism and that
the content of American nationalism is a faith in democracy.

Nationalism and Technology

If the link between American nationalism and democracy is well-
established and obvious, that between nationalism and technology is
perhaps less so. An 1847 article in the *Scientific American* argued that
Americans have made the machine their adopted child (earlier in the
century they admired British machine technology) because they have a
genius for practical science. But rather than keep their inventions to
themselves, they should share them with Europeans. The link between
American nationalism and technology is as strong as that between
nationalism and democracy. Commenting upon this article and other
statements of that time, Leo Marx appropriately remarks, "By now the

image of the American machine has become a transcendent symbol: a physical object invested with political and metaphysical ideality. It rolls across Europe and Asia, liberating the oppressed people of the Old World – a signal, in fact, for the salvation of mankind."[96]

Of all the power machinery for which Americans had such a mania, the railroad was the most awe-inspiring. The railroad was, a French visitor claimed, the "personification of the American."[97] The railroad was, of course, the means for westward expansion. Daniel Webster was one of the most eloquent spokesmen for the railroad, defending it simultaneously as a source of progress and as a means for sustaining the pastoral ideal. Even major writers like Emerson and Whitman provided images of an industrialized version of the pastoral ideal. Technological progress had to be reconciled with yeoman virtue.[98] Nathaniel Hawthorne, Henry David Thoreau, Henry Adams, and William Morris notwithstanding, most writers embraced the promise of technology.

From the beginning of the Republic there was a tendency to associate technology with democracy. Technology was touted as a means of achieving political, social, and even economic equality. Concurrently, the freedom and equality inherent in a democratic system provided the opportunity for technological experimentation. In 1812 Thomas Jefferson in a letter to Thomas Cooper maintained that useful science such as that practiced by Benjamin Franklin performed a democratic service by improving the material existence of the common man.[99] Jefferson realized that technology could not be hoarded by the wealthy even if they so desired, but instead would be made available to virtually every class. Technology was the great equalizer. Both Franklin and Jefferson promoted public education, which was to have a decidedly technical emphasis. Tocqueville noticed this American tendency for the practical and technological, suggesting that extreme social mobility was the perfect climate to stimulate a technological mentality.[100]

Some technophiles even suggested that the factory could be made into a model Republican community. Early in the nineteenth century, Americans, while in awe of English machine technology, were critical of the English factory system. With this in mind, some early American manufacturers wished to establish factories in rural areas and maintain them under strict moral guidance. The history of Lowell, Massachusetts, however, belies the intentions of manufacturing idealists. The factories there resembled those in England in which workers were reduced to the status of inmates in what increasingly became a total institution.[101]

If industrial technology could produce a republican community on the local level, why not at the national level? John Higham has argued that in the second half of the nineteenth century, Americans were being unified through technology:

> Technical unity connects people by occupational function rather than ideological faith. It rests on specialized knowledge rather than general beliefs. It has had transforming effects in virtually every sphere of life. As a method of production, technical integration materialized early in the factory system. As a structure of authority it has taken the form of bureaucracy. As a system of values, it endorses a certain kind of interdependence, embodied in the image of the machine. Technical relations are machinelike in being impersonal, utilitarian, and functionally interlocking. Since the Civil War the growth of technical unity has been the most important single tendency in American social history, and its end is not yet in sight.[102]

With a few notable dissenters, Americans believed that this technological unity was perfectly compatible with democratic institutions. During the Progressive period, as we have seen, there was a concerted effort to reform American institutions by making them more efficient. The efficiency expert, preaching the gospel of scientific management, quickly filled the halls of government and business. Not only individual failure but social injustice as well were to be eliminated by social engineering.[103] At the same time, critics began to see a discrepancy between bureaucratic organization and scientific management, on the one hand, and democratic ideals, on the other hand. Reformers went to great lengths to justify the centralizing tendency of technical efficiency.

First, they argued that at the same time that political and business leaders became more efficient by applying scientific principles to each aspect of their work, citizens would become more rational and hence would understand and approve of what their superiors were doing. The faith was in a scientific method that could produce on all levels of society a consensus on the big issues. For even those not formally trained in scientific management could learn enough of the basics through magazines and newspapers to become technically rational.[104]

Second, by equating the participatory aspect of social engineering with freedom, reformers had a ready response to their critics. Democratic social engineering become popular in the United States in the early twentieth century. American social scientists and philosophers such as William James and John Dewey discovered the group to be a microcosm of the larger democratic society and to be the perfect context for education and therapy. Group process or democratic social engineering established the authority of human technique within a group setting.[105] The purpose of this method is to *adjust* the individual to the demands of a technological society. All the forms of democratic social engineering – self-help societies, scouting, group therapy, recreational groups, and so forth – are in one sense a continuation of what Tocqueville called the American's penchant to join voluntary associations. But actually they were even more a manifestation of the intrusion of technique into every sphere of life.

The most revealing aspect of the link between technology and nationalism is the incredible efflorescence of technological utopianism. Certainly this is not unique to the United States, but in no other country was utopia so completely identified with technology.[106] Prior to the nineteenth century, European writers had perceived America itself to be a utopia. American writers, some of whom were influenced by their European predecessors, began to write about America as a potential utopia, but one totally organized by technology. In research on American technological utopianism, Howard Segal examines the work of 25 writers, all of whom shared common ideas:

> The technological utopians aimed at accurate prediction of the future, not at idle visions of a world someday somewhere. Moreover, the world they foresaw so specifically represented no break with the existing one – the world of 1883 – 1933 – and many of the technological changes they predicted were, by 1883, already being discussed and, in some cases, developed. The difference between their utopias and the present was not qualitative but quantitative: they multiplied what they saw as the outstanding contemporary trend and predicted the greater and greater advance and spread of technology. This was not to be a sheer proliferation of machines and structures but an increasing use of technology in establishing and maintaining an entire society.[107]

Edward Bellamy's *Looking Backward* was the most popular American utopian novel. If the other writers did not achieve the same level of popularity, this is probably due more to their second-rate literary skills than to the content of their stories. At the heart of all such novels lies a devotion to efficiency. The individual is supposed to be efficient in all his activities and concomitantly be a cog in the machine of society. Work is all important in the utopia and it is often compared to play.[108] Individualism is downplayed in the interest of cooperation and therefore freedom becomes participation in the group. Politics, based upon conflict and compromise and thus inefficient, is virtually eliminated in the utopian society.

Technological utopianism in literature ran parallel to the various reform movements begun in the Progressive period insofar as both

stressed scientific management, believed in progress, and thought that
America could be transformed into a real utopia.[109] The actual utopian
communities that sprang up in the United States differed more from the
utopian literature than did the reform movement. The reason is that the
small utopian communities were reactionary in their attempt to recreate
an idealized past and thus not primarily interested in efficiency, whereas
the utopian literature and reform movements were committed to
technological efficiency and progress.

The content of American nationalism has been democracy and
technology, each of which has been defined in terms of the other. By the
late nineteenth century it was evident that the nation–state was assuming
more responsibility for the expansion of technology and for the care of
its citizens. This was exactly what Tocqueville had foreseen – a
government that controlled its citizens by meeting all of their desires.
The coming together of the nation–state and technology is, as Ellul has
often noted, the single most important fact of the late nineteenth
century. Charles Sanford has observed that the "real stakes of the game
[nineteenth century imperialism] were not capitalistic acquisition,
but national power."[110] For the nation–state to become powerful, it was
a prerequisite that the individual become a "mass man," something both
Kierkegaard and Tocqueville perfectly understood. The individual
needed to identify with the majority (public opinion) and ultimately with
the nation which acts as a surrogate person. As Bertrand de Jouvenel
observed, "the state is the visible expression of the 'nation-person'."[111]
In the nineteenth century, for the first time, society was conceived of as
an organic unity having an identity or personality apart from but
vicariously including the individual citizens who comprise it. England,
France, Germany, America were now hypostatized into organic beings
that could only be visualized in terms of the activities of their respective
governments. Sanford summarizes this series of events perfectly, "mass
man was the creation of machine technology which transferred the will
to power from the individual to the nation."[112]

Nationalism as Religion

The nationalization of success could never have occurred without
nationalism assuming religious dimensions. For nationalism, as Ernest
Gellner maintains, is the major belief system of industrial societies.[113]
Unlike the nationalism of agrarian societies of the past, modern
nationalism replaces the church in societies that have become
homogeneous and anonymous (mass societies) and in which the state
is equated with society itself. The nation becomes the cultural and

psychological counterpart to the state as a structure of power. Nationalism, moreover, becomes the cornerstone of both a literate high culture and popular culture.

Just as the political state became stronger as it became more technical in the twentieth century, nationalism increased its psychological hold over citizens through the technology of the mass media. It is not crucial whether the content of programs and advertisements is overtly nationalistic:

> The media do not transmit an idea which happens to have been fed into them. It matters precious little what has been fed into them: it is the media themselves, the pervasiveness and importance of abstract, centralized, standardized, one to many communication, which itself automatically engenders the core idea of nationalism, quite irrespective of what in particular is being put into the specific messages transmitted. The most important and persistent message is generated by the medium itself, by the role which such media have acquired in modern life. The core message is that the language and style of the transmissions is important, that only he who can understand them, or can acquire such comprehension, is included in a moral and economic community, and that he who does not and cannot, is excluded.[114]

If the nation-state became sacred in the nineteenth century, then it had to have been expressed in myth; for the sacred is always set forth in myth and symbol.[115] This was indeed the case. The myth of progress, the greatest myth of the nineteenth and early twentieth centuries, contained the nation as its geographic and cultural context. Scientific and technological progress was set within the nation-state and would lead to its increasing greatness. The identity and fate of the United States lay in technological progress. Success was then not just a cultural value but more precisely a mythological symbol (see the following chapter for a fuller discussion of this).

Most of what has been discussed about nationalism and technology in America applies to other western countries as well. England and technology had long been equated before America's late nineteenth-century advances. Yet there were conditions in America that made the intensity of the association (between technology and the nation) greater. John Kouwenhoven has put it well: "[Americans are] the first people in history, who disinherited of a great cultural tradition, found themselves living under democratic institutions in an expanding machine economy."[116] America's "democratic-technological vernacular" makes it unique. All other European countries had longstanding cultural traditions that mitigated to some extent, at least initially, the impact of technology upon their culture.

America was, as was previously discussed, a conscious experiment from the beginning for both the Puritans and the founding fathers of the Republic. That America was a Christian country at its inception is true only if one finds no irreconcilable differences between Enlightenment thought and Christianity. It would be equally correct to say that America represents an Enlightment experiment. It is little wonder that America saw in technology and progress an image of itself – practical reason. It is not enough, then, to say that America had no great cultural tradition, for one must immediately add that America's cultural tradition was already fully open to the experimentation of science and technology.

Vicarious Success

Collective (technical and national) success not only took place in reality but also in imagination, in fantasy. Vicarious success is a major industry whose chief purveyor is sports. Earlier in the twentieth century, participants often compared the world of sports to that of business, which acted as a model for the development of the virtues of self-reliance, competitiveness, and success. Today this has been reversed: businessmen compare business to sports, using sports metaphors to describe their activities. ("We have to red dog the opposition!") Sports is more "real" today than business insofar as reality has become for many that which is on television.[117]

Largely because of television, sports has become spectacle. It is not enough that the game be well-played; there must be additional drama to that which is on the field – pep bands, gymnastic cheerleaders, dancing girls, marching bands, and the increasingly violent gesticulations of the participants. All of this aims to work the fans into a state of ecstasy so that they mirror psychologically the violence in the arena. The spectators vicariously experience the success or failure of the team they support.[118]

Sports enthusiasts and critics appear to agree that winning is the "nucleus of the sport."[119] Most often cited is the remark of Vince Lombardi, former coach of the Green Bay Packers, that "winning is not everything – it's the only thing." There is little disagreement about this in the ranks of coaches and players today.

No better indicator of the supreme emphasis on winning exists than the decline of sportsmanship. One sees this especially in the sports that draw the largest audiences – soccer worldwide, and football and basketball in the United States. Players are taught how to get away with certain rule violations, and when to use them strategically: intentionally injuring the other team's star player or feigning injury to receive an additional time out. The spectators' behavior too is sometimes frenzied. In American football the fans attempt to drown out the signals called by the opposing team's quarterback and in basketball fans try to distract a player shooting a freethrow and routinely boo the other team's players upon introduction at the start of the game. Coaches only reprimand the fans when a penalty appears imminent. Coaches and players alike play up to the crowd, referring to it as the 12th man or 6th man (depending on the sport) and even crediting it with the victory. Gary Gumpert argues that the television replay plays a part in the effacement of sportsmanship by emphasizing and normalizing rule infractions (whether intentional or unintentional).[120]

Fan identification with a team can readily become politicized, especially in international competition. The success of a sports team or even that of an individual performer in an international event is a national success akin to a military victory. It is well known that the Olympic Games are a thinly veiled opportunity for national rivalry so intense that even the judges are influenced by national sentiment. Janet Lever's study of soccer in Brazil demonstrates quite clearly that the Brazilean national soccer team and its star Pele were for many Brazilians a source of identity, purpose, and vicarious success.[121] Some even suggest that for the most devoted fans soccer becomes a cult, a political religion. Consequently sports both encourages and is encouraged by a rampant nationalism.

Modern sports is technique-driven at the same time it is politicized. The incessant experimentation with superior training techniques, better equipment, more efficient organization of practice, and more complete control of athletes' minds and motivation are indicative of a preoccupation with winning and with records. Under these circumstances the distinction between amateur and professional is blurred. At an ever younger age children are subjected to professionalized sports instruction. For both political and technological reasons sports is no longer a game; it has been transformed into a technique of production and a technique of consumption – a political spectacle.

Success or Survival?

After decades in which success was almost taken for granted, sometime in the 1970s the issue of survival began to receive serious consideration. Like success the term *survival* has acquired a number of meanings, the recent history of which will help us put it into proper perspective.

In the cold war period the problem of nuclear war captured the attention of the world. Survival in a nuclear age became a widely-debated issue. Each war fought with conventional weapons was fraught with the possibility of becoming a nuclear war, if only because the United States and the Soviet Union might be drawn into the conflict.

The anti-nuclear war movement was soon joined by the broader anti-nuclear energy movement. The latter movement was obviously connected with the rising concern for the environment. Pollution of air, water, and soil, the disruption of ecosystems, and the threat of "normal accidents,"[122] that is, the breakdown of technological systems such as nuclear power plants and chemical plants, began to be widely discussed in the 1960s and 1970s. Books such as *Blueprint for Survival* and *Staying Alive* became commonplace. When economic disadvantage and unemployment would ensue from measures to curb pollution, however, there was no consensus about what to do. Economic success appears to be at odds with physical survival in modern societies.

The issue of success versus survival is related to the fact that technological growth is out of control and thereby destructive. It creates enormous political, economic, and environmental problems at the same time as it solves other problems. Survival pertains both to a sense of crisis and to the need to repair those sectors of society and the environment that have been damaged.[123]

For a time the problem of overpopulation appeared as though it would dwarf all other problems of survival. Paul Ehrlich became a national spokesman on the dangers of overpopulation. When to this are joined the problem of rapidly diminishing nonrenewable resources, such as metals and fossil fuels, the damage to ecosytems, and the rapidly growing populations of Third World countries, the resulting admixture seems devastating. Groups such as the Club of Rome have been routinely forecasting catastrophes in which an enormous number of people will die from famine, pollution, and disease.

Economic survival began to rival physical survival as an issue in the 1980s. Pressures of international competition, a slowdown in the rate of growth in the US economy, and the cost of technological innovation and implementation made some American businessmen talk more about survival than success. The Japanese penchant for economic planning and long-term profits contributed to such talk.

A spate of books about business appeared with the word *survival* in the title. Economic, political, technological, and environmental uncertainty created a climate in which the businessman had to worry more about keeping the organization afloat than about the size of the profit. Pessimism in the business world can be devastating with so much dependent upon investor and consumer psychology. Not everyone succumbed to this kind of talk, however. One corporation runs an ad that expresses the dilemma aptly: "We don't want just to survive; we want to succeed."

This suggests that the two belong on the same continuum: success is maximum survival, just as survival is minimum success. Survival is emphasized when the perception of crisis abounds. Elias Canetti has defined survival (and by extension success) as the "moment of power."[124] I survive, the other does not; I succeed, the other does not. This brief definition is as perfect as it is ominous. For if success and survival are paramount mythological symbols, then we have turned power itself into a value. Linked together inexorably, the nation-state and technology are the foremost manifestations of power today. Increasingly, however, the power of the nation-state itself resides in technology.

3

A Morality of Happiness and Health:
Advertising as Mythology

The cultural values of happiness and health that became pronounced in the eighteenth century eventually became institutionalized in advertising's liturgy of consumption. If success and survival as values were transformed into collective outcomes, happiness and health filled the void for the individual. To a certain extent individual success was redefined in terms of well-being: happiness and health (security is implied).

The modern notion of well-being has nothing in common with the Greek idea of eudemonia or happiness. The latter makes happiness a consequence of moral action and character, a harmony one achieves with oneself and others; the former eventually turns happiness and health into material values: bodily pleasure through consumption on the one hand and the technical perfection of and enjoyment of the body on the other hand. By the end of the nineteenth century, a complementary definition of health and happiness as adjustment, more precisely, a mental state that ensues from adjustment, had become established.

The modern sense of well-being has its origin in the decline of Christendom in the late fourteenth century. The aristocratic values of fighting, hunting, and courtship had barely been held in check by a Christian social morality even in the best of times. Into the moral space vacated by a Christendom in decline slowly entered the value of possession. The "pride in being rich" was the specific source of the "desire for happiness" that accompanied the admission of wealthy businessmen to the ranks of the aristocracy. The urban aristocracy in central Italy appears to be the first class to profess the value of material well-being.[1] By the middle of the fifteenth century bankers and cloth merchants in Florence could be viewed as a distinct class of bourgeoisie. Sombart maintains that the middle class respectability we associate with the seventeenth and eighteenth centuries is already found in the fifteenth century.[2] Alberti's *On the Government of a Family* is an earlier, Italian version of Benjamin Franklin's *Poor Richard's Almanac*. Respectability and material well-being went hand in hand.

Indirect support for the thesis of an early emphasis on happiness and health (well-being) comes from literature. Dante, the last major Christian writer to employ the Christian figural view of reality, subverted this interpretive scheme by his vivid and even seductive imagery. The human world is portrayed in such an exciting way that "the image of man eclipses the image of God."[3] The world of pleasure is becoming an end in itself.

The present chapter begins with a description of the European bourgeoisie and the history of consumption. Subsequently there is an examination of two related phenomena in the United States from the late nineteenth century to the present: advertising as the institution of well-being and the emergence of a therapeutic ethos of adjustment.

The Values of the Bourgeoisie

What had begun as a tolerable aberration – the love of material well-being – in the confusion of the late Middle Ages became normal in the eighteenth century with the increase in the number and prestige of the middle classes. The European bourgeoisie both was and was not a unitary class. One can certainly speak of it as a class over against the working class on the one hand and the nobility on the other hand; yet concurrently at the lower reaches there was an over-determined attempt to distance itself from the working class, just as at the upper reaches with the mobile, financial and business bourgeoisie there was a concerted effort to emulate the nobility. The presence of a negative or a positive model at the lower and upper sectors of the bourgeoisie made for a different emphasis. As a unitary class the bourgeoisie[4] held three major values: spiritual and material well-being, respectability and assimilation, and the family.[5] For the lower middle class trying to distance itself from the working class the issue of respectability and acceptance into legitimate society was the foremost concern. By contrast the upper middle class rapidly transformed spiritual comfort or well-being into what Tocqueville called material well-being in its efforts to possess the trappings of nobility.

Although most of the bourgeoisie remained Christian in name (few of the *Philosophes* became atheists), the Christianity they retained was emasculated. There were differences, of course: Bernard Groethuysen maintains that Catholics were somewhat less influenced by the secular, materialistic values of capitalism than were Protestants.[6] Whatever the case, Christianity became consolation and justification, a *means* to ends purely human. For instance, God was turned into a "tender father," whose primary mission was to make "honest folk happy" in this life as well as the next.[7] God became, in effect, Father Christmas. Just how ephemeral God eventually became to the bourgeoisie is evidenced by the tendency to take Him seriously only in time of crisis.[8] God had been transformed into the "high god" of traditional societies. Planning and moderation supplanted God's Providence. The bourgeois "applied calculation to the data of experience," with the result that "Divine Providence had no place in this expertly regulated and ordered life; the end-of-year balance sheets were in the nature of manuals of experimental science, drawing out mystery."[9] The law of probability assumed the form of moral obligation.[10] Unable to control death and disease through planning, the bourgeois turned to religion to deal with the unexpected crisis. Just as the high god of traditional societies plays little if any part in day-to-day living, the high god of Christianity takes second place to a "strong faith in the visible world."[11]

In their great desire to appear respectable and to master the world, the bourgeoisie placed business and religion into mutually exclusive categories, turned Christianity into a morality, and, finally, created a secular morality. Religion now became a private matter: It was reduced to a domestic ritual in which parental authority and familism found validation and it was restricted in its moral obligations to family and friends. Business occupied the public sector as an autonomous set of practices that contained their own moral obligations.[12] By the nineteenth century the hyperbolic statement that one was a Christian on Sunday and a businessman the other six days had largely come true.

Turning Christianity into a moral system is a way of doing away with God by objectifying his will. The "infinite demand" of God is turned into a finite set of obligations that become interchangeable with the moderation and probity that characterize the actions of the prudent businessman and citizen.[13] Being a Christian means avoiding the serious (mortal) sins. Kierkegaard has described the life-style of the bourgeois Christian:

> . . . a secularized life, avoiding major crimes more out of sagacity than for the sake of conscience, ingeniously seeking the pleasures of life – and then once in a while a so-called pious mood.[14]

The most audacious achievement of the bourgeoisie with respect to religion and morality was the establishment of a set of virtues largely related to success in business. Prudence, industry, frugality, honesty, and temperance were prominent among the virtues demanded by a business economy. The distance between business and virtue was closed in the nineteenth century when, in Sombart's words, middle-class virtues were turned into "objective principles of business methods,"[15] or, in other words, technical rules.

Of the remaining virtues reserved for the private sector, familism[16] was the most significant. Familism here refers to the tendency to justify any action that enhances the status or power of one's family. The family principally referred to the nuclear unit. Underlying this familism was the value of the family as the locus and source of emotional gratification and compensation, a "haven in a heartless world."[17] For the nobility the family's chief value consisted in its symbolic status as evidenced in the importance of lineage. The historical contribution of one's ancestors to the life of the community was commemorated in the hereditary titles of the nobility. Lacking such symbolic resources, the bourgeois family turned in upon itself.[18]

Affectionate relationships among family members – conjugal happiness and the parent-child relationship transformed into friendship – were made *obligatory*. A doting wife and admiring children made the success of the middle-class father worthwhile and his occasional failure bearable. What the bourgeois family lacked in status it made up for in emotion. It turned emotion into moral status and called it respectability. The respectable family was the family without conflict, the family that appeared to be happy, the family that thereby could act as a moral unit according to the principle of familism.

How did happiness and health fit into the bourgeois scheme of things? By the early eighteenth century an ethic of happiness was clearly in place. It "oriented man to the possible goods of the world, be they conceived in terms of the full realization of his potential abilities in work well done, of respect and esteem by his fellow men for his achievements, or of wealth and the pleasures and comforts of the flesh."[19] Happiness was rescued from the pitfalls of contingency. As one eighteenth-century bourgeois wrote, "I have seen that happiness walks in the footsteps of religion, religion in those of reason, reason in those of education, so that happiness depends entirely upon ourselves."[20] The self-help movement begins here.

The nobility's notion of happiness by this time tended toward luxury, extravagant living, and physical pleasure. Because the nobility led its life largely in the public eye in court society,[21] its consumption was for public display. Although the bourgeoisie imitated the nobility in consumption for public approval, for instance, in home furnishings, its opportunities for display were necessarily limited. The occasional display notwithstanding, the lifestyle of the bourgeoisie remained rather austere until late in the nineteenth century.[22] The bourgeoisie at both extremes – upper and lower – were less ambivalent toward the nobility than the middle ranks were. The mobile, financial and business bourgeoisie attempted to emulate the exaggerated lifestyle of the nobility; the lower middle class, without real opportunity of even appearing to be noble, traded respectability and moral resentment for hope; the regular bourgeoisie were caught between emulation and disapproval. Few, however, escaped the attraction of a more comfortable and exciting lifestyle at the same time they condemned "extreme sensual gratification."[23]

At the same time, however, that the bourgeoisie was emulating the nobility, the reverse was occurring.[24] This was not just a consequence of more members of the bourgeoisie having become aristocrats, but mainly the result of the fact that the bourgeoisie in action and attitude were more in line with the major developments of a capitalistic and technological civilization (as Marx clearly understood).

Health and physical well-being (security) were important dimensions of the middle class definition of happiness. The bourgeoisie were preoccupied with the physical security of their homes and family members just as they were with job security. Health in the eighteenth century was the base upon which happiness was built.[25] Only later would health come to rival happiness as an independent value.

Berdyaev perceptively noted earlier in the twentieth century that the bourgeois was a psychological type universal in all civilizations but was only made a predominant social type in modern times.[26] Extending this argument, Ellul maintains that the bourgeoisie have won a total victory, involuntarily to be sure, so that all modern and modernizing societies are bourgeois.[27] Capitalism, socialism, and communism as ideologies all promise their true believers the good life of happiness, health, and general prosperity.[28]

Happiness Goes to Market

The spiritual happiness of the eighteenth century that consisted of "good health, good sense, and good conscience,"[29] was slowly being transformed into a material happiness. If the extravagant life-style of the nobility had been a model at first only for the upper middle class, the increased consumption that industrialization both provided for and demanded democratized this ideal.

By 1800 England had become the first consumer society.[30] The transformation had begun early in the second half of the eighteenth century,[31] so that the industrial revolution and the consumer revolution went hand in hand. Consumption here obviously refers to more than the consumption of necessities for survival; it points as well to luxuries and to stylized, improved, and novel necessities so that the distinction between necessity and luxury becomes blurred.[32] There is a conjunction of reasons why England rather than France first achieved this status. That such a heavy concentration of the population lived in London (by 1800, 16 percent of the population either lived in or had lived in London) allowed it to be a highly effective "windowshop" for the country. The increased income of many sectors of society (the rate of increase was highly differential) meant an increased ability to spend money. This in turn led to the recognition of the increasing value of the home market.[33] But England of course was just the first of a host of western societies to increase their rate of consumption in the nineteenth century.

Certainly a reduced ability to produce one's own goods comparable in cost and quality to those that were being mass produced led to an increase in consumption.[34] Of greater importance, increasing over time, were motivational factors born not out of necessity but out of desire. Social emulation of the nobility by the bourgeoisie and of the bourgeoisie by the working class had become a reality through mass consumption. One could now buy the appearance of higher status and increased respectability. Whether for purposes of emulation or not, however, the act of consumption was essentially an individualistic act.[35] What was being unleashed here was more than emulation – it was the desire to be happy, to make the power of the product one's own.

To tap the hidden recesses of consumer desire, merchants had to "sell consumption."[36] The display of goods produced a rhetoric of its own,[37] an advertisement for consumption. Prior to the establishment of advertising as a gigantic industry, the world of goods had to be put on display in major cities. The major ways in which this was accomplished included expositions and fairs and large department stores. The mail-order catalogue, the "first American kind of book," was created to reach those in rural areas.[38]

After the Crystal Palace exposition of 1851 in London, a series of international expositions about the latest technological innovations (tools, machinery, products) were held in Paris in the second half of the nineteenth century. They were designed to attract as many visitors as possible. At first the emphasis was on educating the public about new technologies and the science behind them; later the displays were designed more to entertain. For instance, the 1867 exposition featured a Palace of Industry that was organized precisely to teach people about recent scientific and technological breakthroughs in such areas as aluminum and petroleum distillation. By 1889 the exposition's main attractions were the Gallery of Machines and the Eiffel Tower. Williams describes these two wonders:

> The two focal points of the 1889 fair were the Gallery of Machines, a long hall with a vault nearly 400 feet across where sightseers could gaze from a suspended walkway at a sea of spinning wheels, clanking hammers, and whirring gears, and the Eiffel Tower, a monument once scientific, technological, and aesthetic, the architecture of which was derived from that of iron railroad bridges; at its summit was an assortment of apparatus for meteorological, aeronautical, and communications research.[39]

At the exposition in Chicago in 1893, the featured attractions were the Transportation Building and the Ferris Wheel on the Midway.

By 1900 the "sensual pleasures of consumption" had taken precedence over the intellectual pleasure of learning.[40] More and more the exposition was becoming a spectacle. From "La Parisienne," a sexy goddess in tight skirt and coat of imitation ermine that sat atop the Monumental Gateway, to the exposition to the Trocadero, that part of the fair devoted to the exotic material culture of colonial peoples (Algeria, China, Japan, Cambodia, Sudan), a primitive version of Disney's Epcot Center, the emphasis was on the visually spectacular and sensually pleasurable. A contemporary observer described the Trocadero as a collage of "Hindu temples, savage huts, pagodas, souks, Algerian alleys; Chinese, Japanese, Sudanese, Senegalese, Siamese, Cambodian quarters . . . a bazaar of climates, architectural styles, smells, colors, cuisine, music."[41] Expositions and fairs had become miniature cities of consumption, whose utopian rhetoric was that each consumable object contained within itself the power of bliss.

The department store was, outside of advertising, the greatest force in making consumption a way of life; it represented the institutionalization of the exposition (in its later stages). Michael Miller's study of the Bon Marché Department Store in Paris is wonderfully illustrative. Founded in 1869 this great store, rivaled only perhaps by the Louvre, became in a short time a behemoth of consumption. The building itself was enormous and its architecture histrionic; it had the appearance of a theater and even at times of a temple.[42]

The interior of the building appeared even more spacious than it was because of the use of columns and glass. Large galleries and three grand staircases contributed to the overall impression of vastness. The large crowds, exacerbated by bargain counters near entrances, were matched by the huge number of employees: from 1,788 in 1877 to 4,500 in 1906.[43]

The Bon Marché had something for everyone. There was a reading room on the second floor with a multitude of newspapers and periodicals; nearby was a gallery that exhibited the work of contemporary artists. Most astonishing, however, was the scheduling of house concerts and shows. It was here that the selling of bourgeois culture reached its apogee. There were even scheduled tours of the building, suggesting not only that it was a living museum but also that it was becoming a major symbol of consumption. Evidence for the latter point is provided by the enormous number of illustrated cards the Bon Marché gave away – invariably with its image somewhere on the card. Pamphlets, calendar books, and catalogues provided still more images of the store. Almost any part of the building or phase of the operation could be the topic for illustration.[44]

But the real star after all was the merchandise itself. Its organization and mode of display titillated the appetites:

> Everywhere merchandise formed a decorative motif conveying an exceptional quality to the goods themselves. Silks cascaded from the walls of the silk gallery, ribbons were strung above the hall of ribbons, umbrellas were draped full blown in a parade of hues and designs. Oriental rugs, rich and textural, hung from the balconies for the spectators below . . . White sales, especially, were famous affairs. On these occasions the entire store was adorned in white: white sheets, white towels, white curtains, white flowers, *ad infinitum*, all forming a single *blanc* motif that covered even stairways and balconies.[45]

The store's clientele were mainly bourgeois; their purchases from among the gallimaufry of objects on display represented the materialization of a middle class identity. The larger implication of this was not lost on the owners and promoters: middle class identity needed to be renewed in novelty.

Displays in the various departments depicted the bourgeois life-styles. There were scenes of women wearing "coats for visit, coats for travel, coats for ball, or coats for the theatre."[46] There were many family scenes as well: the family at the beach, in the countryside, at dinner. Children were not neglected, for there were entire departments devoted to their needs and life-style. The store's catalogues, calendars, and illustrated cards reinforced and added to the ideal image of bourgeois life that the various departments promoted: "The Bon Marché showed people how they should dress, how they should furnish their home, and how they should spend their leisure time."[47]

The department store in the United States never reached the grandeur of the Bon Marché or the Louvre; still it was grand enough to be referred to as a palace. Not an American invention, the department store nevertheless took deeper root in America than anywhere else. In keeping with the democratic sentiments of its customers, the American department store emphasized "show windows," large windows at ground level that were used to display merchandise. " 'Window-shopping' was the name for a new and democratic popular pastime."[48]

The uniquely American contribution to consumption, however, was the mail-order catalogue. This proved a boon to the farmer and other rural dwellers. Montgomery Ward and Sears, Roebuck and Company were the largest and among the earliest mail-order companies. Between the early 1880s and the early twentieth century the size of each company's circulation grew prodigiously, e.g. Sears's circulation went from just over 300,000 in 1897 to over three million in 1907.[49] The mail-order catalogue became known affectionately as the "Farmer's Bible." This secular Bible promised a different kind of joy – the happiness of consumption. Boorstin describes its religious significance:

> It was not merely facetious to say that many farmers came to live more intimately with the good Big Book of Ward's or Sears, Roebuck than with the Good Book. The farmer kept his Bible in the frigid parlor, but as Edna Ferber remarked in *Fanny Herself* (1917), her novel of the mail-order business, the mail-order catalogue was kept in the cozy kitchen. That was where the farm family ate and where they really lived. For many such families the catalogue probably expressed their most vivid hopes for salvation.[50]

The treatment of consumption in the novel (from the early nineteenth century onward) is sure sign of the cultural significance of consumption. For illustrative purposes I have chosen three novelists whose work provides both rich descriptions of consumption and insights into its variegated meanings. Balzac could rightfully be called the chronicler of consumption. From a bourgeois background he repeatedly showed how desire unleashed in competitive emulation and acquisition was the downfall of otherwise decent people. He had a sensitive eye for the detail of consumption (as Henry James had an ear for the detail of conversation) by which individuals distanced themselves from or identified with others – "the way a cravat was tied, how shoes were polished, the type of cigar smoked."[51] Even more impressive was his understanding of the images and objects of consumption. In his novels the protagonists are invariably "looking at each other and looking in the mirror" to the point that they have become images, life-styles reduced to projecting an image. At the same time the characters consume the various objects of display and desire, they are reduced to servants of their objects.[52]

The American counterpart to Balzac was Sinclair Lewis. Writing in the early twentieth century, Lewis's most detailed study of consumption is *Babbitt*. Each scene contains a virtual catalogue of consumer goods and services from clothing and furniture to the automobile. Each object symbolized something about either the inner or outer person and her social rank. Lewis understood, as Baudrillard later did, that the disparate objects of consumption formed a symbolic system.[53] His description of the automobile hierarchy is to the point:

> A family's motor car indicated its social rank as precisely as the grades of the peerage determined the rank of an English family – indeed, more precisely . . . There was no court to decide whether the second son of a Pierce Arrow limousine should go into dinner before the first son of a Buick roadster, but of their respective social importance there was no doubt.[54]

For Lewis unlike Balzac the tragedy of modern consumption is that both collective meaning and personal identity are inscribed in the objects of consumption.[55]

Don DeLillo, a contemporary American novelist, provides a humorous and incisive critique of consumption in *White Noise*. In a sense the main characters in the novel are television and the supermarket. DeLillo's insights into consumption are contained in this passage:

> Babette and the kids followed me into the elevator, into the shops set along the tiers, through the emporiums and department stores, puzzled but excited by my desire to buy. When I could not decide between two suits, they encouraged me to buy both. When I said I was hungry, they fed me pretzels, beer, souvlaki. . . They were my guides to endless well-being. People swarmed through the boutiques and gourmet shops. Organ music rose from the great court. We smelled chocolate, popcorn, cologne; we smelled rugs and furs, hanging salamis and deathly vinyl. My family gloried in the event. I was one of them, shopping, at last. . . I began to grow in value and self-regard. I filled myself out, found new aspects of myself, located a person I'd forgotten existed.[56]

From the beginning of the eighteenth century consumption has been presented as the cornucopia of happiness. Certain astute observers, advertising agents, and novelists perceived that the relationship between the self and the object of consumption was becoming a deeply symbolic and emotional one. Initially consumer goods were sold as a means of achieving middle-class status. The principle at work here is social emulation. One must not restrict this idea to that of upward mobility, for the ephemeral aspect of consumption, constantly shifting goods and styles, meant that one's status required frequent renewal. Set within the swirl of changing fads and fashions, the individual was at a loss to discern what the demands of status were; hence the consumer turned to the department store and the catalogue for the most up-to-date models of status.

Because the "rhetoric" or form of display of consumable objects makes a fundamental appeal to desire, the act of consumption is an individual one. In discussing the implications of Lewis's novels about consumption, Harris notes that the world of objects is not so much about obtaining status as it is about forming an identity.[57] Colin Campbell ties the ethic of consumption to the Romantic definition of the self as infinite possibility: the unending search for new and intense experiences.[58] He concludes that "it would be just as true to say that the self is built through consumption as that consumption expresses the self."[59]

Yet it is just this distinction between status and life-style on the one hand and identity on the other hand that consumption blurs. In commenting on how the purchase of a Bon Marché tablecloth entailed the acquisition of bourgeois status, Miller explains that "images and material goods were coming to constitute life-style itself."[60] When life-style is reduced to consumption, the consumption of life-style becomes the consumption of consumption. This represents consumption taken to its logical and absurd conclusion.

In any society where consumption becomes an end in itself, the meaning of life, the human being is persuaded to become an image/object. This happens in two ways. First, there is an implicit pantheism in the rhetoric of consumption: I become what I consume; the powers of the objects of consumption become my powers. Second, the reified human being becomes a mere role player who puts himself on display for others to consume. The human personality has become an object for others to consume.[61] Finally, consumption fragments the individual into multiple selves and roles, each realized in a different commodity.[62] Debord calls the moment when everything becomes a commodity the time of the society of the spectacle (the image/object).

The reason for the ascendancy of consumption as a source of meaning is that "the consumer is filled with religious fervor for the sovereign liberty of the commodities."[63] "Every single product represents the hope for a dazzling shortcut to the promised land of total consumption and is ceremoniously presented as the decisive entity."[64] The object of consumption has been transformed into a fetish. Just as with failed magic, the consumable object does not realize its promise. But as Debord observes, there is always another object that contains the same hope. Thus the emptiness of present consumption is compensated for by the fullness of the future promise.

The Liturgy of Advertising

When liberally defined, advertising can be dated to the onset of civilization itself. Advertising only becomes a major force in the life of society late in the nineteenth century at which time its symbiotic relationship to the mass communications media is forged. Although most of the discussion to follow is about American advertising, the important points are applicable to other modern societies. Daniel Boorstin has called advertising the "omnipresent, most characteristic, and most remunerative form of American literature." It was "destined to have an intimate popular appeal and a gross national influence without parallel in the history of sacred and profane letters."[65] Without a long-standing cultural tradition and the emergent identification with technology and experimentation, the United States embraced advertising with a vengeance.

The rise of advertising to a prominent position in society was aided by the newspaper. New techniques for printing and a growing readership provided fertile grounds for the growth of advertising. For a time newspaper advertising was held back by the tiny size of the agate type that had long been mandatory. Large department stores, which were the largest employers of newspaper advertising and were already using display presentation and illustration techniques in their in-house brochures and flyers, were pressing newspapers to do the same.[66] Joseph Pulitzer with the acquisition of the New York *World* in 1883, and William Randolph Hearst with his newspaper chain permanently changed the form and content of newspaper advertising. The display presentations in advertising aped the sensationalistic headlines: the newspaper and its ads were becoming one. Expenditures on advertising, largely in the print media, increased from $15 million in 1870 to over $140 million in 1908.[67] Newspapers claimed the largest share of advertising revenue.

Magazines, however, shortly began to rival newspapers in the competition for advertising income; indeed some magazines were expressly created for the purpose of advertising.[69] Religious periodicals, numbering around 400 in 1870, dominated the periodical advertising market for at least a decade and received a large percentage of advertising revenue. The N.W. Ayer and Son advertising agency was established by profits from the solicitation of advertising for religious magazines. With no sense of irony, Frank Presbrey observes that at the same time these periodicals often rejected patent-medicine ads they accepted those from insurance companies. The latter industry proved to be the major advertiser in religious periodicals.[70]

By 1890 women's magazines had surpassed religious periodicals in the acquisition of advertising. Cyrus Curtis, founder of *Ladies' Home Journal*, did more to promote magazine advertising than any other publisher. By 1888 the *Ladies' Home Journal* had at least twice as much advertising as its women's magazine competitors; by 1892 its circulation exceeded that of every other periodical whatever the subject matter.[71]

In 1897 Curtis acquired the *Saturday Evening Post*, a literary magazine from the early nineteenth century (which even earlier had ties to Benjamin Franklin's *Pennsylvania Gazette*). Freely mixing popular culture with high culture (as in his claim to have the "best poems in the world" and "great speeches of famous Americans" side by side with stories of "American money kings" and "practical sermons by the great preachers") Curtis increased the circulation of the *Post* from 2,000 to 200,000 in three years. By 1928 the circulation had risen to nearly three million and its advertising income exceeded $48 million.[72]

Just as Pulitzer and Hearst had helped narrow the difference between news and the ads by making each spectacular, so did Curtis with mass-market magazines. But it was more than headlines and personal interest stories. As Wilson has demonstrated,[73] the very *tone* of the popular magazine was that of advertising. Creating an amalgam of "plain talk" and "tall talk" the mass-market magazine effectively used a simple, direct yet persuasive style that resembled a "pitch." Concurrently there was an editorial emphasis on stories that "glamorized" the commonplace and everyday, that in effect created a "romance of real life."[73] The advertising style present in the *Saturday Evening Post* and the *Ladies' Home Journal* found an eager group of imitators in the magazine trade.

Radio advertising had to await the formation of national networks of affiliated stations to take off. The percentage of weekly programs that had regular sponsors followed the increase in radio stations that became nationally affiliated. Between 1937 and 1947 the percentage of stations that were members of a network increased from 46 to 97. National ad agencies and the largest businesses effected this dramatic change and until 1941 controlled radio programming directly.[74] The radio soap opera, a tremendously popular genre, was the brainchild of advertising agents who realized that people were bored with information presented all day in a matter-of-fact way. The use of music in both programming and advertising further cemented the relationship between communications media and advertising style.[75]

Of course nothing captured the public's attention more than television. As it became apparent that people read less and watched more, that they took their news from television, and that the visual image was a more effective advertising tool than the written or spoken word, advertising agents and advertisers found a variety of ways to realize television's enormous potential as an advertising medium. None of the other media was able to make its stories or programs so completely blend into the style and content of advertising as effectively as television.

Even more than television soap operas, game shows exploited the very tendency toward consumerism that advertising preyed upon. But Leiss concludes that it is the common style even more than content that has united advertising and television: camera angles, dialogue, acting, and music. "Advertising uses television programming as a system of reference; returning the favor, programming uses advertising as its framework and in some cases its exemplar. 'Sesame Street' adapted the pacing of advertising to the task of teaching preschoolers."[76] The reverse is that some television advertisements imitate the music video format with its fragmentation of time and space and resultant dream-like mood.[77]

The movement of new media into the arena of advertising did not pit medium against medium in a winner-take-all war for advertising revenue. On the contrary, each time a new communications medium took hold, there was a sizable increase in the total amount advertisers spent for advertising. Magazines, radio, and television successively added to the overall fortunes of advertising agents and the communication media.[78]

If the overall amount spent on advertising by advertisers increased, so did the reliance of the mass communications media on advertising revenue. Today radio and television (except for the public versions) are almost totally dependent on advertising money for their operating expenses; newspapers receive about 75 per cent of their income from advertising and magazines between 60 and 100 per cent.[79]

The advertising agencies rationalized the relationship between advertisers and the communications media. Until 1875 the agencies' clients were the media, they assisted in the location of advertisers. Once the power of advertising was widely recognized, the ad agencies found clients among the advertisers.[80] After 1875 the shift in clientele was more or less complete: now the agencies worked for the advertisers. At the bidding of the major businesses, agencies helped the media better understand their respective audiences and shape the form and content of programs to sell products more efficiently.[81] At the same time the agencies explained to businesses what media under what circumstances best served their needs. The agencies were information brokers between two clients: the first (the paying client) had a manufactured product or consumer service to sell; the second had an audience and a communication medium to sell to the first.

Undoubtedly the most profound change in the ability of advertising to persuade people to consume more was the increased reliance on the visual image. After 1910 there was a steady decline in the text and a great increase in display and illustration in print advertising.[82] In his study of magazine advertising between 1920 and 1940, Roland Marchand identified the "visual cliché" as the critical form of advertising appeal. The visual cliché is a set of visual images that form a familiar scene at once both idealized and desirable. By associating a product with the scene, advertising encourages the viewer to transfer the qualities of the scene to the product. The earlier "parables" of the advertising text, such as the "democracy of goods," were being translated into "more emotional, icongraphic forms."[83]

The great advantages of the visual image over the word, as Leiss points out, include: emotional impact, memory retention, and ambiguity.[84] The visual image makes a fundamental appeal to our emotions, not our minds, and is retained in memory longer than is discourse. The full ambiguity of a visual image permits it to be associated with an enormous range of products and services. Television allows for the most complete use of visual images in advertising because of the speed at which it disseminates them and because of its ability to dramatize them more effectively than print media.

As noted earlier Boorstin has called advertising America's most omnipresent and influential form of literature. Jules Henry has termed it a philosophical system, in that it contains an ontology of life.[85] Yet Boorstin's later and more general comment that advertising is a folk culture is the most appropriate depiction.[86] The distinction between high culture and popular culture is well-known. High culture was the culture of the aristocracy and the literate – the culture of higher learning, great literature, art and music, refined manners, and noble virtues. The high culture was centralized and highly formalized. Popular culture was the oral culture of the peasants or the folk. It included local traditions, songs, dances, stories, and, of course, common sense. Popular culture was decentralized and flexible. What held both high and popular culture together was a common religion and a sense of continuity with the past.

Advertising and the programs and stories of the mass media (recall the blurring of the distinction between the two) have become the American popular culture. This popular culture, however, is centralized and rationalized and thus manufactured.[87] One might argue that it is the *only* national culture today, especially in light of the fact that the ruling class is more a technical class than a cultural class.[88] The high culture of the past survives as nostalgia, rather than as a living culture that informs everyday existence.[89]

But there is another even more important difference between advertising culture and previous cultures: novelty and experimentation. Advertising and the attendant mass media create a world of the eternal present, a world in which everything is constantly changing, a world in which our purpose as consumers is always to seek new experiences. Advertising culture, like the technique that gives rise to it, destroys the past by making it irrelevant to moral life yet still permitting it an ephemeral existence in nostalgia and a static existence in history.[90] Is a culture of "self-liquidating" ideals actually a culture? Perhaps only as a "material culture," one whose values are fully reified in consumption.

Mythological Values in Advertising

The values of advertising culture have been identified by a host of researchers. Advertising poses to and answers for the consumer the fundamental question: "How can I be happy through consumption?"[91] Advertising sells "well-being and happiness."[92] Happiness is the paramount value of advertising culture and as such is the most general; it implies and is related to all the others. Happiness is portrayed in advertising as pleasure, increased consumption.[93] Leisure time is the opportunity for consumption and pleasure; hence leisure activity predominates over work in advertising.[94] Happiness is located in the ecstatic expressions on the faces of the actors or models. Even the family when portrayed in advertising is the locus of or background for paradise.[95]

"Advertisements were *secular* sermons, exhortations to seek fulfilment through the consumption of material goods and mundane services."[96] As Marchand concludes, "the cumulative crowning parable of advertising amplified the American dream by proclaiming, 'you can have it all.' "[97] Marchand's choice of the terms "sermons" and "parables" was not by chance, for he realizes that advertising is a liturgy in the multitude of consumer religions.

Second only to happiness and directly related to it in the general idea of well-being is health.[98] Allied to the value of health are those of beauty and youth. All three refer to dimensions of the human body: Health refers to the perfection of the body or at least its general maintenance; beauty refers to its pleasing external appearance; youth, to a combination of health and beauty, to a perfected state of existence. In advertising, youth is reality.[99] As Andren observes, "women are the chosen victims of the 'youth cult,' "[100] in part because they were identified earlier in the twentieth century as the major consumers.

Success and high status as advertising values appear less frequently than the above values. Even here, because of the prepronderance of leisure over work in the ads, high status and success are realized in consumption.[101] Leiss argues that after 1965 there was a marked emphasis on life-style in advertising.[102] The life-styles portrayed are, of course, those of successful and higher status people engaged in activities rather than merely using a product. The activities are leisure activities and are thus presented as consumer services.

Friendship and love appear even less frequently than status and success. If one makes a distinction between sex and love, this finding is not surprising. After 1930 the sensual appeal of products received much greater attention,[104] as did the use of sex to sell the products. Then, too, love and friendship are subtle qualities, difficult to visualize. They are not well matched with the medium of television.[105]

Advertising depicts freedom in two related ways: the free world with its plethora of goods, and the enormous number of choices consumers have.[106] A Wendy's commercial of the 1980s plays this to perfection. In the ad, a small group of Russians sit watching a fashion show in which a stout woman stylelessly attired wears the same garment to show the audience the latest in day-wear, beach-wear, and night-wear. Quickly the scene changes to the United States where freedom is shown to be choosing what to put on your burger while at Wendy's.

Happiness symbolizes the rest of these cultural values and thus provides a basis for their variegated relationships. The reason for this is that happiness is most directly related to the central message of all advertising: increased consumption brings maximum happiness.[107] The advertising ideology or, more precisely, the advertising mythology that makes sense of these values is that of technological utopianism, which is intimately related to the myth of progress. The technological utopia is the future state towards which progress is moving.[108]

This utopian narrative is straightforward. Science and especially technology are leading us to a utopia of maximum production and consumption. Technology insures our collective survival and success in allowing us more efficient control of life and providing solutions to all our problems. This promised land is likewise a world of total consumption. In it people have perfect health, are beautiful, eternally youthful, free to do whatever is pleasurable, and thus completely happy. The myth of technological utopianism is promulgated through the liturgy of advertising. This myth (in the strong sense of the term) is as much a myth as that of any archaic people.

Technological Utopianism

The myth of technological utopianism is equally present in the structure or logic of advertising. I refrain from calling this a narrative structure because of the predominance of visual images in advertising.[109] Neil Postman has exposed this logic most admirably in his interpretation of a classic ad, "The Parable of the Ring around the Collar." The ad typically finds a married couple who normally get along well in a commonplace setting, a restaurant; the waitress notices the husband's dirty shirt collar and calls attention to it. The husband is upset and the wife embarrassed. The next scene shows the wife using the correct detergent that eliminates the unseemly ring around the collar. Finally the couple returns to the restaurant enveloped in ecstatic rapture.[110]

In Postman's analysis there is a narrative in the ad that takes this form: problem, solution, ecstasy. The problem is the dirty collar along with the husband's anger over the social embarrassment; the solution is the advertised brand of detergent; ecstasy is the satisfied expression on the faces of the couple in the aftermath of the solution.

I think, however, that there are two distinct but closely related logics at work in this single ad. Moreover, I maintain that all ads contain either one or the other and often both of these logics. Finally, I suggest that these two logics illustrate perfectly the two dimensions of the myth of technological utopianism: the objective power of technique and its subjective impact upon the consumer.

The two logics are: problem to solution and discontent to content. The problem – solution logic was dominant in advertising until the early twentieth century in a product information format.[111] These earlier advertisements, still relying on the text, described how a product worked more efficiently than its competitors or simply how effective it was. The ad was like a scientific demonstration.

After 1925 advertisers began to use approaches that directly appealed to desire; the consumer was viewed as much an irrational being as a rational being. The visual image became the dominant force in advertisements; the text became its adjunct. Visual images were better suited to demonstrate consumer satisfaction than product efficiency.[112]

Leiss has identified three other advertising formats besides that of product information. The "product image format" provides the product with a number of symbolic qualities by placing it in a natural or human context; the product comes alive. The "personalized format" suggests that the product and its use make you more of a person – happier, admired, respected, and so forth. The "life-style format" associates the product with a collective style of life that includes friends, activities, and satisfaction. These latter three formats – product image, personalized, and life-style are all stressing the relationship between the product and people, that is, the satisfying use of the product over against the mere utility of the product.[113] Yet all four formats continue to be used, for they comprise a unity.

This brings us then to the second logic: discontent to content. Sometimes the discontent is explicitly shown, as in "The Ring Around the Collar" ad. The husband is angry, the wife is embarrassed; both are humiliated. The use of the correct detergent produces emotional satisfaction if not ecstasy. Often, however, the discontent is only intimated. Andren has called this phenomenon the "Hollywood Set." In such an advertisement there is an idealized world, but off the set is the real world of anxiety and discontent. This is one reason, he maintains, that there is so much use of the nostalgic representation of the past.[114]

The two logics, problem-solution and discontent-content, correspond to the two major story-lines of the myth of technological utopianism. Techniques solve all our problems objectively (success) while simultaneously providing us with maximum subjective pleasure through consumption (happiness). Therefore each logic implies the other, whether made explicit or not in the advertisement. The overall myth unifies the two logics.

If the world of advertising is truly a mythological world, then it exists outside of the dialectic of truth and falsehood as understood in a scientific sense. On this level true and false refer to whether something is factual or not. But the world advertising creates is not actual but only possible. As with all mythologized rituals, advertising can withstand the negative test of reality for there is always a next time: the possibility of perfection and total fulfilment in the newest commodity.

The Therapeutic: Happiness and Health as Adjustment

Running parallel to the definition of happiness and health as the sensate well-being promulgated in advertising and achieved in consumption was a definition that made happiness and health a psychological condition acquired through mental adjustment to the environment. Happiness and health as adjustment has its origins in nineteenth-century popular psychologies, whether religious or secular.

Prior to the transformation of happiness into a psychological state, it had assumed political and economic forms in the United States that were a direct consequence of Enlightenment thought. Inspired by the British utilitarians and the French *philosophes*, Jefferson, Madison, and other American founding fathers made happiness to be either a condition of a society with a democratic form of government or a consequence of individual competition and achievement in business.[115] Fortunately for eighteenth century thinkers one could have it both ways. In the nineteenth century American happiness as business success was complemented by the Emersonian idea of happiness as self-fulfilment. This romantic view reached its culmination in William James near the turn of the century but now with a greater emphasis on the psychological exploration of the self and on adaptation to the environment.[116] In little more than a century, happiness had begun to withdraw from the world of politics and business, the public sector, and find refuge in the persona of the individual, the private sector. By making individual psychological adaptation an end in itself, Americans ran the risk of turning adaptation (an active relationship to environment) into adjustment (a passive relationship to environment).

Happiness and health as adjustment first surfaced in the United States in the form of "mind cure," a form of popular religious psychology. Acting on the insight that Americans had become nervous and even anxiety-ridden and that medicine provided neither interest nor remedy, popular psychologists, such as the Reverend Warren Evans, began to provide self-help treatments, as in his 1869 book *The Mental Cure*. Some of the devotees of mind cure were former patients of Phineas Quimley, a practitioner of "mental suggestion."[117] In the beginning mind cure was overtly religious. Pantheistic mind cure enjoined the patient to "think the thoughts of God." Whether through placing one's unconscious in touch with God's thoughts or through auto-hypnosis, better known as positive thinking, the patient was to act freed of anxiety and insecurity. The aim was to produce a trouble-free human being.

Women were the chief customers of mind cure; they also formed the majority of its therapists. In the late nineteenth century women were perceived to be both sensitive and weak. Being sensitive they were experts in emotional relations. Because love was the ultimate form of religious action, women were expected to handle the religious and moral education of the children. But being weak (a necessary concomitant of sensitivity) women stood in need of mind cure.[118] It was no accident, then, that the founder of Christian Science was a woman, Mary Baker Eddy.

Mind cure never became fully respectable; it smacked of a stationary medicine show. Religious groups such as Christian Science and the Unity Church were often perceived as cults, and the secular practitioners of mind cure faced the opposition of medical practitioners. Only when mainline Christian groups and business professions adapted psychological adjustment as a tacit but paramount goal did positive thinking gain wider acceptance.

After 1900 there was a glut of books for businessmen on how to be successful through the power of positive thinking. Dale Carnegie's books and courses were the most popular. (This was discussed in a different context in the preceding chapter.) The point here is that much of the literature claimed an affinity of happiness for success. It was not so much that success brought happiness, as that happiness or health (as adjustment) was a prerequisite for success. Now men needed psychology as much as women. Some forms of positive thinking were advocated as a cure for not being successful! George Beard's nineteenth-century forecast that health might become an end in itself because modern civilization was becoming too stressful was coming true. The pains of becoming successful, or of maintaining success, or of living with the fear of failure, were all too evident.

Concurrent with the growing respectability of popular psychology in business was that in mainline religion. A study of popular religious books between 1875 and 1955 indicates the strong influence of psychological technique. Central themes in this literature are wealth, health, and earthly happiness.[119] The latter theme, happiness in this life, was a dominant topic "almost to the exclusion of any alternative."[120] Although the authors draw a distinction between earthly happiness that is promoted as a consequence of religious commitment and earthly happiness that is independent of religion, both kinds appear in the literature. The distinction, however, is less important than the similarities, for even when religion is associated with happiness it is reduced to the status of a *means* to the end of happiness. The religious literature advocating health, wealth, and happiness succeeded in inverting New Testament teachings about the suffering and rejection that a witness to Christ would necessarily encounter.

No one achieved greater fame in this field than Norman Vincent Peale, a Protestant minister. Like other advocates of auto-manipulation his central message was to reject depressing and obsessive thoughts and accept positive thoughts. *The Power of Positive Thinking* stayed on top of the best seller list for two years beginning in 1952. In this book and related ones like *A Guide to Confident Living, The Art of Real Happiness,* and *Inspiring Messages for Daily Living*, Peale reduced religious advice to the form of cliché. In *Inspiring Messages for Daily Living*, for instance, Peale set forth forty "health-producing, life-changing, power-creating Thought Conditioners," a set of "spirit lifters," and even motivator words. Meyer describes Peale's objectives:

> Peale wanted any given section of his manual read though first, then one thought – a spirit lifter, for instance – was to be read each day. It was to be repeated as often as possible, the patient "savoring its meaning and feeling it drive deep within your nature." At night, before sleep, the booster words were to be repeated: "The Spirit Lifter that I read and committed today lies deeply embedded in my mind. It is now sending off throughout my thoughts its healing, refreshing effects."[121]

Peale had reduced word magic to its lowest form – a technique that mocked common sense.

The popular religious literature underwent several related changes after 1940. The theme that religion makes one successful in terms of wealth declined, although the televangelists have demonstrated that it is resilient. As we saw in the previous chapter, this change corresponds to a redefinition of success as consumption and to a greater emphasis on the success of the organization. This latter emphasis necessitates the *adjustment* of the individual to the organization.[122] Therefore happiness (or health) as a consequence of consumer activity is indirectly linked to happiness as adjustment through this two-fold redefinition of success.

The demise of individual economic success notwithstanding, secularization, which had been latent in the literature up to this point, became manifest. The secularization takes two forms. In the first, religion promotes certain ends that, while spiritual (peace of mind), are not so in a way specific to Christianity; in the second, religion is employed as a means to achieve material ends, such as health, wealth, and happiness. As part of this larger process of secularization, the inspirational religious literature began to emphasize adjustment in a self-conscious way that bordered on fatalism. Adjustment to environment, one's peers, the workplace, was viewed as inevitable. Related to this was an increased reliance upon professional psychology and psychiatry.[123] In the attempt to borrow from the "helping professions," organized religion found itself despoiled. For the tacit question was always present: If religion and the helping professions both promote health and happiness, what is the difference?

The helping professions often preferred to talk about mental health rather than happiness, but the referent was invariably the same – adjustment. In a review of definitions of mental health by practitioners and theorists in several countries, Barbara Wootton concludes that the concept of adjustment is "particularly prominent" and is always implied in those definitions that do not mention it by name.[124] The following is a fairly typical example:

> Let us define mental health as the adjustment of human beings to the world and to each other with a maximum of effectiveness and happiness. Not just efficiency, or just contentment – or the grace of obeying the rules of the game cheerfully. It is all of these together. It is the ability to maintain an even temper, an alert intelligence, socially considerate behavior, and a happy disposition. This I think, is a healthy mind.[125]

In addition to its boy-scout-like quality, this definition links happiness to mental health. Wootton notes that "mental health tends to be equated with happiness."[126]

A study of American mental health conceptions concluded that following the Second World War, the majority of Americans used the idea of psychological adjustment as the criterion for judging the stability and contentment of themselves and others.[127] Maurice North's incisive analysis of professional social work in Great Britain and the United States discovered that social workers' major stated objective was the adjustment of their clients to the environment.[128] Paul Halmos has extended the argument beyond what are specifically referred to as the helping professions to include many personal service occupations. These occupations include, among others, teachers and the clergy. His argument is that any occupation whose function is health, welfare, or education and whose members establish a personal relationship with their clients, qualifies as a therapeutic occupation.[129] Never before were so many preaching and teaching adjustment under the guise of health or happiness or both.

Howard Mumford Jones's history of the conception of happiness in the United States from the eighteenth through the mid twentieth century concludes that the closer one gets to the present, the more dominant is the equation of happiness with adjustment.[130] The happiness peddlers include popular psychologists, newspaper columnists, religious leaders, and professional therapists. It is clear, then, that in the twentieth century happiness and mental health had largely become synonymous, for both concepts were defined as adjustment.

The publication of Philip Rieff's *The Triumph of the Therapeutic* in 1966 was the springboard for a debate on the reality of a therapeutic culture. Goethe was apparently the first to have intimations of a "hospital culture;" Kierkegaard too saw it coming. Rieff's shocking insight was that this imagined state was now a reality: an entire culture was organized in the pursuit of therapeutic goals. A therapeutic culture, in brief, is one in which a "sense of well-being has become the end, rather than a by-product of striving after some superior communal end."[131] A spate of books and articles followed. Some disagreed with his explanation, others with his evaluation, but most agreed that he had called attention to an exceedingly important cultural phenomenon. Christopher Lasch's *Culture of Narcissm* in 1979 became a best seller; he revived the debate but this time from the perspective of the Left.

At the same time some historians began to refer to advertising as a part of the therapeutic ethos equal to if not more important than psychological therapy in the narrower sense.[132] Common to both is the attempt to move the consumer from discontent to content. I have chosen to use *therapeutic* in a narrower way, using the term to refer to the psychological techniques that concentrate on adjustment. This is not to suggest that the similarities between psychological techniques of adjustment and advertising technique are not important. The distinction I wish to draw is a subtle one. In commenting on happiness as psychological adjustment, Jones notes that the issue is posed as "the problem of adjustment between the primitive subliminal urges of our hidden selves and the drab and practical necessities of every day."[133]

Reality can never completely satisfy our desires; at best, it can do so only momentarily. Our desires and needs have to accommodate reality. Psychological techniques develop to help people handle stress and the failure of life to go according to one's expectations. Like religion, therapy is comfort for the misery of living. By contrast, advertising does not promote adjustment but rather unlimited desire and unlimited aspirations in regard to consumption. The mythological world of advertising and the mass media, as we have seen, is a utopian one in which our unlimited desires are perfectly fulfilled. Here is the crux of the matter: therapy and advertising are moving us in opposite directions. One tells us to scale down our desires, the other to enlarge their purview. Moreover, the more that consumption fails to deliver on its advertised promise, the more the consumer is disappointed and anxious and thus in need of therapy. Inadvertently, then, advertising has promoted the demand for therapy well beyond its direct impact through specific commercials about therapy.

And yet these two opposing forces in regard to desire – advertising and psychological techniques of adjustment (therapy) – are brought together in two ways. The first is to turn the psychological techniques of adjustment from self-help books to private therapy into a form of consumption. As consumer services the psychological techniques of adjustment have a rightful place in the mythological world of advertising. The second is to allow the psychological techniques to envelop themselves in the symbolism of happiness and health and in this way to partake of the myth of technological utopianism. The techniques of adjustment, then, are forms of magic[134] to the extent that objects of consumption are talismans: magical practices and magical objects.

The Mythological Symbolism of Happiness and Health and Success and Survival

More than philosophical or even common-sense concepts are happiness, health, success, and survival symbols.[135] All myths contain a set of interrelated symbols. For instance, Mircea Eliade has demonstrated that for archaic peoples the sun, moon, sky, water, rocks, and so forth were symbols that formed a larger system in that each particular symbol implied all the others.[136] The reason is that each symbol was part of a unifying myth. In Eliade's examples the mythical narrative was invariably one about the creation and renewal of nature. The sun, moon, sky, water, and rocks all have a part to play in nature and its creation.

Analogously, I am suggesting that happiness, health, success, and survival are symbols, each one of which implies the others, that are held together by the myth of technological utopianism. You may have noticed, especially in the discussion of happiness and health, how slippery these terms are. This is the way of real symbols. This is not to say that they are vague and meaningless. Just the opposite. They overflow with meaning because each symbol is related to and involves every other symbol.

Happiness and health each has two distinct sets of meanings. Happiness refers both to consumption and to adjustment; health refers to the well-being and perfection of the body and to adjustment (mental health). Happiness and health have a common meaning in adjustment. At the same time happiness as consumption and health as the perfection of the body have a common meaning in physical well-being. Happiness and health, then, have two overall meanings: physical well-being and emotional well-being (adjustment). But these two overall meanings are related. For as Jones has noted, physical health is a persistent theme in definitions of happiness, including adjustment.[137] Moreover, advertising suggests that a consumption-oriented life-style is necessary to be adjusted. Consistent with the myth of technological utopianism, emotional well-being (adjustment) is contingent upon physical well-being.

Success and survival are related to each other and imply happiness and health as well. We saw in the previous chapter that individual success was redefined in terms of consumption and happiness. Moreover, collective success demanded the adjustment (happiness or health) of employee to the organization. The idea of survival contains the notion of adjustment. Success and survival are mythical symbols that are related to technique in its *collective productive* capacity, whereas happiness and health are related to technique in its ability to provide for *individual consumption*. The myth of technological utopianism unites the two sides of technique and thus assures that the four mythological symbols mutually imply one another.

The social setting for the collective success or survival that technique guarantees is the nation-state. In the nineteenth century, the nation-state was able to combine a myth of origins with the myth of progress that promised a utopian future. As technological utopianism grew stronger in the twentieth century, the nation-state, while still sacred, was reduced to the context within which the utopia would be realized. More important was the technological nature of the utopia. Technique is experienced as sacred today.[138] The relative shift in emphasis from nation to technique is reflected in two related ideological changes. The first is that every major political ideology in the second half of the twentieth century – socialism, communism, and capitalism – made technological growth the cornerstone of its system. Second, just as it became clear that nationalism was a stronger force than the more general political ideologies, it was equally apparent that nationalism was really not an ideology (in the strict sense of the term) anymore. Nationalism today simply means the *power* of the nation-state, an absolute minimalist ideology.

Now this places the nation-state in perfect harmony with technological utopianism. This myth is about the two sides of technique: its productive power as *means* and its outcome in consumption as *object* (goods and services). But technique is, after all, only power. So nationalism and technological utopianism are perfectly matched, for both have turned power into a value.

If the nation-state is committed to technological growth, a constantly changing utopia, reality does not easily accommodate it. Not only is there the destructive political and economic competition for technological growth, but the growth itself is destructive. Baudrillard has observed that technological systems appear to go through cycles of growth and repair. Growth in technological systems is uneven; moreover, the areas of greatest growth eventually demand the most damage control.[139] We have devastated our physical environment in the quest for ever more sources of energy and wealth; now we must repair the damage.

Therefore success (as technological growth) and survival (as technological repair) stand in contradictory relationship. Analogous to this is the relationship of physical health to happiness as consumption. We have discovered that many of the things we consume are injurious to our health. This explains in part why there is a national obsession with physical health. Daily advice in the media about cholesterol levels, alcoholism, diet, and nutrition is omnipresent. Not all the advice and interest in health, however, is purely defensive and survivalist in orientation. Some of it is concerned with the technical perfection of the human body – advice about beauty, muscle development, looking young. This latter advice is more in keeping with the idea of growth and consumption. Therefore contradictions in the real world of technology – growth and repair – are reflected in the ambiguity of these mythological symbols.

Now that we have examined the mythological values or symbols that form the basis of the modern morality, we turn to the forms of prescription and proscription in which these values are expressed. The first and most important form of moral imperative is *technique*.

4

From the Moral to the Technical:

the Necessary

Morality is comprised of mythological symbols (values) and a sense of direction as expressed in paradigms, guidelines, limits, rules, or imperatives. The latter realize the former, make them concrete, and put them into practice. The four symbols I have identified – success, survival, happiness and health – make up the fundamental and exclusive domain of value in modern morality. Every other possible value, whether it be love, security, freedom, or justice, is a variation of or combination of these basic symbols. The main problem in respect to these symbols or values is that they have made power itself into a value – success and survival as collective power, and happiness and health as the individual power of consumption.

Equally striking, however, are the forms that morality (or its absence) has assumed today. One of these, and the most important, is technique. As I pointed out in chapter 1, modern morality is organized around three major dialectics: the necessary and the ephemeral; the necessary and the compensatory; and within the necessary, manipulation and adjustment. The ephemeral and the compensatory will largely be dealt with in chapters 5 and 6, the necessary in this chapter.

Technique is the necessary. By this I mean that it is the single most important factor in the organization of modern societies. It is so significant that one can rightfully speak of modern societies forming a technological civilization.[1] Ellul's definition is apt: "Technique is the totality of methods rationally arrived at and having absolute efficiency

(for a given stage of development) in every field of human activity."[2]
This concept of technique is historical, for it recognizes that technique
prior to the nineteenth century has little in common with the technique
after this period. Certainly technique is a universal dimension of human
existence; humans have always discovered means to confront the
dilemmas of existence. Before the nineteenth century, technique was not
dominated by the goal of efficiency. The techniques of the past were
concerned as much with aesthetic expression as with efficacy. Moreover,
they were integrated into the larger culture and thus symbolically related
to other activities. Because these techniques were imbued with moral
and religious significance, they did not dominate the culture.

In the nineteenth century the great reversal begins: technique in the
sense of efficiency becomes an end in itself. The myth of progress
provides the impetus to unleash technological growth. As the number of
techniques proliferate at a dizzying rate, the attempt to integrate them
into the larger culture becomes futile. Because modern technique is a
rational and logical substitute for symbolically mediated experience and
tradition, those domains of culture not subject to technique become
suspect and are thus put on the defensive. Technique ultimately comes
to dominate (and even eliminate) culture by the mid twentieth century.[3]

Efficiency is the first characteristic of modern technique; holism is the
second. Holism refers to the conscious effort to find multiple
applications for a technique beyond its intended usage but especially
to the rational coordination of techniques. Technique (as the totality of
methods) tends to form a system.[4] The computer permits the
coordination of technique by calculating and processing an enormous
mass of information. This technological system, as we will see later, is an
open system, but one without true feedback (self-regulation).

Both Ellul[5] and Mumford[6] have seen that modern technique includes
more than machines; there are both material and non-material
techniques. The former are obvious, the latter, more subtle. Non-
material techniques have as their object the control of human beings.
Although material techniques are sometimes applied to humans, as in
surgery, non-material techniques' exclusive domain is the organizational
and psychological dimensions of human existence.

Techniques of organization or administration and psychological
techniques make up the two main categories of non-material technique.
Organizational technique refers to bureaucracy and related techniques of
administration such as human relations. Psychological technique
includes advertising, propaganda, human and public relations,
therapeutic techniques, and the plethora of "how-to" manuals for
"effective" relationships (*Parental Effectiveness Training* and the like).
Clearly there is an overlap here, for the technique of administration

draws upon the vast reservoir of psychological technique. Both kinds of non-material technique (from this point on we will refer to them as human techniques) have as their goal the *manipulation* and *control* of human beings. It is historically apparent that the more technology has been used to exploit the forces of nature, the more it was necessary to turn the same technical logic to the organization and control of the human environment.

Much of the action that was traditionally motivated and regulated by ritual, manners, and social morality is now encapsulated in human technique. The symbolically mediated experiences embedded in ritual, manners, and morality provided a flexibility to these cultural forms; human technique is by intent inflexible, for it represents the search for the "single best method." Moreover, it is a mistake to think of moral norms largely in terms of logical concepts and rules.[7] While it is true that they could become atrophied into abstract, rigid rules, concrete moral norms had a rudimentary metaphorical dimension, thus permitting their analogous application to a variety of contexts. At the level of everyday reality, then, social morality was a loose amalgam of dialectical concepts, that is, concepts whose meaning came in part from their context of application.

Human technique as a set of objective rules and procedures reduces its recipient to an abstraction; it denies the individuality of its object. Human technique makes everyone equal by ignoring individual differences. If parents use Parental Effectiveness Training (a technique of child-rearing) to raise each child, they in effect reject the real individual differences between their children. When salesmen use a standardized selling technique, they make each customer the same. Bureaucratic rules have the same effect: the reduction of the individual to an abstract object.[8] At the same time human technique denies the subjectivity of its object, it suppresses that of the subject as well. In depending upon technical procedure instead of personal experiences, one is denying one's own subjectivity. Technique respects the individuality of neither user nor recipient.

Finally, human technique destroys meaning. Technique, as we have seen, is preoccupied with efficiency, with the most effective means. In other words, technique is exclusively a means of power, autonomous with respect to moral ends. Insofar as meaning arises from the collective attempt to limit and symbolize power, technique thus lacks meaning. All attempts to infuse technique with meaning are futile, for technique is not integrated into the larger culture; rather it suppresses culture by rendering symbols ephemeral.[9]

In summary, the differences between traditional lived morality and human technique include the following: morality is flexible, intersubjective, and meaningful; human technique is rigid, objective, and meaningless (or to put it another way, makes power itself a value).

Organizational Technique: Bureaucratic Rules

As one of the two major forms of human technique, organizational technique is usually referred to as bureaucracy. We should keep two points in mind: bureaucracy is a form of technique; and as such it employs psychological techniques that are in use outside the organization as well.

What is the nature of technical rules? As previously indicated technique is a logical procedure whose sole purpose is efficiency. Or in other words, technique contains a set of "effective procedures," that is, rules that guarantee a successful outcome. Effective procedures can be contrasted with the "state-transition" rules in a game that permit the player a range of choices in moving from one state to the next. In chess, for instance, players have a number of possible moves from one play to the next within the limits of how a piece may be moved.[10] Technical rules as effective procedures permit no choices, for they purport to be the single best method. Technical rules are effective procedures for making a decision or acting.

Both technical rules and state-transition rules can be contrasted with traditional moral norms. The former are general and thus abstract.[11] They constitute a logic; a set of technical rules is a closed logical system, a set of state-transition rules, an open system. Moreover, their meaning is direct and fully rational. By contrast, moral norms are symbolic in terms of meaning and dialectical in terms of form. That is, traditional moral norms have an indirect meaning that links them to other moral norms as part of a larger cultural narrative such as a myth. Moreover, moral norms are expressed as dialectical concepts because their meaning arises in part from the context to which they are applied. Hence they are less general and abstract than logical rules that have a fixed meaning no matter what the context.

Technical rules are rapidly supplanting moral norms by making them irrelevant. A technological civilization is one in which the means absorb the ends. Traditional norms place limits on power; technical norms are a form of power. And yet technical norms participate in the myth of technological utopianism whose chief values include success, survival, happiness, and health. In this sense they are moral norms for they have an indirect or symbolic meaning. At the same time, however, this meaning is a false meaning because these mythical values, as previously indicated in chapter 3, are only expressions of power itself. Therefore both the form and "meaning" of technical norms is power.

Bureaucracy and its rules appear to be omnipresent. From the sixteenth century onward the uninterrupted growth in the power of the state has been accompanied by the bureaucratization of government, which, in turn, aided the later bureaucratization of the economy.[12] All modern societies today are heavily bureaucratized. James Q. Wilson, however, contends that the United States uses rules to eliminate discretion more than any modern democracy.[13] But even more than eliminating discretion, rules proliferate to deal with various inefficiencies.[14] The cardinal sin of a technological civilization is, of course, inefficiency. Street crime, alcoholism, obesity, depression, and ignorance make for communities unfit for business and industry and an undisciplined work force. The proliferation of civil, criminal, and administrative law continues unabated as does that of human techniques designed to eliminate such destructive behavior. Never before has any civilization been subject to such a maze of bureaucratic rules, laws, and human techniques.

Formal rules generate paperwork that is unaffectionately known as red tape. The paperwork becomes a rough index of the quantity of rules. Federal administrative agencies produce more than 50,000 pages of regulations (in preliminary and final form) each year. An estimation of 100,000 pages was made for 1980. Congress gives birth annually to at least 1000 pages of public laws.[15] Just keeping track of the rules in a single governmental agency is a monumental task. The proliferation of rules in the corporation has occurred apart from governmental regulation because the modern corporation is itself heavily bureaucratized.[16] Yet the relationship between the political state and the corporation, even in the United States, grows increasingly symbiotic.[17] Today, ignorance of the rule is the fate of every man. Before analyzing the different kinds of bureaucratic rules, let us briefly look at three case studies, one in the private sector and two in the public sector.

The first is Elinor Langer's study of the Commercial Department of the New York Telephone Company, a division of AT&T. Ms. Langer became a Customer's Service Representative, who handles complaints and calls for new equipment and services, not to pursue a career but to discover how lower-level employees, experienced industrialized work; she was a participant-observer from the outset. Like so many other companies, the New York Telephone Company used a rigid system to train employees. The training program established a number of work-related rules that were repeated in instruction and in the correction of errors in training sessions until the employee became (in Langer's words) a machine. She summarizes the three rules governing a referral when the representative lacks expertise: get immediate control of the contact; always express interest in the case and indicate willingness to help; get his consent to this arrangement.[18] The first rule suggests that one is not to allow the customer to divulge too much extraneous information – such as feelings at being inconvenienced or worse. Instead, one lets the customer know that the Customer's Service Representative is a capable professional, albeit not a therapist. The second rule, which is actually a commentary on the first, contradicts the first rule. Once the customer has allowed the representative to take charge of the relationship, only then does the representative show concern. At this point the representative elicits more information, but only that sufficient to decide whether the customer needs to be referred to someone else. Finally, the representative is required to obtain the customer's consent to the referral. The object of this burlesque of common sense is to manipulate the customer into thinking that the representative is a confident professional, that the representative actually cares about the customer, and that professional expertise consists in knowing to whom to refer the customer. The representative must never appear weak or stupid, for she represents the New York Telephone Company.

Ms. Langer describes the 18 rules for handling a request for a telephone cord:

Fact-finding:
1   Business or residence
2   New or existing service
3   Reason for request
    (a)   handset or mounting cord
    (b)   approximate length
4   Type of set or location
5   Other instruments in the household and where located
6   Customer's phone number

Then you get:
Off the line where you
1   Get customer's records
2   Think and plan what to do
3   Check reference materials
4   Check with supervisor if necessary

Then you return to the line with a:
Recommendation:
1   Set stage for recommendation

2   Suggest alternative where appropriate or
3   Accept order for cord
4   Suggest appropriate length
    (a)   Verify handset or mounting
5   Present recommendation for suitable equipment that "goes with" request including monthly rental (for instance an extension bell).
6   Determine type of instrument and color
7   Quote total non-recurring charges
8   Arrange appointment date, access to the apartment, and who to see.[19]

Even the trainees, imbued as they were with the company's ideology, sensed the absurdity of it all.

The second example is drawn from William Gibson's account of how the Vietnam War was administered.[20] Secretary of Defense McNamara, employing what is sometimes known as systems analysis,[21] attempted to run the war as an exercise in statistical management. Every object, person, and behavior must be quantified so that the ratio of cost to benefit can be calculated. Henry Kissinger's view of American foreign policy formed the backdrop for McNamara's deadly management game. Kissinger claimed that "*technology plus managerial skills*" gave the United States the wherewithal to make the international political and economic system conform to its reality. Anticipating Baudrillard, Kissinger understood that technology was itself creating reality by first simulating it. In short, the United States could impose its (technical) version of reality anywhere.[22]

Gibson describes a nightmare in which managers in the Defense Department imposed a set of rules and productivity norms upon soldiers in the field that were out of touch with a reality that could not be bent to fit their mathematical models. There were two sets of rules of engagement, each written on a card and distributed to the soldier: one in regard to the civilian population, the other in regard to the enemy. The former was called the "Nine Rule" card:

1   Remember, we are guests here. We make no demands and seek no special treatment.
2   Join with the people! Understand their life, use phrases from their language and honor their customs and laws.
3   Treat women with politeness and respect.
4   Make personal friends among the soldiers and common people.
5   Always give the Vietnamese the right of way.
6   Be alert to security and ready to react with your military skill.
7   Don't attract attention by loud, rude or unusual behavior.

8 Avoid separating yourself from the people by a display of wealth or privilege.
9 Above all else you are members of the U.S. Military Forces on a difficult mission, responsible for all your official and personal actions. Reflect honor upon yourself and the United States of America.[23]

The latter card was referred to as The Enemy in Your Hands card and contained five rules:

1 Handle him firmly, promptly, but humanely.
2 Take the captive quickly to security.
3 Mistreatment of any captive is a criminal offense. Every soldier is personally responsible for the enemy in his hands.
4 Treat the sick and wounded captive as best you can.
5 All persons in your hands, whether suspects, civilians, or combat captives, must be protected against violence, insults, curiosity, and reprisals of any kind.[24]

The treatment of prisoners, then, is supposed to approximate that of civilians.

At the same time that these normative rules were in effect, productivity norms were being stringently enforced. The "war-managers" believed the Vietnam War could be conducted according to sound management principles and cost-benefit analysis. Body count was among the most important forms of production. Using the ratio of American and Republic of Vietnam dead to Viet Cong dead, or sometimes merely the number of enemy dead, war-managers "measured" the skill level of combat units. Because a high body count was necessary for promotion, high-ranking officers often established productivity norms for their underlings.[25] As the pressure on the United States to win the war as quickly as possible mounted, the war-managers voraciously demanded higher body counts. This consequently led to "systematic falsification of battle reports, routine violation of the rules of engagement and regulations covering treatment of prisoners, and systematic slaughter of Vietnamese noncombatants."[26]

The theoretical rules of engagement in regard to civilians and the enemy were reduced to one *practical* rule, the " 'Mere Gook Rule': 'If it's dead and it's Vietnamese, it's VC.' "[27] It was not just that civilians were counted as Viet Cong, but that air strikes that produced high body counts became more indiscriminate. At the same time the South Vietnamese civilians became expendable, so did American and Republic of Vietnam troops. Because of pressures for high body count and the conviction that "artillery, jet fighter-bombers, and helicopter gunships" were the chief means of victory, the soldiers were "seen as a kind of migrant labor force of only marginal importance."[28] Clearly the need to run the war efficiently was the only issue. Imbued as we are with the idea that there are no rules convening modern warfare, we are still shocked by the cynical "expenditure" of our own troops and South Vietnamese civilians. Bureaucratic administration left to itself turns all moral issues into technical ones and thereby makes success/survival the ultimate value.

The third example is drawn from Thomas Scheff's study of the legal processing of mental patients in a large urban area in a midwestern state.[29] After a temporary admission (with a psychiatric intake examination) to a state mental institution, there was a judicial hearing (usually within a week) to determine whether the patient should be involuntarily committed. Solicited for review in the judicial hearing were the examinations of two court-appointed psychiatrists.

There are in general two legal grounds for involuntary admission: (1) that the individual is a clear danger to himself or others, and (2) that the person is incapable of caring for himself. Twenty-five hospital psychiatrists, those who conduct intake exams, were asked a series of questions about the most recent ten consecutive patients each had admitted. Roughly two-thirds of the admitted cases did not satisfy either of the two legal criteria for involuntary admission.

At the same time, the research team observed 116 judicial hearings; in 86 cases the court-appointed psychiatrists did not establish the mental illness of the patient. Moreover, there were 48 cases in which the patient appeared to be completely normal. There was not a single instance, however, in which the release of the patient was recommended. They examined another 80 cases, only to find the same result – no recommendation for release.

The psychiatric examinations of patients, it turns out, averaged ten minutes. Psychiatrists made a decision on only the skimpiest of evidence and often seemed to prejudge the cases. The examinations were in the main "careless and hasty."[31]

The researchers were confronted with a discrepancy between the intake psychiatrists' tacit admission that most patients did not satisfy either legal criterion for involuntary commitment and the court-appointed psychiatrists' apparent assumption that all sick patients are mentally ill. Now the law is clear that the court starts with the presumption of sanity so that the burden of proof is on the psychiatrist and other court officials to conclude otherwise.

Scheff discovered three major reasons for the court-appointed psychiatrists' assumption of insanity: pecuniary, ideological, and political. I think a fourth factor is implicit in his analysis – efficiency. The court-appointed psychiatrists were paid on the basis on how many patients they examined, hence the brief examination. By itself, however, this does nothing to explain the assumption of insanity, for one could just as well conduct brief examinations with the assumption of sanity. The key to understanding the assumption of mental illness is the psychiatric ideology:

1   The condition of mentally ill persons deteriorates rapidly without psychiatric assistance.
2   Effective psychiatric treatments exist for most mental illnesses.
3   Unlike surgery, there are no risks involved in involuntary psychiatric treatment: it either helps or is neutral, it can't hurt.
4   Exposing a prospective mental patient to questioning, cross-examination, and other screening procedures exposes him to the unnecessary stigma of trial-like procedures, and may do further damage to his mental condition.
5   There is an element of danger to self or others in most mental illness. It is better to risk unnecessary hospitalization than the harm the patient might do himself or others.[32]

The fifth proposition about the danger the mentally ill pose to the community is both a reflection of and stimulus to the political pressure on court-appointed psychiatrists not to release anyone suspected of being insane, for the media love to call attention to recidivists. The psychiatric ideology and perceived political pressure meant that psychiatrists would assume those they examined were mentally ill.

It appears, however, that the demand for efficiency plays an important part in the handling of the mentally ill. The court-appointed psychiatrists operated according to a set of rules that were more than tacit:

1   Spend as little time as possible on each case.
2   Assume insanity.
3   Find one piece of evidence to substantiate this assumption.

Certainly the contractual arrangements with court-appointed psychiatrists (paid by the number of patients processed) encouraged a high productivity rate. But this entrepreneurial efficiency is set within a larger public efficiency that engulfs the entire court system. It is sometimes called bureaucratic justice.

Abraham Blumberg's study of a metropolitan criminal court called attention to how an overburdened court used guilty-plea negotiation as a way of processing the accused efficiently.[33] A trial is an expensive and time-consuming activity; the ability to pressure the accused into pleading guilty at a rate of 90% or higher enabled the court to handle a large number of cases rather quickly. Blumberg suggested that the court-appointed defense attorney usually acted on behalf of the system rather than the client.[34]

Erving Goffman's reflections on the necessity of mental institutions puts the matter into the most general perspective.[35] He argues that mental institutions are essentially bureaucracies set up to control the largest number of inmates with the smallest number of staff. Virtually everything that is done in the institution is done in the interest of institutional efficiency rather than rehabilitation. Yet this institutional efficiency is set within a larger societal efficiency:

> Mental hospitals are not found in our society because supervisors, psychiatrists, and attendants want jobs; mental hospitals are found because there is a market for them. If all the mental hospitals in a given region were emptied and closed down today, tomorrow relatives, police, and judges would raise a clamor for new ones; and these true clients of the mental hospital would demand an institution to satisfy their needs.[36]

Mental patients are those against whom there are complaints or who complain too much themselves; they create havoc for the rest of us.[37] As societies because more heavily technologized each remaining inefficiency seems more problematic.[38]

From work to war to the control of deviant behavior, technical rules reign supreme. The examples could, of course, be multiplied indefinitely. Of special note is the distinction between the formal work rules at the New York Telephone Company and the informal rules of the Vietnam war and of processing the mentally ill. The "Mere Gook Rule" and the assumption of insanity rule (and related rules) are informal rules that violate certain legal or moral norms that govern the organization. This is perfectly in accord with our thesis: under the pressure of organizational efficiency, moral and legal norms are negated in the interest of technical rules. Not all informal rules, however, are in the interest of organizational efficiency. In the following chapter we will look at peer group norms that run contrary to organizational efficiency. Langer's study of the New York Telephone Company indicates that administrators can prevent informal work rules from developing if they are able to exercise enough psychological control over employees and keep them under effective surveillance.[39] To prevent the emergence of informal norms, then, requires techniques that themselves may well violate moral and legal norms, leading to ever more complex situations.

Students of organizations have documented some movement away from bureaucratic centralization. Charles Perrow's classic statement is that the decentralization of power can occur efficiently when there is a centralization of psychological assumptions about work and the organization.[40] Shoshana Zuboff's study of several organizations indicates that information systems can lead either to decentralization or greater centralization of power.[41] Decentralization sometimes leads to a diminution of rules, in other instances to a proliferation of rules, but with employee participation in their continual revision. The primary question, however, is whether decentralization actually increases the organization's hold over its employees. If the answer is yes, then we can safely conclude that the transformation of moral norms into technical rules is even more complete with decentralization.

In exploring this issue we need to distinguish among those rules primarily about work, those about the organization, and those about the worker. Such a distinction has to be qualified with the realization that all three types of rules are tightly related. The simplest and most direct way of controlling work next to personal surveillance is the establishment of productivity norms. This is in keeping with the intent of Taylorism – to separate the laborer from his labor.[42] The measurement of "output" becomes a means to increase productivity. Although some analysts maintain that the establishment of productivity norms for complex tasks eventually leads to a corruption of the quality of performance, the measurement of productivity continues to be used even in regard to highly skilled and intellectual labor. Ida Hoos's acerbic analysis of systems analysis and the Public-Programming-Budgeting System (PPBS) indicates that the effort to measure virtually every human outcome continues unabated.[43] Even universities feel compelled to measure faculty productivity. Related to productivity norms are work rules that cover such behavior as absences, tardiness, smoking, drug use, gambling, theft, and the destruction of company property.[44] Direct surveillance, productivity norms, and work rules make up a large part of what Perrow calls first-order controls. They are, in his view, the means for "disciplining a labor force in low-complexity organizations existing in a favorable labor market."[45] They are still used in more complex organizations under different labor market conditions, but have been partially supplanted by more sophisticated forms of control, ones designed in part to elicit less resistance on the part of workers.

Rules that center on the organization itself are rules of coordination. Specialization (one of the major characteristics of bureaucracy) is the other side of the totalization that is maximum efficiency. Totalization is a consequence of the coordination of all the various specialized functions in the organization.[46] Hierarchy, which is supposed to assist in coordination, complicates efficiency by adding a vertical flow of information to the horizontal one.[47] The source of hierarchical power is the control of information.

Horizontal coordination involves reconstructing a task or set of tasks into a linear logic of behaviors. This is, of course, the essence of the factory system and Taylor's theory of scientific management. For tasks that can readily be quantified and can be more or less temporally and spatially segregated from other tasks, a linear system can be constructed. Perrow uses the term "tight coupling" to refer to a system with a large number of time-dependent processes and invariant sequences that results in the "one best way" being programmed.[48] Tight coupling works best in a linear system.

Complex systems, on the other hand, involve multiple interactive subsystems (of tasks and operations) that are dependent upon one another for information. Complex systems cannot be fully understood because not all the complex interactions can be anticipated.[49] Prime examples of a complex system are a nuclear power plant and a university. The former is a tightly coupled complex system, the latter a loosely coupled one. A system that is loosely coupled is one that is flexible in its decisions and procedures. Bureaucracies tend to be complex systems in part because they require both horizontal and vertical coordination simultaneously. They differ tremendously, however, to the degree they coordinate activity in a "loose" or "tight" manner.

With the onset of the computer have come management information systems and the ability to coordinate rapidly a large number of subsystems within and between organizations. Shoshana Zuboff's massive study of the use of information technology in several industrial plants and corporations clearly demonstrates that management information systems can either reinforce bureaucratic authority or subvert it. The logical conclusion of information technology is the creation of an "informated" workplace in which workers have equal access to information; incorrectly used, information technology produces an "automated" workplace which only reinforces the hierarchical control of information.[50]

The computer allows for the establishment of an "electronic text" in which the organization's entire spectrum of work, including both procedures and practical knowledge, can be made visible and even quantified. The creation of a single electronic text means, of course, that the text is both a comprehensive logic and a system of specialized information. This leads to what Zuboff calls a "radical centralization" of power.[51] This power is not, however, one based on human experience and cultural tradition; rather it is the abstract and impersonal power of technique. If the electronic text invariably centralizes power, it can concurrently lead to a decentralization of power. If all employees have access to the computer system, then hierarchical authority (that which is based on the control of information and communication) is made superfluous. Computer or information systems used to their fullest potential contradict the hierarchical dimension of bureaucracy.

Zuboff's forecast about the workplace of the future includes a model of the informated organization.[52] Workers will have both the computer skills to master the entire program and make changes in it when necessary and have full access to the program. Instead of manager/employee relationships there will be collegial relations. She envisages the workers organized (symbolically if not spatially) in a series of concentric circles around the center: the electronic text, the data base. One's distance from the center is a direct reflection of the "range and comprehensiveness" of responsibility and the extent of one's accountability to the organization. All in all the informated workplace will blur the distinction between blue-collar and white-collar worker as everyone becomes a computer programmer to a greater or lesser extent.[53] The worker's skills based on practical knowledge decline, while his computer-based skills increase. The opportunity for mutual participation in the system's operations and for common learning will produce a shared sense of responsibility. Zuboff claims that this will produce an "anticipatory conformity" to avoid being shamed by one's peers.[54]

The informated workplace is already being experimented with. As one might expect, the resistance of middle managers is enormous.[55] They much prefer to have an automated workplace. This is one in which humans are turned into machines; that is, they are given a minimum of information (only what is necessary for the specific task), little if any flexibility in the performance of the job, and no chance to alter the system. Such an inflexible system is called an expert system; it contains a set of decision-rules or effective procedures that represents the experience of successful practitioners reduced to calculative rationality. Barbara Garson has documented the use of expert systems that in effect automate the workplace (without the replacement of personnel by machines). For employees at McDonalds to airline reservationists to stock brokers and estate planners, expert systems have rendered trivial their contribution to work.[56]

Stockbrokers, for example, have a number of expert systems for financial planning from which to choose: Pathfinder, College Builder, and Home Builder. Garson reports on an interview with a young Merrill Lynch broker:

Jeff showed me a College Builder plan. This particular printout, many times longer than the original questionnaire, anticipated costs of over $300,000 to send three specific children to three specific universities in the years from 1998 to 2009. College Builder calculated the annual savings necessary to pay the projected college bills if the parents began investing right now in TIGRS (pronounced "tigers," the acronym for Treasury Investment Growth Receipts) to be held in tax-saving custodial accounts for each child.[57]

The final end of modern management, according to Garson, is to reduce the labor of the worker to a fully objectified technique, for the performance of which he can be held accountable at all times.[58]

Whether modern organizations turn in the direction of an automated or informated workplace, the use of information systems allows information to assume a normative cast. The rules of the bureaucracy come to rest in the information system in one of two ways. The first is the expert system, which contains decision-rules (effective procedures) and makes decisions when fed the proper information. The second case is a data base with decision-rules subject to modification. And yet even here (Zuboff's informated workplace) the tendency will be for the informated workplace to approximate an automated (expert system) workplace. How can any individual have complete abstract knowledge about the work of a complex organization in relation to the *world beyond the computer*? This is the crux of the matter: each individual worker is supposed to master the electronic text, but no individual can have sufficient knowledge about the work of an entire complex organization to prevent the information system from becoming largely automated. Partial knowledge is dangerous, for it may change in the context of the knowledge of the whole. Therefore, the tendency will be to defer to the extant information system and to alter it only in minor ways. Zuboff's informated workplace only makes sense in regard to organizations that are relatively small and produce a material product.

The introduction of the computer into business and government in the 1950s resulted, among other things, in an indiscriminate generation of data and a proliferation of data collection systems.[59] The result is an enormous increase of information. This kind of computer-generated information is radically different from the information used in traditional societies. The latter is practical knowledge, knowledge gained from experience and made meaningful in the context of tradition, myth, and ritual. The former is a kind of theoretical knowledge, the purpose of which is to enable us to adjust to or manipulate the world for technical purposes.[60] In modern technological societies, truth and reality become one: "truth becomes success in relation to reality."[61] The purpose of this "service-information" is to better enable us to adjust to what is and to manipulate reality according to what is possible. The what is and what is possible refer to a purely quantitative reality – a reality of objects, material images, and reified qualities. The truly symbolic eludes the domain of service-information and the computer. Information systems are therefore normative in respect to a reality reduced to power.

The third type of rule is that which centers on the worker herself. These rules may be either explicit or implicit and are part of a larger set of psychological controls. Perrow's analysis of the centralization/ decentralization paradox suggests that an organization can safely decentralize authority when it controls the premises or the assumptions employees make about their work and the organization.[62] This is both the most subtle and most effective form of control. It would appear to work best on managers, most of whom have been imbued with the business ideology in college. The implicit rules of the ideology include the following: (1) never criticize the organization in public, and (2) do whatever is necessary to allow the organization to succeed or to survive.

For employees who are not managers, more explicit forms of psychological control are required, anything from the old human relations to the new "humanized management." The human relations and participatory democracy approaches to employee control are merged in the quality circle technique that originated in Japan in the 1960s and spread to the United States. A quality circle is a "small group of workers in the same area of production, usually led by a foreman, who 'shares with management the responsibility for locating and solving problems of coordination and productivity.' "[63] The aim of the quality circle, apart from its ideological defense, is to increase the productivity of workers by convincing them that the company genuinely cares for them so that they will begin to pressure one another to meet quantitative and qualitative standards as satisfied team players.

Guillermo Grenier's study of quality circles at Ethicon-Albuquerque, "a suture-making subsidiary" of Johnson and Johnson, demonstrates humanized management in practice. Although Ethicon-Albuquerque used the quality circle technique in part to prevent the plant from becoming unionized, it also thought it could improve worker morale and increase productivity. Facilitators (who worked for management) dominated the meetings that had become mandatory for members of each production team; they controlled the agenda but still needed to appear open to worker suggestion.[64] Team decisions never affected the distribution of power in the plant, nor were they ever important to either management or labor.

According to Grenier, the humanized management that creates the trappings of participatory democracy as a way of manipulating workers

is a "method of de-bureaucratizing control" that possesses "greater sophistication, efficiency, and subtlety" than typical bureaucratic control. And yet this technique of psychological control is set within a larger bureaucratic structure. It is a case, once again, of the centralization/decentralization paradox. Grenier describes the seven characteristics of de-bureaucratizing control: (1) personalized authority of a manager who is "one of us;" (2) spontaneous creation of rules as threats to the organization's goals develop; (3) managerial latitude to chastise workers for deviant acts unrelated to work efficiency; (4) mandatory participation; (5) preventing team decisions from being effective; (6) the attitude that peers are responsible for one another's performance as a justification for actual peer pressure; and (7) the fiction that the difference in power between workers and managers is offset by their common commitment to corporate culture.[65]
Informal rules thrived in this climate:

> It was a rule that team members interview potential employees and evaluate their capabilities and ability to fit into the team concept. It was a rule that team members evaluate each other on a wide range of issues, not all clearly related to production. It was a rule that team members discuss personal difficulties at meetings to help the facilitator decide whether and what intervention was required. It was a rule for peers to control and regulate each other. It was even a rule that workers had to belong to a team and attend team meetings.[66]

These rules were necessary because without them participation in the quality circle program would have vanished. The workers knew to a greater or lesser extent that they were being manipulated, but the ideology of quality control made it difficult for them to articulate their grievances. How can one effectively oppose participatory democracy for the worker without appearing to be anti-labor and even anti-American?
Both the use of the computer to create an informated workplace and the use of psychological techniques such as quality control permit a certain measure of decentralization, but invariably at the expense of greater centralization: a centralization of information in the former instance, a centralization of assumption and attitude in the latter case.

The Bureaucratic Mind

Both Karl Marx and Max Weber made reference to a phenomenon termed "the bureaucratic mind," recognizing not only that every organization produces a psychological mode of adaptation, a mind-set so to speak, but also, and more importantly, that the bureaucratic mind-set is a near total one. Moreover, this bureaucratic mind is split between seemingly contradictory attitudes: "the deification of authority and consideration of the world as a mere object of bureaucratic action."[67] In a more general technological context, this mind-set views life *exclusively* in terms of adjustment to and manipulation of reality. When one makes reality, a purely material reality of objects and power relations, the ultimate criterion for action, then there are only two possibilities: an ethic of manipulation (world as an object of bureaucratic action) or an ethic of adjustment (deification of authority). Both are demanded simultaneously, however, and both consist of technical rules. As C. Wright Mills observes, "To the bureaucrat, the world is a world of facts to be treated in accordance with firm rules": rules of manipulation and rules of adjustment.[68]

The equation of reality and truth is the most pernicious aspect of the onslaught of technology and bureaucracy. It is not enough to say that science has become the arbiter of truth in the modern world, for the value of science today lies in technology. Technology has become truth.[69] This represents the materialization of truth. Perhaps this is what Heidegger meant when he called technology the metaphysics of the twentieth century. Truth is success in respect to reality; technology is that which guarantees success. As we have seen previously, success and survival are more or less interchangeable in the sense that both represent the moment of power. Their main difference now becomes clear: success is manipulation, survival is adjustment. Technology allows for the manipulation of the world but simultaneously demands our adjustment to it as object, means, and knowledge. The cycle of manipulation and adjustment in attitude and behavior produces contradictory feelings: a feeling of enormous power and a feeling of powerlessness;[70] a sense of absolute freedom and a sense of fatalism. For reasons we will go into later (chapter 7) the feelings of powerlessness and fatalism are stronger than those of power and freedom. The former feelings are expressed in the "obedience to authority" syndrome.

Stanley Milgram called attention to the phenomenon in *Obedience to Authority*. Originally Milgram wanted to investigate why so many Germans had become acquiescent in the hideous Nazi "experiment." Turned down by the German government, he conducted a series of experiments in New Haven, Connecticut. The experiments' real purpose was to determine how far an individual (the teacher) would go in applying an electrical shock to another individual (the learner) who was purportedly attempting to learn a language or some other body of knowledge. The teacher was led to believe that the experiment was about the effect of pain (punishment) on learning; he was unaware that the electrical shock inflicted on the learner who missed her questions was only simulated. Each time the learner missed a question, the teacher was told to increase the dosage of the electrical shock that the learner was only pretending to receive. The teachers in the experiment were under no compulsion to inflict pain on the learners except for the orders to do so. (The experiment had been designed so that the teacher could quit at any time; moreover, the monetary inducement was rather minimal.)[71]

The results were startling: almost two-thirds of the subjects followed orders even to the point of giving to their learners what they thought could prove a fatal dosage. As Milgram emphatically notes, however, the subjects were not "monsters" but ordinary citizens from varied occupations and social classes. At this point Milgram compares the results of his study to Hanna Arendt's conclusion that Adolf Eichmann personified the banality of evil.[72] Eichmann's defense that he was only following orders, that he was a mere "cog in the machine," was not the defense of a diabolically evil person but that of a normal person. As Arendt notes, this normality is "terrible and terrifying" because it signals that there is a large number of people who are unaware that they are doing anything wrong by simply following orders no matter what their content. More recently, of course, Colonel Oliver North invoked the same argument in the Iran-Contra affair. Milgram's results indicated that a certain number of teachers later experienced remorse about their actions when they discovered that though they had not inflicted pain on anyone, they had been willing to risk killing someone in the name of science. The guilt that some experienced was contradicted by the sociopathy of the obedience to authority syndrome.

One of Milgram's most incisive insights was that specialized technical tasks are incompatible with a broader view of context and consequences that moral decisions require.[73] To become fascinated with factual details or the details of the logic of a set of procedures is hypnotic in that it turns life into a game. A bureaucracy thrives upon specialized tasks. Obedience to authority has become obedience to technical authority. No specialist can be the master of technical authority, the parts of which form a logical system. A moral agent takes the broader view; the technician never gets beyond his narrow specialization.

Bureaucratic organizations not only produce and make use of the obedience to authority response but also that of conformity to the peer group. The distinction between obedience and conformity is often made on the basis of hierarchy versus equality. Authority is hierarchically structured, formal, and explicit; the peer group is based upon equality (in principle), and its norms are informal and often implicit.[74] The modern organization collapses the social distance between the two.

Shoshana Zuboff has demonstrated that a reliance upon information systems produces "anticipatory conformity." Information systems make work more visible; the computer contains traces of accountability. If the workplace is informated rather than automated, then the universal access to information creates maximum transparency: everyone's work is fully visible to others. If, on the other hand, managers retain control of information, then either workers will direct their anticipatory conformity toward their superior or they will alter the information they enter into the system to protect themselves. Information systems lead as well to the integration of production, thereby making workers more functionally interdependent; moreover, they reduce the psychological distance between the worker and the organization insofar as informated work requires continuous learning that, in turn, demands greater personal involvement than does automated work.[75] Consequently, obedience to the manager is supplanted by the anticipation that one's peers will disapprove of shoddy work.[76]

Zuboff maintains that as organizations become more dependent upon information systems, rationality replaces authority. In her words, "truth is the information system."[77] The implications seem plain enough: authority is vested in the information system; obedience to authority takes the form of obedience to information. Therefore, information systems concomitantly produce obedience to authority and anticipatory conformity. Bureaucratic authority is decentralized only to the extent that it is rationalized and centralized in the information system. The price is an ever greater blurring of the distinction between the individual and the organization.[78] Only individuals, however, are capable of acting as moral agents.[79]

The bureaucratic mind is ultimately cynical, for it reduces everything to power: adjustment to and manipulation of reality. Modern cynicism has been discussed in a variety of contexts: television,[80] politics,[81] art,[82] and even everyday life.[83] Cynicism's easy conscience and cover-up is idealism in all its forms. Realism keeps on the narrow path between cynicism, which excludes everything but power, and idealism, which glosses over the various manifestations of power. Cynicism spills over into scorn and derision at times. Take, for instance, modern humor. From television shows like *Monty Python* and *Saturday Night Live* to individual comedians like Roseann Barr and Sam Kinison, humor has become extremely aggressive. It's not enough to point out the foibles and incongruities of human existence and to laugh with the other; instead one must show contempt for the stupidity and absurdity of the other. The other is a failure; I, the scorner, am a success.

The most telling form of cynicism, the one that best explains the compelling nature of the bureaucratic mind, is technological fatalism.

Now it may appear paradoxical to call our faith in technology fatalistic, for modern technology is an expression of supreme confidence in our ability to direct the future. But as we have already seen, technology concurrently produces a sense of power and powerlessness. Traditional fatalism also gives rise to a similar dualism of power and powerlessness. The differences between nature and technology, however, create a different dialectic in each case.

For traditional societies nature was the life-milieu,[84] the absolute value that served as a model of emulation. The power of humans was small over against the immense power of nature. One's fate was tied to that of nature. The exercise of human power in the face of powerlessness assumed two major forms: the symbolization of nature and the attempt to discern the cycles of nature in advance. Ritual was a way of appeasing and harnessing the forces of nature.

It is only with the rise of a sense of history and of the ability to make history that fatalism begins to recede. Technology as our life-milieu reintroduces fatalism in several ways: it destroys the efficacy of symbolic experiences and creates an eternal present. Shared experiences and a sense of the past are a motivation to conserve what is the best and to avoid the harmful in creative ways that actually make history. In a technological civilization time becomes repetition – the repetition of the past in the future. As Hans Kelsen observes, "Whatever is grasped of the future by means of knowledge is, at bottom, merely the past."[85] Technology aims to predict the future, but ends up chaining us to the present.

Technological fatalism is different from traditional fatalism in that it enlarges the scope and quantity of human power. At first glance it should enhance our sense of power, diminish our sense of powerlessness. But for the most part it has just the opposite effect. Technology exacerbates our sense of powerlessness in two major ways. First, to the extent that technology becomes a system (see chapter 7), power becomes objectified and abstract. Moreover, as organizations tend to supplant institutions,[86] they become the technological context of our lives. Whatever technical power one might possess as an individual is dwarfed by the extent to which one is subordinate to organizational rules. Second, the more technology is applied to nature and society, the more life becomes unpredictable. The complex interactions of technology as they bear upon nature and society create an ever larger number of unintended consequences. No mathematical model is sufficient to get at all the variables; many of the most important can't be quantified. Furthermore, the use of systems analysis (as with information systems) actually militates against the flexibility required to deal with that which is unexpected. We are thus double victims of our own logic.[87]

This increased powerlessness to predict the future and solve the problems technology creates is not clearly recognized; our unlimited faith in technology clouds our perception. In traditional societies the negative outcomes never proved the ritual wrong (the ritual must have incorrectly performed); in modern societies the negative outcomes never prove technology wrong. It only means that we need more and improved technology. No matter how irrational, our wager is on technological growth. At this point the prisonhouse of technological fatalism is sealed; we have no choice but to obey technological authority.

Obedience to authority is reinforced by psychological fragmentation: the development of multiple selves in which the individual becomes a mere role-player. The reasons for this fragmentation include both the rise of technology and the decline of common meaning. The writings of Dutch psychiatrist J. H. Van den Berg[88] have devoted more attention to the latter cause, whereas those of Erich Kahler[89] and Arnold Gehlen[90] have emphasized more the former cause. Differences notwithstanding, for all three authors the two reasons are interrelated.

Van den Berg has reinterpreted Freud's concept of the unconscious by placing it in a historical and sociological context. Freud's discovery that sexual repression was at the center of unconsciousness, he argues, was related to the way in which sexuality was defined in the Victorian period. Van den Berg is able to define the unconscious without the additional concept of repression. For him unconsciousness means unawareness. When cultural values become multiform and multivalent, and when people become divided into special interest groups whose competition with each other is not mitigated by a larger unity, a culturally defined hierarchy, the result is that social contacts become vague and dangerous. In this situation, my knowledge becomes your unconscious and your knowledge becomes my unconscious.[91] Van den Berg's view of the unconscious is intimately related to the development of multiple selves.

He sees both the unconscious and multiple selves not as a permanent feature of human nature but rather as an epiphenomenon of the nineteenth century: the decline of a moral community. As a common morality declines, our relationships to others become more vague and ambivalent; moreover, our knowledge of ourselves becomes progressively uncertain. If my self understanding is to a great extent molded by the reactions of others to my actions and attitudes so that, for example, I think of myself as humorous because others laugh at my jokes, then ambiguous relationships will leave me in doubt about my own self, about what I do well and even what I believe. Without a moral community the various groups I belong to tend to become mutually exclusive. In each group a different part of me is called upon; consequently, I have as many selves as groups to which I belong. Yet because I employ only one self in any situation, my other selves remain unconscious. Therefore my unconsciousness (unawareness) of others is accompanied by my unawareness of my multiple selves. The social psychological concept of the human as a role-player is an ideological reflection of this.[92]

The fragmentation of the human personality is simultaneously the result of the reification of the human being. After Marx, reification has referred less to the transformation of a concept into a thing and more to the objectification of human abilities and needs. If the nineteenth century witnessed the reification of the human through private property, "the extent of the power of money is the extent of my power,"[93] the twentieth century has seen this process of objectifying what is truly subjective linked more to consumption.[94] As the number of consumer goods and their advertising images expand, consumer objects appear to be autonomous. These objects are linked together in a logical process – technique. The individual becomes merely one more object set within the layer universe of objects.

Moreover, the relationships between humans are mediated by technique. As mentioned earlier, both as a user and an object of technique, one's subjectivity is denied. My use of technique objectifies my abilities, just as the other's use of technique reduces me to an abstraction, to an object. Simultaneously technique fragments the personality because of the multiplicity of techniques. Each technique draws upon a different self; each technique employed by the other turns me into a different object, a different abstraction.

The implications of this for the obedience to authority syndrome are fairly obvious. The more one's self is fragmented, culturally and technologically, the less one is able to resist obeying technical rules – no matter how absurd, no matter how immoral. Only a unified self, a moral self, is capable of placing *specific* rules into a more *general* moral context. Man the role-player is man the servo-mechanism.

Contemporary American literature since the Second World War vividly portrays the fragmented self. Indeed Josephine Hendin finds this to be the central theme of American literature. Holistic fiction and anarchic fiction, to use Hendin's terms, perfectly mirror the fragmentation due to cultural disintegration and to technical reifica-tion. Holistic fiction dramatizes the plight of the individual who mechanically approaches life as a role-player and for whom life is a series of logical choices. Anarchic fiction, by contrast, highlights the disintegration of the human personality in the inability to find meaning in life. The nihilist often escapes cultural fragmentation by plunging into random sensations, a life devoted to ecstatic and mystical experiences.[95] Both holistic and anarchic characters have failed to achieve an ethically-unified self and thus remain fragmented. Thomas Pynchon and Don DeLillo, among others, demonstrate both tendencies in their novels.

Psychological Technique

The other major type of human technique is psychological technique. As indicated earlier, psychological technique includes advertising, propaganda, human and public relations, therapy, and the full range of "how to" manuals for the manipulation of human action. Because the mass media will be dealt with in chapters 5 and 6, I shall focus attention here on human techniques that work on a personal and an interpersonal basis: therapeutic technique, "how to" manuals, techniques of persuasion, and the pervasive use of groups such as self-help groups, support groups, and "life adjustment" groups. Previously we have examined a work group based on the human relations model as a part of organizational technique; therefore there is no sharp distinction between organizational and psychological technique. Just as with organizational technique, psychological technique comprises a set of logical rules – effective procedures – that result in (or at least promise) a successful outcome: manipulation or adjustment. The basic thesis is that psychological technique employed in relation to the self and the other has largely supplanted traditional manners and morality. Daily life is encapsulated by psychological technique.

A few preliminary distinctions are in order. The first is between internal (techniques of the self) and external (techniques of information and action). The former technique refers to those in which one is altering one's personality or one's bodily image in order to manipulate the other, e.g. to sell something. The latter technique refers to all those techniques in which one learns a set of behavioral rules to control the other (as in Parental Effectiveness Training). This distinction, however, quickly falls apart because the internal techniques objectify the self, that is, make it external and the external techniques demand at least a change in attitude if not in personality. Among the external techniques there are those that are used by an individual and those that involve group participation. Among the group techniques we can distinguish between those that are task-oriented, such as work and educational groups, and those that are therapeutic, including self-help groups, support groups, and life-adjustment groups. Clearly the growth and proliferation of therapeutic groups is the single most important form of psychological technique apart from advertising and propaganda, for it now covers every aspect of life from birth to death. All of life is now a problem to be solved technically.

Let us briefly look at five case studies, divided between internal and external technique. The first is Arlie Hochschild's study of how airline stewardesses and stewards learn to package their emotions. Her analysis is based primarily on observation and interviews with Delta Airline flight attendants and trainers as well as a perusal of airline literature and training manuals. All of the airlines expect the attendants to help sell the airline to customers by selling themselves as friendly, concerned commodities. The training of attendants aims to transform an individual into someone who can express friendly emotions in more than a superficial way. Hochschild's distinction between surface and deep acting is helpful here. Surface acting entails feigning certain feelings toward someone else with full consciousness that one feels otherwise; deep acting involves a more complete assimilation of the role to the self (at least for the duration of the deep acting) through repeated commands to the self (a kind of self-hypnosis) or by imaginatively constructing the desired emotions internally. Deep acting is more tiring because it temporarily requires a greater transformation of the self, but it is more convincing. For this reason the airlines attempt to turn airline attendants into deep actors who are always friendly and compassionate toward the customers no matter how unlikable and obnoxious they become. Neither surface nor deep acting is spontaneous and sincere.[96]

The training of flight attendants begins with the smile. The rule to smile always is an analogue of the Sermon of the Mount admonition about prayer. As one trainer said, " 'Your smile is your biggest asset – use it.' "[97] The smile is the beginning and the end of emotional warmth.

In order to facilitate the smile and other forms of deep acting the trainee is urged to imagine the cabin of the plane as her living room and the passengers as her guests, even as potential friends, and, when rude, as naughty children. When the guest's rudeness, however, makes it impossible to regard him as a guest anymore, there are rules for dealing with one's anger: invent an excuse for the passenger's behavior; or if that fails, sublimate the anger in some innocuous way, e.g. "by chewing on ice." Recurrent training programs for veteran attendants concentrate on dealing with anger. Prolonged periods of deep acting appear to create resentment. Finally, the airlines attempt to control the attendants' peer groups, a potential source of unity against the company, by invoking a rule against talking to fellow attendants when one is angry with a passenger. Such talk, it is believed, will only fuel the anger.

The attendant's physical appearance or image is a matter of great concern as well. Stewardesses especially are expected to keep at their ideal weight – a pound over can bring recriminations; moreover, their make-up, hair-length, and wigs are regulated. The rules about physical appearance have been relaxed in recent years but remain formidable.[98]

One well-known psychological technique to control one's image is related in John Molloy's *Dress for Success*. Following the correct rules (technical) for dressing can bring, among other things, business success and success with women, can improve the image of one's corporation, and, in general, can allow one to better sell one's self. In the chapter "How to Use Clothes to Sell Yourself," Molloy lists a number of rules about man's dress that are either obvious or banal, and invariably exploitative:

1   If you have a choice, dress affluently.
2   Always be clean. . .
3   If you are not sure of the circumstances of a selling situation, dress more . . . conservatively than normal.
4   Never wear any item that identifies any personal association or belief, unless you are absolutely sure that the person to whom you are selling shares those beliefs. . .
5   Always dress as well as the people to whom you are selling.
6   Never wear green.
7   Never put anything on your hair that makes it look shiny or greasy.
8   Never wear sunglasses, or glasses that change tint as the light changes. People must see your eyes if they're to believe you.
9   Never wear any jewelry that is not functional, and keep that simple.
10   Never wear any item that might be considered feminine.
11   Wear, do or say something that makes your name or what you are selling memorable. . .
12   If it is part of your regalia, always carry a good attaché case.
13   Always carry a good pen and pencil, not the cheap, junky ones.
14   If you have a choice, wear an expensive tie.
15   Never take off your suit jacket unless you have to. It weakens your authority.
16   Whenever possible, look in the mirror before you visit a client. . . you'll be surprised at how many flaws you'll catch this way. . . .[99]

Almost all of these trite rules can be reduced to one norm: dress like a successful person. This, of course, is the crux of the matter; if you dress like a successful person, then the client will associate your product with success. From the manipulation of one's emotions and one's physical appearance (internal technique) we now turn to the external techniques, those that involve a logic of external actions beyond personality and appearance.

The first of our examples is drawn from the technique of selling insurance, which is, for all intents and purposes, the selling technique in essence. Guy Oakes's revealing *The Soul of the Salesman* is our main source. As he notes, "For fully trained agents, life is a series of technical challenges that are attacked in a certain sequence and solved by means of certain preferred methods."[100] This is largely a consequence of the training program that breaks down an agent's life into parts each one of which can be technically reconstructed for efficiency and that keeps the agent under virtually total surveillance.[101]

Oakes identifies the five technical steps in selling insurance: (1) techniques for identifying prospective clients; (2) techniques for getting prospects to agree to a sales interview; (3) techniques for conducting an interview about their financial security needs and ability to meet them; (4) techniques to motivate prospects to sign an application for a policy and to pay for it; (5) techniques to keep the client within the fold so that he continues to meet his premiums.[102]

For example, as part of the crucial second group of techniques, those to motivate the prospective client to agree to an interview, there is a technique for dealing with the bereaved. The objective is to convince the prospective client of one's sincerity and to establish a bond between the two of you. This is done in a number of ways depending on whether one actually knew the deceased. If the agent did know the deceased, then he should recall or invent a "pleasant memory" to share with the bereaved, thereby strengthening his relationship with her. If the agent did not know the deceased but only a member of the family, then he should construct a pleasant memory from second-hand experiences or, again, make one up. Finally, if the agent knows neither the deceased nor the bereaved, then he should pick out some attributes of the bereaved, such as courage, sensitivity, or optimism, and infer that these are indirectly a consequence of the bereaved's relationship with the deceased. First the agent sells himself, only later the insurance.

The relationship between agent and prospect is an especially delicate one when the prospect is a friend. The training literature explicitly urges the agent to regard his friends as a pool of prospective clients. The literature attempts to allay the anxiety of the agent by equating "good ethics with good business."[103] The justification for manipulating friends into buying life insurance is the ideology of financial security: one can never have enough life insurance. The point is not so much that agents will sell friends and other clients inappropriate insurance, for the agent must not be seen as disreputable, but that the agent poses as an expert who knows best. Moreover, the manipulation of clients to achieve their financial security is a variation of the end justifies the means argument. Ultimately, however, the ideal of financial security is so open-ended as to be utopian, for no one can be guaranteed protection against all of life's contingencies. Perfect financial security belongs to the myth of technological utopianism as a means to full happiness and health.

Comparisons between the flight attendant and insurance salesman immediately jump to mind, but with one important difference: the flight attendant has a life beyond deep acting emotional concern; because the life insurance salesman has to regard every situation in life as a potential opportunity for sales, he literally becomes his role.[104]

It is no accident that all three examples so far have involved sales, for increasingly we are all enjoined to sell ourselves – in job interviews, in politics, in friendships and family life – every woman or man's plight is that of the airline attendant if not the life insurance agent. The message is: to manipulate the other one must first manipulate the self.

Our next two examples come from the ever-expanding world of group technique. They represent opposite approaches both in terms of method and philosophy; yet there is paradoxically a deeper commonality. The first is *est* (Erhard Seminars Training). Although this form of group therapy is now discredited, it was a popular therapeutic technique in the 1970s and 1980s. By 1980, in San Francisco, the home of *est*, it is estimated that one out of nine college graduates, had taken *est*.[105] Like so many other group therapies of the 1960s and 1970s, *est* used a host of techniques to break down the consciousness and resistance of the group members.[106]

Long days (often sixteen hours), one meal, few breaks for a drink or a trip to the bathroom, the trainer's confrontational behavior, the frequent admonitions to fantasize, and the emotional sharing of experiences by fellow group members work to produce emotional stress and fatigue. The goal is to get group members to acknowledge how pitiful their lives are and to accept *est*'s rules for living. While not as confrontational as some encounter groups, *est* has a set of procedural rules that permit no deviations, all the way from sitting in a chair most of the day to not talking to fellow participants.

Est articulates rules for living: one general rule, so vague as to be meaningless, and two "specific" rules, that appear to contradict the general rule. The general rule is that you should do "whatever works for you," that is, whatever produces the greatest experience of "aliveness."[107] Despite "aliveness" having little if any content, there are specific rules to achieve this state of bliss. The first is to make your life work, or, in other words, realize your social and economic goals: work, education, leisure. The second is to follow the rules of life: the conventions of society, bureaucratic rules, contractual rules, etiquette, and even the dress code. The trainer repeatedly admonishes the trainees that they should follow these rules not because they are naturally good or possess transcendent value but because they are as intractable as reality itself. Not to follow the rules of life will leave one with no sense of "aliveness.'

This utterly banal message of obedience to authority promises "aliveness" through adjustment. History and literature of course would seem to suggest just the opposite: one's sense of self, of being alive, comes more from resisting the rules than from following them slavishly. *Est* is a kind of organized "banality of evil," a secularized and vague Nazism.

The final example, Alcoholics Anonymous, is chosen because it has been the model for a large number of self-help groups. Alcoholics Anonymous is the opposite of *est* in almost every conceivable way: it avoids the jargon of *est*, does not operate in an authoritarian manner, and promotes unselfishness. The famous "twelve steps" of recovery constitute a psychological technique. The original articulation of the steps of recovery by one of the co-founders, Bill, was briefer:

> You admit you are licked; you get honest with yourself; you talk it out with somebody else; you make restitution to the people you harmed; and you pray to whatever God you think there is, even as an experiment, to help you to do these things.[108]

There are three key rules in the process whatever the number of steps. First, you must see yourself as you really are – powerless and pathetic – and repent of your evil to a "greater power" beyond one's self; second, you must tell others of your plight and join with them for sustenance; third, you must reach out to other alcoholics and help bring them voluntarily into the fold. Only in following this third rule is one recovered, for the unselfish act of helping someone else actually helps one become more committed. Alcoholics Anonymous is highly effective, at least for those who admit what they have become and find solidarity with members of their local group.

Despite the great differences between *est* and Alcoholics Anonymous there is an underlying similarity: both are psychological techniques and as such justify themselves in terms of efficacy; in the former case, adjustment to reality leads one to become "alive"; in the latter case unselfishness and commitment to others leads to one's own recovery. It appears that for Alcoholics Anonymous the power beyond oneself (a vague concept) is none other than the power of Alcoholics Anonymous itself.

Alcoholics Anonymous is now just one of a growing number of self-help groups, many of which are based on the same twelve-step program. It involves the recognition that one's addiction has left one miserable and powerless. Self-help groups now include those for: drug addiction, work addiction, sexual addiction, anorexia, bulimia, romance addiction, gambling addiction, shopping addiction, negativity addiction, emotional addiction, and relations addiction.[109] From the profound to the banal, self-help groups cover the full range of human addictions.

Support groups often resemble self-help groups except that the former groups don't center on addictions or self-inflicted problems but rather on the members' status as "victims." There is considerable overlap, however, for there are both bereavement self-help groups and bereavement support groups, cases where the label is different but the substance is the same.

The fullest expression that life has become one vast series of therapeutic problems is the proliferation of life adjustment groups. These include everything from groups for children on how to be a sibling, to groups for parents on how to relate to their children, to groups for those about to retire, to groups anticipating death (the "happy death movement"). The following is taken from a brochure for a workshop on "parenting alone;" it includes specific workshops and their descriptions:

1   "Appropriate Discipline for Pre-Adolescents" (description: Every child will sometimes misbehave and make mistakes in judgment. Discipline can help the child learn from his or her mistakes).
2   "Help! These Kids are Driving Me Crazy!" (description: Finding strength and support while raising children as a single parent is difficult. This workshop will teach you skills to help you through the tough times).
3   "Maximum Parenting: Influencing Kids' Self-Esteem at Home and School" (Learn how you can influence kids in positive ways. You will learn how to identify "high-risk" kids and the essential steps to developing healthy self-esteem).
4   "Don't Worry! Be Happy!" (description: We spend a lot of time worrying, being angry, discouraged, scared, sad, and frustrated. For most of us happiness is not a priority. How we feel is a choice and happiness may be the most practical choice of all).
5   "New Relationships/Blended Families" (description: Children often react negatively to their parents beginning a new relationship or entering into a permanent relationship with someone new. They may worry about whether their parents still love them or if they will ever see their parents again).

The brochure does not just promise a chance to share one's concerns as a single parent, but successful techniques. Workshop #4, "Don't

Worry! Be Happy!," is suspect in its use of exclamation points alone; beyond this it is a denial of reality. Can anyone actually believe that "happiness is not a priority" in light of the advertising industry and its exclusively aesthetical approach to life?

How do these psychological techniques work? When successful they work because they are expressions of common sense (sometimes beneath a jargon-studded veneer), because they are forms of magic, or because they are methods of coercion. A particular technique often combines more than one of these approaches. Psychological techniques that do not involve the use of drugs or surgery are verbal techniques. As such they require the subjective belief and assent of the client. Psychological technique, then, is not technology in the strong sense of the term: an *objective* logical method that guarantees an efficient outcome.

Anthropologists and psychologists have compared modern forms of psychological therapy with traditional forms of magical healing.[110] There is a great similarity. Levi-Strauss's classic study of sorcery, "The Sorcerer and His Magic," demonstrates that the sorcerer's magic is born out of trust: the community's confidence in the sorcerer becomes his ability to heal, just as his ability to convince them his healing powers are divinely guided becomes their confidence in him.[111] He notes that those being healed suffer from psychosomatic maladies. Jerome Frank's analysis of modern psychotherapy concludes that those patients who are "cured" are those predisposed to trust others, who accept the "symbols of healing" (belief in the method), and who identify with an enthusiastic therapist. The method is less important than the subjective states of both patient and therapist and the chemistry between them.[112]

The difference between Levi-Strauss's example of the sorcerer's ability to heal and Frank's example of modern psychotherapy is the presence of community in the former and its absence in the latter. Victor Turner provides an example from Africa of a successful Ndembu doctor ("ritual specialist") who involves the community even more than does Levi-Strauss's sorcerer. This ritual specialist interprets psychosomatic illnesses as a consequence of dissension in the community; his job is to mediate the conflict. A "cure" is effected when he can get both the patient and his antagonists to admit their grievances toward each other in a public confession before the community. The ritual specialist with the full assistance of the community restores good will among neighbors.[113]

Group therapies would appear to have a greater chance for success than individual therapy in that they provide the clients with a ready-made community. But this is the crux of the matter: modern therapeutic communities are both artificial and transitory. Unless group therapies can provide clients with a permanent community their curative effective is as transitory as the group itself. This explains, then, the great success of self-help groups. To the extent that they provide a permanent group, one that assumes many of the functions of a real community or family, their cure too is long-lived.[114]

Perry London's exhaustive study of techniques of human control indicates that traditional ritual healing and comparable forms of modern therapy are among the least coercive forms of control. Gradually more intrusive forms of control – hypnosis, conditioning, electronic devices, drugs, and surgery – have supplemented the former.[115] "Harder" technology drives out softer technology when the latter is not effective. But even here it is not so clear-cut. Authoritarian group therapies like *est* and behavioral conditioning techniques rarely have more than an ephemeral impact because their hold over the client is partial and temporary. When the therapy is finished, the client often reverts to previous ways of behaving. Self-help and support groups are more effective because like traditional ritualistic practices they provide the client with both a community and a belief system, a belief, however, in technique itself.[116]

At a societal level, the various helping professions and their attendant psychological techniques represent the increasing technologization of life from birth to death. At the very moment traditional morality, manners, and common sense are declining, factual and technical knowledge fill the void:

> A moral law removes a phenomenon to a place where the existence of the phenomenon is known but the details of the phenomenon can be ignored. Knowledge of the immoral is complete once we know it is wrong. Details become titillating, suggestive, occasionally seductive, but they remain forbidden. On the other hand, a phenomenon that is a technical problem does more than simply allow knowledge of its details; a technical problem compels analysis and requires detailed knowledge of its fine structure. . . Moral rules used to exclude; one might be inside moral laws or outside them. Now everyone lives on the inside since the "essence of morality" lies in a technical truth about life as a system . . .[117]

The system is the collection of more or less interrelated techniques. The aforementioned selling techniques show the side of technology as rules of manipulation; the therapeutic techniques (for the client) demonstrate the inverse side – rules of adjustment.

The Therapeutic Mind

If there is a bureaucratic mind that is a direct reflection of organizational technique, so too is there a therapeutic mind as the mirror of psychological technique. There are three major aspects of the therapeutic mind: dependency, the interiorization of life, and the fear of others.

When life ceases to be symbolically meaningful (in a holistic sense), when it ceases to have a common moral purpose (in the traditional sense), then life is transformed into a never-ending series of technical problems. The increased technologization of life on the sociological level is matched by the need on the psychological level for information and techniques to deal with other people in everyday situations. But because technology, as we have seen, is a denial of subjective experience, it creates in us a great dependency on experts.[118] This is Ivan Illich's main thesis. Becoming too dependent means passivity, self-doubt, and decreased freedom. Just as importantly, it means that the expert tells me what my needs are. Of course for the expanding health and well-being industry the "need" of the therapist is that the needs of the client increase rather than diminish.[119] There is a conflict of interest, then, for the therapists: on the one hand, they wish to help clients overcome their debilitating problems; on the other hand, they reserve the right to define as needs or problems aspects of the client's life previously untouched. There must always be a large reservoir of unrecognized and undefined needs just waiting to be siphoned from client to therapist. There is always an expert waiting to tell us, "Don't Worry! Be Happy!" or to tell us if we are happily married. We are in danger of becoming like DeLillo's characters Babette and Jack Gladney in *White Noise*,[120] unable to make a decision for ourselves.

The issue of the interiorization of life has been raised by J. H. van den Berg and Philip Rieff in somewhat different ways.[121] Both, however, attribute the development of an inner self to a decline of the reality of a moral community. I shall follow van den Berg's analysis here. The triumph of a positivistic worldview, a view that only facts could be known objectively, eventually led to the subjectivization of ethical and aesthetical meaning. Common meaning becomes personal meaning: each individual has to discover meaning for herself. In a moral community, there is less a difference between the inner and outer self; common meaning obviates the need for constant experimentation in regard to meaning. There are fewer serious external differences among people, less need for a fully developed inner self to come to grips emotionally with the conflict that a proliferation of external differences (in function, status, and power) in the absence of a common morality engenders.[122] At the levels of meaning and emotion, then, the loss of common moral purpose leads to a completely interiorized, subjective reality. More and more in the modern life the individual has to spend time coming to grips with her emotions, her meaning, her relationships. What van den Berg calls the "factualization of understanding" creates a subjective world of emotion to which we are enslaved, because it is here that the meaning of life now resides. No wonder we turn to therapeutic technique for assistance.

External differences between individuals, morally unmediated, create a more problematic existence. Not only does the loss of meaning make vague my relationships to others, but it makes them more dangerous. I do not know what to expect of the other, especially as he becomes more externally different. Soren Kierkegaard understood this very well when he talked about the basis of association in modern civilization as fear and envy. Karen Horney's still timely *The Neurotic Personality of Our Time* allows us to better understand how competitive human relationships have become. She attributes this in part to capitalism, but competition is inevitable to the extent the moral basis for cooperation begins to decline.[123]

In her reformulation of Freud, repressed hostility lies at the heart of the unconscious. The unconscious hostility toward others is an expression of the basic anxiety (shared to different degrees by both the neurotic and the normal) of modern life: the "all-pervading feeling of being lonely and helpless in a hostile world."[124] Capitalism not only exacerbates competition but leads to the treatment of the other as a commodity. Horney notes that all relationships today, including those of friend and family, are competitive and manipulative. As Horney notes, the less real love there is, the more talk of love abounds as compensation for the loss. The basis of self-esteem then is not unconditional love but success. One feels good about one's self when one succeeds; one feels lousy about one's self when one fails. Success, because it is so unpredictable and infrequent, proves a "shaky basis for self-esteem."[125]

There are a number of ways of protecting one's self against the unconscious feeling of loneliness and helplessness: other people are as hostile to me as I am to them. One of these is submissiveness; "the motto is: if I give in, I shall not be hurt."[126] It is exactly here that we can see the dialectic between the bureaucratic and therapeutic minds. The obedience to authority syndrome is reinforced by feelings of submissiveness, a sense that authority is likely to exceed its limits. The need to obey is conscious; the fear of not obeying is largely unconscious. Feelings of submissiveness combined with feelings of dependency produce an explosive contradiction: a need for the very authority (bureaucratic or therapeutic) one fears.

Organizational technique and psychological technique are interrelated; not only do organizations make greater use of psychological technique in lieu of traditional bureaucratic authority, but also psychological techniques are used by practioneers who for the most part work for large organizations. Yet an important difference remains: organizational technique is more tied to the symbol values of success and survival, psychological technique to the values of happiness and health (as adjustment).

As indicated in chapter 2, success has been redefined in collective terms, the organization and the nation. Behind both is technology. Happiness and health make a fundamental appeal to the individual. Happiness and health have two distinct meanings: physical well being and consumption on the one hand, and adjustment (emotional well-being) on the other hand. The psychological techniques of the mass media and advertising (chapters 5 and 6) appeal primarily to the former, whereas the psychological techniques outside the media are more related to the latter.

Organizational technique can only work to the extent that the individual is adjusted. Moral problems for both the group and the individual give way to the technical rules of organization and psychological adjustment. Technology thus represents the necessary side of modern morality. In the following chapter we examine public opinion, which forms part of the ephemeral side of this morality.

5

From the Moral to the Normal:

the Ephemeral

The normal has supplanted the moral (in the traditional sense) in itself becoming the moral. We are speaking here of statistical normality, a statistical average. The two major forms this statistical morality assumes are public opinion and peer group norms. In the former instance, the norms are abstract and impersonal; in the latter, they are concrete and personal. Yet public opinion increasingly informs the attitudes and behavior of the peer group. What the majority of people do and say tends to become normative.

There are three principle reasons, all related, for the triumph of normality. First, the growing prestige of science from the seventeenth to the nineteenth centuries elevated the status of the fact. The mission of mechanistic science was to break objects down to their ever smaller constituent parts. This atomistic approach produced a plethora of facts. For those positivistic scientists and laymen there was a one-to-one relationship between the fact and its referent in the real world: perception was possible without the contaminating influence of preconception.[1] With the gradual dissolution of the belief in the objectivity of religious and moral values, objectivity took up temporary residence in science. Objectivity lay in the laws of science that were a mirror of the laws of an autonomous nature. That part of natural law that spoke to the normative dimension of human existence eventually was seen as subjective. Facts were now objective, values subjective.

Scientific theory has come to be seen to have a merely formal relationship to reality, arbitrary in its conceptual substance, but realistic in terms of the mathematical relationship between concepts and of conceptual parsimony.[2] This further elevates the status of the fact, this time at the expense of theory. Atomistic science has produced in effect a universe of random facts. These facts both in and out of science can be disseminated to the public as fascinating information.[3] Witness the incredible interest in books and games of facts, such as the *Guinness Book of Records* and Trivial Pursuit. We are fascinated with the most intimate details of a person's life (the television talk shows) and in the exotic details of nature. The reason is clear: facts and reality are one, and our approach to reality is purely aesthetical. We are detached consumers of interesting facts. Reality is the sum of all facts but is known one fact at a time. Therefore reality is experienced as both fragmentary and interesting.

The view that nature is ordered according to lawful relations amenable to scientific explanation is eventually applied to society as well. A growing immanentism (a belief that the world is a self-contained material reality), which cannot be attributed to science as such, rather to the use of science as a worldview, encouraged the elimination of the dualism of nature and society. There had been a longstanding idea in western civilization that the laws of both nature and society were normative, but that those of society could be violated by humans. Freedom implied the possibility of transgressing God's laws. By the nineteenth century, however, immanentism was well in place, as understood by Nietzsche in his "death of God" proclamation. If science could be used to discern the laws of nature, there was no reason they could not be used with respect to society. The rise of the social sciences in the nineteenth century attests to this belief. As Comte understood it, the laws of sociology, statistical norms, would replace outmoded moral norms. The normal supplants the moral.

Traditional morality, moreover, is reduced to the status of ideology. The distinction between what ought to be and what is gives way to that between ideology and reality.[4] Morality becomes a screen behind which the self-interests of the group and the individual are played out. Marx's theory of ideology is, in this sense, only a reflection of the decline of a belief in the objectivity of moral norms in western civilization. Marx's materialism is but one form that radical immanentism has assumed.[5]

What finally saves immanentism and scientism from total relativism is the theory (myth) of progress. Continuous improvement in all domains of life and all undertakings is the cornerstone of this doctrine. The normal is justified both because today's normal is relatively superior to that of the past and because it is necessary to future improvement. The normal contains the promise of perfection. But not everything is equally successful. The tension between the average and perfection suggests two conceptions of normality: what is and what is successful.

Emile Durkheim called attention to this in his critique of Adolphe Quetelet's concept of the normal as the statistical average.[6] As Durkheim pointed out, when one places the normal into an evolutionary perspective, then at certain key moments what is statistically abnormal may prove to be essential to the survival (success) of a society. Moreover, what is abnormal now may prove normal later on. Therefore the normal as the statistical average may prove in certain instances to be completely at odds with normality as success. The two conceptions of the normal tend to become one, however, to the extent that technique dominates life; for modern technique's sole purpose is a successful outcome.

Arney and Bergen, for instance, speak of certain medical textbooks that propose "optimal life trajectories," that is, technologies of behavior from birth to death that maximize one's chances for a long, healthy, and happy life.[7] Over against these norms of technical perfection can be charted the patient's actual life-style. From this utopian perspective the individual becomes a collection of deviations from the multiplicity of technical norms.[8] The task of modern medicine and related helping professions is to bring the individual's normal behavior closer to the perfect life-style as defined by medical technology. The theory of progress assures us that the normal and the technical will someday be one.

Public Opinion

The term *public opinion* is sometimes used to refer to behavior as well as to attitude. What people actually do, at least as reported in surveys, and their attitudes, as reflected in opinion polls, constitute public opinion.[9] There is good reason for including both: as the distinction between what is and what ought to be becomes blurred in a morality of the normal, behavior and attitude tend to become one. The distinction between behavior and attitude must still be maintained, however, because public opinion can be weak or strong, uncrystallized or crystallized. The weaker the public opinion expressed, the less normative it is in regard to behavior. At the same time, behavior that is collectively of great consequence can eventually lead to a change in attitude.

The rise of public opinion as a major force in political life is concurrent with the centralized state's perceived need to collect statistical information about its citizens in the eighteenth century. Population growth, the emergence of a mass society, and the impetus toward equality meant that the political state had to take the public seriously. One way it did was by compiling statistics on births, marriages, homicides, suicides, and diseases. The growing need to exercise control over the unruly masses is expressed in the expansionistic definition of health (to include the moral) and the definition of illnesses as epidemics.[10] It would take some time, however, before social scientists began to ferret out virtually every form of behavior for analysis. Equally important as the data themselves were the categories used to organize the data. Whereas some categories were those of common sense, others were a fabrication of the human sciences.[11] As Foucault has pointed out, the political state and medicine became staunch allies in the eighteenth century, thereby paving the way for the growth of the positivistic human sciences and helping professions in the nineteenth and twentieth centuries. A market for the continual surveying of human behavior had been established.

In the seventeenth century several notable writers, such as Locke and Descartes, call attention to the phenomenon of opinion; by the eighteenth century interest had changed to amazement. David Hume believed that the foundation of the modern state was public opinion. His optimistic view of opinion is based on the assumption that love of fame, or what Adam Smith would call the "need for the approval of others," exercised a beneficent influence in society.[12] In the public arena citizens contend with one another for excellence in practical and virtuous matters; those who excel are recognized and admired by others. In this way opinion will solidify around the recognition of those leaders best qualified to govern. Hume's view is extended by Adam Smith in the *Theory of Moral Sentiments*. Anticipating most of the late nineteenth and early twentieth century work on socialization, Smith argues that in becoming spectators to the moral actions of others we realize that others judge our actions in turn. Once one anticipates the evaluations of others, the "impartial spectator" is born. Because we desire the approval of others (the pleasure of being in harmony with another), we approve of all actions that don't violate our inherent sense of justice. On the basis of empirical generalization, that is, generalizing from our own experiences, morality emerges. Morality becomes, for all intents and purposes, public opinion. For this reason and because of the "invisible hand of God" in the marketplace, Smith could be sanguine about self-interested action.

James Madison accepts the optimistic view that public opinion is ultimately beneficient, but he differs with Hume about its dynamics. He understands common opinion to work not so much as a result of the positive competition for fame in which one willingly identifies with the winners, but more as a fear of the consequences of nonconformity – the strength of one's opinion is commensurate with the number of those with whom one agrees.[13] Despite this reservation, Madison and Thomas

Jefferson extol public opinion as the voice of a democracy. The French *philosophes* tended to be even more optimistic than certain British empiricists and utilitarians with their belief that man was naturally good and could be easily educated, thereby paving the way for an informed participation in political affairs.[14]

Of course, there were the naysayers: those who, based on classical or Christian preconceptions, took a bleaker view of human nature and public opinion. Conservatives such as Edmund Burke and Alexander Hamilton distrusted common opinion because it represented a clear threat to hierarchy, to cultural authority. There were others, however, whose criticism went well beyond a defense of cultural authority. Perhaps the most incisive of such critics are Alexis de Tocqueville and Soren Kierkegaard.

In *Democracy in America* Tocqueville exposes public opinion as a power that recognizes no limitations. In an age of equality, he argues, men have little confidence in the opinion of another individual but unbounded confidence in the view of the majority. Equality leaves the individual both independent and weak. At the same time that equality frees one from the authority of others it destroys the reciprocal moral obligation that authority engenders. One's relationship to others becomes vague; in not knowing what to expect of others, one fears them. In this state of weakness one more readily turns to the collectivizing forces of government and public opinion to control others.

The independence that equality produces leads to individualism, even an exaggerated sense of one's own importance. Yet, as Tocqueville notes, equality diminishes individualism by making individuals more similar; consequently, the image of the crowd or the public is the only identity that stands out as unique. Hence one's individual identity is insidiously transformed into a collective identity: one can become an individual only through conforming to the will of the majority.

Tocqueville makes a number of acute observations about the collectivizing influence of public opinion. Because the origin of power in a democracy is in the will of the majority, and not in that of a distant royalty or an aristocracy, citizens do not perceive a danger in granting the majority unlimited power. Because equality promotes the "idea of the indefinite perfectibility of man" and because religion in America is less authoritative as "revealed doctrine" than as an expression of public opinion, he raises the possibility that "trust in common opinion will become a sort of religion, with the majority as its prophet."[15] As he notes, "the majority lives in a state of perpetual self-adoration."[16]

In his famous essay, "The Omnipotence of the Majority," Tocqueville notes that once public opinion is settled on an issue, those in opposition to the view of the majority become silent so as not to be ostracized.[17] He contrasts this "tyranny of the soul" with the situation in Europe where the king's view never stifles dissent. He goes on to suggest that the majority's unlimited power poses the greatest threat to individual freedom in America, where already "there is less independence of mind and true freedom of discussion" than in any other country with which he is familiar.

Kierkegaard's views on public opinion are in most respects strikingly similar. Tocqueville and Kierkegaard both view it as a serious threat to freedom and a source of the fear of others; moreover, both writers anticipate the concept of a mass society, a society that promotes both collectivism and the individual simultaneously. When it comes to religion, however, they part company. Tocqueville argues that religion's main social function is to place moral restrictions on self-interest; it would be useless in this endeavor if it assumed a fully oppositional position to public opinion. Religion, he argues, should only oppose public opinion when it contradicts revealed doctrine. By contrast, Kierkegaard's position is totally critical. Kierkegaard does not believe that Christianity should become a social institution and control agent as it had with Christendom; furthermore, Christianity is for him not so much a doctrine as a decision and set of practices. A Christianity that radically sets the individual against the world is invariably at odds with public opinion.

Among Kierkegaard's most penetrating insights is the idea that the public is formed not only by the mass communications media (the newspaper and pamphlet in his day) but also by individuals becoming detached observers of others.[18] This condition of being an onlooker to life involves a complex of intellectual and psychological processes:[19] reflection, envy, and moral ressentiment. Kierkegaard opposes reflection first to passion, then to action.

In a period of moral dissolution, relationships between individuals become ambiguous in that the aesthetical interests of each party are in conflict and yet remain partially concealed both to self and other. It is not polite to admit one's selfish motives. This leaves the individual in a state of "reflective tension." Rather than an inward relationship regulated and given meaning by moral qualities such as trust and self-sacrifice, the relationship has become external. In Kierkegaard's formulation, passion can only be expressed by those whose relationship to others is inward, that is, ethically qualitative. With the decline of inwardness and passion, one's relationship to the other becomes concurrently that of aesthetic possibility and ethical indifference. As such the relationship must necessarily become abstract, the object of theoretical reasoning (reflection). Life in a "reflective age" assumes the characteristics of a game in which one plots one's moves in advance in order to maximize one's chances for success.

Reflection itself, Kierkegaard maintains, is not the problem, but rather reflection that does not result in action, reflection that becomes an escape from action. When reflection is not accompanied by inward moral commitment, envy ensues. The powers of reflection are at the disposal of selfish desires. One envies others, their possessions and accomplishments. "Selfish envy" actually deters the individual from decisive action; instead time is spent ruminating about one's possibilities or what it would be like to be someone else. At this point Kierkegaard draws a startling conclusion about the modern reflective and passionless age: "*envy* is the negative unifying principle."[20] This envy has both individual and collective manifestations, for the envy within the individual has its counterpart in the envious attitudes of others. As we shall shortly see, the chief way in which this collective envy is expressed is through public opinion.

When the envy that is present in reflection as aesthetic possibility is not punctuated by decision and action, it spills over into moral ressentiment. Assuredly ressentiment is present in every age but what makes it different in the modern era is "levelling." By this Kierkegaard means the attitude that no one is better than I am. Because of a lack of moral character the individual denigrates and even ridicules those who have distinguished themselves. It is not enough to admire and envy the other; one must tear him down. Levelling to be effective must be done in concert with others; it is essentially a collective phenomenon. Whereas it was once the province of a social class or occupation, in a reflective and passionless age it is accomplished by the public. The public is an abstraction in that the members do not interact with one another; therefore, the public's opinion must be expressed through the mass media. Because moral ressentiment takes the form of levelling in a time of passionless reflection, and because levelling is expressed through public opinion, public opinion both creates and is an expression of the "negative unity of the negative reciprocity of all individuals."[21] Kierkegaard's brilliant insights help us to better understand the tendency for the media, even more so today, to "level" every politician, movie star, and celebrity. And, to follow Kierkegaard again, because we have become onlookers to life, we can't get enough of the exposé, the scandal, and the conspiracy. The individual has become a "fractional part" of the public and as such delights in levelling.

Public opinion, in Kierkegaard's formulation, expresses desire (positive up to the point of selfish envy) and ressentiment (destructive envy that desires less to imitate the other than to see him brought down to one's level). The paradox of public opinion is that it is at once both aesthetical and ethical. Public opinion is normative; it has the weight of morality, but its content is aesthetical – desire and possibility.[22] For both Kierkegaard and Tocqueville public opinion is a threat to individual freedom and independent thought. Tocqueville, however, was less wary of it than Kierkegaard. He thought it possible that the lack of administrative centralization, an aristocratic legal profession, and the jury system might act to keep the tyranny of the majority in check. Kierkegaard, by contrast, realized that beyond the sociological context Tocqueville observed there was a decline in the qualitative side of life and therefore in moral character itself. In his view public opinion was more than a threat to individual freedom. At the mercy of envy and moral ressentiment, it was an expression of the impending collapse of community.

Eighteenth and nineteenth century thinkers struggled to understand public opinion at a time when its importance had begun to increase enormously. The historical meanings of the term *opinion* tell us a great deal about its valuation. Until the rise of liberalism, opinion was at best associated with uncertainty, at worst linked to error. Opinion as a form of subjectivity was suspect over against doctrine and Church teachings. By the eighteenth century opinion had moved from the private sphere to the public sphere. Now opinion was defined in terms of power. No ruler could afford to ignore it. By the nineteenth century, with the strengthening of democratic sentiments, public opinion acquired the meanings of wisdom, even truth.[23] The movement of historical meaning in opinion from error to truth illuminates the last six hundred years of Western cultural history. Of special impact for our purposes is the transition from public opinion as power to public opinion as truth. This is not so much a change of meaning as it is an addition of meaning. Radical immanentism equates power with truth whether that power be scientific knowledge, technology, or public opinion.

Before discussing some contemporary issues about which public opinion is in various stages of formation, let us examine the characteristics of public opinion. First, it is based on second-hand knowledge rather than on experience or readily intelligible facts.[24] Public opinion is a necessary component of a mass society; it is a substitute for interpersonal knowledge that arises from practical, everyday life in the context of intense familial and friendship relations. The mass media provide us with ersatz experiences upon which opinion rests. If, as Boorstin notes, personal knowledge is phenomenal, public opinion is epiphenomenal;[25] it is concerned with what most of us know little about through experience or serious thought. Therefore public opinion is secondary both in regard to its source – the mass media – and its type of knowledge – epiphenomenal.

More obvious than public opinion's artificial character is its fragmentation.[26] There is no coherence nor continuity to the totality of opinions. A sure sign of fragmentation is the inconsistent if not contradictory quality of many opinions. For example, American opinion supports preserving the environment and economic growth simultaneously. Opinions are always out of context, for issues are presented to the public consecutively as self-contained entities; they resemble facts that appear to be autonomous. The fragmentation of opinion is a reflection of the fragmentation of information conveyed through the media.[27] Infatuated with the new and the sensational the media unintentionally destroy the memory of the past.

In part as a consequence of fragmentation, public opinion is based on simplified issues.[28] Complex and profound problems can only be resolved, and even then only rarely, through long and arduous discussion. Because opinion forms (or is pressured to form) on an enormous number of issues, many of which are outside of most people's personal expertise, the media must simplify the issue. Only then can public opinion emerge. Criticism of American politicians, for example, sometimes centers on their tendency to simplify issues, when the problem is actually much more a result of the mass media that can only operate profitably through simplification and the public, which, no matter how well educated, due to technical specialization, is ignorant about most issues. Inefficient bureaucracy, for instance, comes under attack from the political right in its assault on bloated government, when the evidence is rather strong that bureaucracy under certain circumstances is highly efficient and that big business is itself highly bureaucratized.[29]

A prevalent form that simplified opinion assumes is that of the stereotype.[30] Stereotypes need not be "negative;" indeed, they are just as often "positive." In a time when we are expected to have an opinion on everything and everybody, generalizations based on limited experience and a handful of cases abound. Stereotypes in a mass society permit people with limited time to place people and events into a manageable set of categories. Whether the stereotypes are negative, e.g. women are poor drivers, or "positive," e.g. women are sensitive, depends on the prevailing ideology and the historical period. Keep in mind that for the same category, as in the previous example, the stereotypes may be both positive and negative. All stereotypes are negative, of course, in the violence they do to the individual.

If public opinion is knowledge (albeit simplified and secondary) at one level, it is desire (and fear) at another. Kierkegaard's nineteenth–century remarks about envy and moral ressentiment are still pertinent. Public opinion is ultimately about that which one desires to occur or that which one wishes to be eliminated or controlled. This is evident in the very terms under which opinion is solicited – "agree or disagree," "yes or no," "approve or disapprove," "like or dislike." Public opinion is founded upon desire, and it is upon desire that it sometimes founders. Public opinion tends to follow the desire that technology's promise unleashes. At the same time, however, public opinion acts to "level" those above us. The paradox is that we are expected to desire the very things that we resent other people for having. Public opinion is about that which makes life more comfortable or more difficult; it is a function of consumerism – happiness and health. Because public opinion is based upon desire, it refers more to the future than the present.[31] Under certain circumstances public opinion can represent an escape from the present. Kierkegaard clearly understood that public opinion was both an expression of desire and a normative form. Public opinion is ultimately a morality based upon desire and an anticipation of the future.

Public opinion forms itself around issues that are unrelated to reality.[32] To a certain extent this can be deduced from its fragmentary and secondary nature. Public opinion is knowledge taken out of historical and cultural context. Just as important is the symbolic dimension of these issues. Public opinion is not created out of common interpersonal experiences; hence those whose views form public opinion must be supplied with a common denominator – mythical beliefs. Now it is true that the interpersonal experiences of those in traditional society were interpreted through a series of myths. There are two differences, neither of which I have the time to develop in detail, between traditional and modern myths. The former myths take us to the past, whereas the latter propel us into the future.[33] The perfection of the future is seen to be far greater than the perfection of the past as understood in the idea of the *origins*. That is, the perfection of the past was much closer in kind to the present reality for traditional peoples. The perfection of the past was the abundance of nature. Technological change is so rapid that the anticipation of the future is without limits. The second difference is that modern myth is centralized in the mass media, which themselves *create* experiences for us. Traditional myths emerged from common experiences with nature; they thus had a greater congruence with experience. For us this is not the case: we have come to expect the utterly fantastic and to live it out vicariously.

Both the political left and the right share a common belief in technological progress, in the ability of technology to solve all problems and to create a cornucopea. Beneath the ideological conflict, then, there exists a mythological unity. In the most advanced technological societies, the myths promulgated by the media reinforce public opinion's tendency to form itself upon simplified issues. All myth simplifies reality to some extent.[34] Given that a technological civilization is exceedingly complex in its inner workings and movements and in the proliferation of specialized information, mythological simplification of issues is just as crucial to the formation of public opinion as is scientific simplification.

Public opinion is decidedly ephemeral.[35] Because it is based upon desire, envy, and fear, public opinion is an aesthetical phenomenon. Its "norms" change as everyday life changes and new objects of desire emerge. Public opinion is tied to current events and technological possibility. Current events are often the least important aspect of political life, but the part most amenable to dramatic presentation in the media. Current events are transformed into political spectacle. I shall argue in chapter 7 that there are two sets of factors that are much more important than current events for a full understanding of political life – the commitment to economic growth and technological experimentation.

The relationship between technology and public opinion rests largely on the titillation of desire. Public opinion, which is founded upon desire, is receptive to technological possibility because technology as illustrated in advertising promises the good life now. Technology modifies desire just as public opinion demands the realization of the desired technological goods and services.[36] It is here, at the level of goods and services, that technology changes most rapidly. At a deeper level, that of a stable structure, technology remains the same. That is, technology changes its appearance, becomes more efficient, gives rise to a plethora of new products and services, but continues to be the chief determining factor in the organization of modern societies.

It is more than coincidence that both public opinion and the mass media have a constantly shifting set of topics and interests. To a large extent the mass media shape public opinion. The propaganda of advertising and political ideology in conjunction with the technology of the media promulgate a consumer-oriented life style – health and happiness – and a technical answer to life's problems – success and survival.

So far I have treated public opinion as if it were a single phenomenon. Many times an issue generates multiple opinions that are at odds with one another. Only under certain circumstances does public opinion become a single view to which virtually everyone subscribes. I have chosen four examples of public opinion that range from settled to partially settled to unsettled opinion: smoking; gender, racial, and ethnic equality; nuclear power; and abortion. These examples illustrate some of the ways in which the values of success, survival, happiness and health come into conflict.

Smoking is an apt example of the public resolution of a controversial issue. Public opinion is now decidedly against smoking. Certainly there are still covens of smokers, but the sentiment against smoking grows stronger all the time. Over the past forty years health groups like ASH (Action on Smoking and Health) and the government have increased the attack upon the cigarette and the smoker. Early on, the criticism centered on the product's harm to the health of the smoker; later, by the 1970s, the criticism of the smoker as an undesirable person whose habit was obnoxious and even harmful to non-smokers was everywhere in evidence.[37] Today banning smoking in public places is on the increase. Here the government has taken the lead in respect to its buildings, but legislation about smoking in grocery stores and department stores has also been enacted.

Earlier in the twentieth century, smoking was represented in advertisements and the movies as both pleasurable and romantic. As early as 1949, however, a Gallup survey found that a majority of non-smokers and smokers agreed that cigarette smoking is harmful to one's health.[38] It was only in 1965, with the Cigarette Labeling Act, that the tide began to turn: health was acquiring a higher priority than happiness. But it is more complicated than this, for the health and the pleasure (happiness) of two parties is at stake. The issue is tacitly defined as the pleasure of the smoker versus the health of the smoker, the health of the non-smoker, and the pleasure of the non-smoker. Still, the concern for health is stronger than the concern for happiness, if only on this issue.

Gender, racial, and ethnic equality is another example of settled public opinion. Here I must insist upon drawing a sharp distinction between public opinion and private opinion and between opinion and action. Public opinion is decidedly in favor of equality even though many individuals may have reservations about it whether with respect to gender, race, or ethnicity. No public official or celebrity can speak against these kinds of equality without a public outcry and the demand for an apology. Just because public opinion has come down on the side of social equality does not mean that discrimination has come to a halt. The extent of the latter is difficult to ascertain.

Movements like PC (Political Correctness) and multiculturalism on college campuses have ruffled the feathers of conservatives, but few of them have been willing to uphold the principle of the inequality of gender, race, or ethnicity. Their objection, it would seem, is to the means employed to realize the end, not to the end itself.

Gender, racial, and ethnic equality today is an issue that goes beyond traditional concerns about how prejudice and discrimination affect equality of opportunity, and beyond the attempt to redress historical inequities. It represents the utopian quest for a perfect equality of power, more precisely, an equality based entirely upon power. This is what sets the current movements for social equality apart from those of the recent past.

Tocqueville has two thoughts on equality that are pertinent to this contention. First, he points out that at certain times the passion for equality becomes insatiable.[39] The more equal people become, the more they notice the still-remaining differences and demand their elimination. Hence the value of equality can never be fully realized. In the discrepancy between actual social equality and the norm of equality, "equality as a social passion takes root."[40]

Second, Tocqueville maintains that every central power "loves equality," for it makes governance easier.[41] Here he is using *equality* in the sense of *uniformity*. For the sake of efficiency central government desires uniformity among its citizens. This is Weber's point as well about equality in a bureaucracy: the same rule applied to all is efficient.

When Tocqueville discussed the passion for equality, he did so in the context of social and cultural equality, which refers more to status and prestige than to power. It includes dress, manners, education, and morals. Moreover, the cultural value of equality and related values such as freedom and justice still exerted some control on the exercise of power. The egoism and individualism in America that he so vividly described were still in their infancy. Therefore even if the passion for equality had become insatiable, the passion was not directed solely or even mainly toward an equality of power. Equality becomes exclusively an equality of power in the face of the decline of all values other than that of power itself.

Dostoevsky's brilliant insights into the equality of power in human relationships are helpful here. In *Notes from the Underground*, he dramatizes the logic of the master-slave relation.[42] For the underground man equality between humans is impossible; his is a world in which one is either a superior or an inferior, a winner or a loser. If one becomes conscious of one's superiority to another, then the pleasure disappears; for superiority can only truly be enjoyed in respect to one's equal. But to triumph over one's equal is to reduce him to the status of inferior, thereby diminishing the enjoyment of one's triumph. At the same time, to demand to become equal in a world of superior and inferior is tantamount to admitting one's inferiority.[43] Dostoevsky's portrait of underground man was not intended to be a metaphysical statement about interpersonal relations but rather a critique of naive and romanticized views of the self and the other.[44] Without either self-sacrificing love or cultural authority, human relations tend to become exclusively competitive. If competitive human relationships are exacerbated by a serious decline in those cultural values that work to control power, then the call for an equality of power readily becomes an excuse to achieve domination.

Martin Luther King Jr. understood perfectly well that racial and ethnic relations would deteriorate markedly if the cultural value of integration declined. Indeed, this is precisely what has happened in the United States. The various gender, racial, and ethnic groups have almost come to occupy mutually exclusive social spaces. Without a common set of shared beliefs and a common morality (in the traditional sense), the struggle for equality becomes a struggle for power – but power left to itself does not recognize equality.

From the perspective of the political state and the technological system, however, equality becomes uniformity. Tocqueville's earlier remark about central powers and equality, when placed in the modern context, can be seen to take in technology as a system. Comparable to Weber's insight that bureaucratic equality had little to do with justice but everything to do with efficiency, Ellul's is about technology (as the basis for the organization of modern society): "All inequality, all discrimination (e.g., racial), all particularism, are condemned by technology, for it reduces everything to commensurable and rational factors. A complete statistical equality for any adequate dimension and any identifiable group – such as the goal of a society having technology as its chief factor."[45]

As we have previously seen, technology is the main guarantor of success in the modern world. All other forms of success, whether of the individual or the group, are secondary. Gender, racial, and ethnic groups become, as it were, special-interest groups competing for a larger slice of the American dream. It is precisely here that the different meanings of equality are joined: uniformity insures the success (efficiency) of the technological system at the same time as an equality of power insures the victory of the special-interest group over its more advantaged competitor.

Placing the issue of gender, racial, and ethnic equality into the context of American values leads to the following interpretation. Gender, racial, and ethnic equality represents *success* to the disadvantaged group and a decline in *happiness* for the advantaged group. John Kenneth Galbraith's *Culture of Contentment* echoes Tocqueville's views on the love of material well-being.[46] The self-satisfied selfishness that the inordinate love of material pleasure produces leads to a decline in civic-mindedness and a sense of moral community. Those who feel most threatened by the possibility of equality – even the normative version – of gender, race, and ethnicity often do so from a position of not wanting to give up certain advantages and privileges. When finally achieved, success brings happiness; moreover, for the individual, success is happiness.

The third issue, nuclear power, represents public opinion that is partially settled. The public opposes building new nuclear power plants, but does favor, in most cases, using extant ones.[47] One study indicates that not all those who oppose the use of nuclear energy do so out of ideological concern; some are opposed out of fear.[48] Whether one can legitimately make a sharp distinction between ideology and fear, there remains ideological conflict about nuclear power. Ideological supporters of nuclear power believe that nuclear energy "will improve the world's standard of living" and that the technical defects of nuclear power plants can be overcome by applied science. Ideological opponents believe that the disposal of radioactive materials threatens the survival of the human race.[49] Related issues include health risks from a nuclear accident such as a melt-down.

While environmentalists have obviously convinced the public that there are serious risks involved in the use of nuclear energy, they have not persuaded them to abandon the use of this energy form. The issue of nuclear power is one of many that pit the economy against the environment. From the public's view this is an impossible decision. So in the case of nuclear energy a compromise, a partial resolution, has been effected. Not to build new nuclear power plants appears to be a negligible economic risk; to end the use of nuclear energy would prove to be, in the short run, an economic disaster. Public opinion is opposed to nuclear energy only up to a point. The mythical values that are embodied in the issue of nuclear power are primarily those of success and survival. The use of nuclear energy represents a technological *success* that concomitantly appears to threaten the *survival* of large numbers of people. Just as happiness and health are opposed in the issue of cigarette smoking, success and survival are at odds in that of nuclear energy.

The fourth issue, which remains bitterly unresolved, is abortion. Because the ideological debate about abortion is omnipresent, the following discussion will be brief. There are, of course, fanatics on both the pro-life and pro-choice sides. For the fanatics (on both sides) abortion is a clear-cut, absolute, and autonomous issue; in other words, it has been rendered irrational. For the pro-life extremists the right to life of an unborn infant is absolute; for the pro-choice extremists the woman's right to choose whether to have the baby is absolute.

Most pro-life advocates are either Catholics or conservative Protestants; for Catholics, at least, the unborn infant has a soul and as such is a human being. According to this belief, abortion becomes an act of murder. This pro-life view appears to a case of moral custom, a vestige of the Christian past. Certain Christian groups, perhaps tacitly aware that they live in a post-Christian civilization, have chosen this issue with which to draw the battle lines over the humanism of modernity. And yet relatively few Christians are fanatically opposed to abortion. If they were convinced that it was an act of murder, more would take the strong view.

This leads me to the highly speculative conclusion that for many pro-life advocates the actual problem is not so much a Christian as a humanistic one. But obviously not the same one the pro-choice advocates have chosen to defend. I think that for many pro-life supporters the regard for the unborn child is part of a larger sentimentalization of the status of child. In the *Feminization of American Culture*, Ann Douglas has documented the changes in nineteenth-century America in the cultural attitudes toward women, children, and life in general.[50] Douglas uses the terms *feminization* and *sentimentalization* more or less synonymously. To sentimentalize something is to treat it in an emotional way that both idealizes it and compensates for the way it is in reality. Rather than providing one with a realistic view necessary to change an actual condition, sentimentalization covers over reality in a pleasant way that renders our opposition to it minimal.

The transformation of the value of children from economic to emotional occurred in the late nineteenth and early twentieth centuries.[51] Children came to be valued aesthetically for their ability to bring pleasure to the lives of their parents. The sentimentalizing of children was performed within the bourgeois family as a "haven in a heartless world."[52] The nuclear family should comfort and provide happiness to the father who faced the cruelties of public life. The more difficult actual child-rearing becomes, however, the more important it is to sentimentalize the status of children.

Many pro-life advocates have a sentimental view of children. By extending the term *child* to include the unborn, one can sentimentalize the unborn. Now the concern is with the "health" of the child (unborn infant), a child who is a future source of happiness to some family. For the pro-choice advocates the issue quite clearly is the happiness of the woman, her right to be free of an undesired responsibility. Both pro-life and pro-choice advocates think and act with the same symbolic universe: happiness and health as physical well-being. As was indicated in chapter 3, the mythical values of modern American morality include success, survival, happiness, and health. These values often come into conflict in the real world as the previous analysis has indicated, not only because they are contradictory in practice but because they are held by groups that are in competition with each other in various ways.

In a certain sense public opinion is exclusively related to happiness and health as physical well-being. Insofar as public opinion is an expression of desire, it turns all issues into aesthetical ones: like or dislike. Our desires have become as ephemeral as consumer goods readily replaced by new products. If advertising is our folk culture, then our desires are fully integrated into a consumer culture. Surveys indicate that as high as 80 per cent of the American population is pursuing the dream of self-fulfilment.[53] No matter how ennobling and idealistic self-fulfilment may sometimes sound, it is really only a thinly disguised variation of the value of physical well-being. It is no accident that self-fulfilment is closely associated with the concept of life-style.

Public opinion is not only transitory, it is also superficial. It requires no commitment nor involvement to express an opinion. There are individuals here and there who take action on an issue, but to have an opinion or to follow it as a form of entertainment demands no real involvement in the lives of others. Paradoxically, it is the ephemeral, superficial nature of public opinion that helps explain moral minimalism.

In her study of the social morality of an American suburb, M.P. Baumgartner used this term to refer to the tendency to avoid conflict in interpersonal relations. One avoids making judgments about the actions of others, or at least expressing them, in face-to-face encounters.[54] The motto is: I don't get involved in other people's lives, and I avoid disapproving of their actions unless it inconveniences me in some important way. Moral minimalism represents a kind of impersonal situational morality, whose chief characteristic is avoidance.

Public opinion is the other side of moral minimalism: one gets "involved" by expressing an opinion as compensation for not getting involved in the lives of those one encounters. Both public opinion and moral minimalism are expressions of the abstractness and vagueness of human relations in a technological civilization.

Peer Group Norms

Tocqueville and Kierkegaard understood that the traditional hierarchy of authority was disintegrating in an age of social and cultural equality. All traditional societies have been hierarchical and holistic.[55] In traditional societies the community (the whole) takes precedence over any social category (the part), such as a specific gender, age, or occupational status. All oppositions within a social category – male/female, old/young, hunter/farmer – are based on the principle of complementerity. Each status needs its opposite and is defined in terms of its opposite, so that both statuses together form a totality – the social category as community. For instance, it takes both male and female to make a human being. The various statuses are complementary rather than mutually exclusive, and a higher status's authority over a lower (male over female) is tightly circumscribed. Louis Dumont defines hierarchy as "the encompassing of the contrary."[56]

Traditional hierarchy is based more on symbolic status than power. It is only when the sense of the whole, the moral community, is called into question that a hierarchy of power appears. Modern societies possess a stratification system of mutually exclusive categories so that power becomes the primary if not exclusive basis of the relation between the various statuses. Under these circumstances authority becomes authoritarian. Tocqueville noted this about French society in his comparisons with America on the status of women and children. But cultural authority turned authoritarian was only a transition to impersonal authority.

Tocqueville's classic essay, "Influence of Democracy on the Family," addresses the question of a changing parental authority. The diminishing authority of the father is on a collision course with democratic government and public opinion. The power of democratic central government and public opinion begins to supplant the authority of the father; it is both a corrosive agent on the authority of the father and an ersatz authority itself. Relations within the family become more equal and more affective; at the same time, however, there is a need for something to re-establish authority. The abstract and impersonal forces of public opinion and government, which permit no hierarchical distinctions, hold father and child equally under their sway. Abstract power begins to replace cultural authority.

The peer group emerges as a sociological entity in the late eighteenth century and becomes formidable in the late nineteenth century. The peer group is important, for our purposes, in two ways: as a conveyor of public opinion and as a political interest group within the organization. The peer group represents an intermediate stage between the personal relations of kinship and community and the impersonal relationship between the individual and the public. Certainly there have always been groups based on age, gender, and occupation. But such groups, at least in traditional societies, were integrated into a hierarchy (in Dumont's sense). The peer group becomes more or less autonomous in a period of social and cultural equality. One's peers are, of course, one's equals. The degree of moral commitment, if not emotional involvement, is more transitory within the peer group. As Tocqueville observed, moral obligation had always been learned within a context of cultural authority.

As authority declines, one's obligations to others become more tenuous, more subject to predilection.

The first peer groups to command attention were those based on similar age and gender, especially the male adolescent peer group. In a time of social and cultural equality, however, there were no limits on possible peer groups. Following upon those based on age were those of occupation and workplace. Perhaps one might extend the term to refer to groups of similar aesthetic interest, what Boorstin refers to as consumption communities. The following analysis is concerned for the most part with peer groups of age, gender, and occupation. Eventually, peer groups will be contrasted with consumption communities.

Until the eighteenth century, Europeans made few if any distinctions among children of different ages. Philippe Ariès concludes that there was no separate linguistic category for those between childhood and adulthood. John Gillis suggests that there was at least an implicit recognition of a separate stage in life after early childhood and before full adulthood – youth. This period, he argues, extended from age seven or eight until marriage, usually in the mid to late twenties.[57] Whatever the case may be, the important point is that adolescence and young adulthood were not perceived as distinct stages of life. Adolescence did not become a separate stage of life until the movement from childhood to adulthood was seen to be discontinuous.[58] The implicit recognition of a hiatus between the two stages created the cultural space for adolescence. And yet the recognition alone did not create adolescence; it was born out of the impact of demographic changes and industrialized upon the extended family and community.

Prior to the onset of industrialized capitalism, youth were bound together either in fraternal organizations or in village youth groups. The former were found in schools, professions, the army, and the clergy; the latter in all villages. Almost all those from age fourteen until marriage participated in village youth groups, a much smaller number in fraternal groups. Both kinds of youth groups, however, were under the control of adults. This is the key. Village youth groups, for instance, had little time to themselves; most of the time their activities took place under the direct or indirect purview of adults.[59]

Traditional youth groups, especially the more common village type, declined in direct relation to the erosion of the peasant economy with its norm of marriage (for men) dependent upon inheritance of the land. In the nineteenth century the mass migration of youth into the cities to search for work created a new kind of youth group – the street gang. These male urban youth groups were stratified by age – a younger group of 14- to 17- year-olds and an older group of 17- to 20-year-olds. Sometimes girls became members of satellite groups affiliated with a male group.[60] The street gang was more autonomous in regard to adult control than the village youth group had been. Preoccupied with the defense of its territory, not unlike its twentieth-century counterpart, the street gang was organized for survival.

Less specific than the urban street gang, the childhood and adolescent peer group, especially in middle-class areas, came into its own with the advent of a culture of consumption. By the mid twentieth century David Riesman maintained it had become a socializing agent to rival the child's parents. The adolescent peer group was now on a collision course with the vestiges of parental authority. In Riesman's formulation, the peer group was a "tutor in consumption." Its basic approach to life was aesthetical – life-style, consumer goods and services, and especially a popular personality. To be well-liked became all important. One in turn became a connoisseur and consumer of others' personalities.[61]

Even though the peer group appears most central to the stage of adolescence, in a time of equality the peer group remains important throughout one's life. The consumer-oriented peer group is a perfect vehicle for the reinforcement of public opinion and a perfect receptacle for advertising propaganda. Public opinion is built on desire, and the peer group realizes desire in the act of shared consumption. Consumption communities become the abstract counterpart to consumer-oriented peer groups. As a form of public opinion, consumption communities are an expression of identification with a product and the kind of person who uses the product. One belongs to a consumption community without having to establish a personal relationship with fellow consumers.[62]

Occupational and workplace peer groups, which have always existed, became more significant in the late nineteenth century for much the same reason street gangs and adolescent peer groups did – the decline of the extended family and peasant community. The father no longer selected the son's occupation, nor worked side by side with him. In contrast to fraternal organizations, labor unions, and professional societies, occupational peer groups were informal and loosely organized. They provided employees with friends and protection against the vagaries of work in bureaucratic, capitalist societies. The informal work group is the bane of bureaucracies, as Weber duly noted. Human relations in the efficient organization should be formal and impersonal. Workers, of course, find this intolerable, and, when possible, establish affective relationships with each other and informal work norms.[63]

The issue of organizational efficiency is exceedingly complex. As we saw in the preceding chapter, informal work group norms are needed to make the organization effective. This suggests that some of the organization's extant rules are ineffective. To some extent the rules of the bureaucracy always lag behind reality. To eliminate discretion, then, is to prevent the organization from being successful. Sometimes, however, informal work group norms militate against efficiency. Alvin Gouldner's study of an industrial bureaucracy reveals that the miners' work groups sometimes performed "bureaucratic sabotage." By conforming to minimum productivity norms (the letter of the law), they could turn them into maximum norms (and violate the spirit of the law).[64] Moreover, the miners often set their own safety rules that rendered them less productive. In one of the following case studies executives form peer groups (or gangs) to insure their success or survival in a climate perceived to be ruthlessly competitive. The success of a group of executives might even be achieved at the expense of the organization's success. Increasingly the occupational peer group acts as a political interest group within the larger bureaucracy.

Because public opinion and its relationship to the values of material well-being (happiness and health) have already been discussed, we will concentrate in the following examples on the peer group's necessary orientation to success and survival. The first example is drawn from Gerald Suttles's *The Social Order of the Slum*. Urban street gangs, in the Addams area of inner city Chicago, included about 50 percent of the boys and were age-graded – oldest (16-18), intermediate (14-16) and youngest (11-14). The boys in the gangs or street corner groups (as Suttles prefers to call them) were usually the most popular in the area and appeared to be no more delinquent than the unaffiliated boys. There were 32 boys' groups (but only 6 girls' groups); the groups averaged 12 to 15 members.[65] The major activities of the boys' groups included fighting, hanging out, drinking, and stealing. The groups were not nearly as cohesive as popular legend would have it. No one was expected to take part in all activities. Groups limited collective action to situations when they believed they could count on a heavy participation. The individual's personal reputation played a major part in determining what group activities he would participate in.[66] The individual's personal reputation, then, did not coincide fully with the group's reputation.

Despite their occasional crimes, street corner groups made several vital contributions to the social order of the neighborhood. Because the groups were segregated by sex, age, ethnicity, and territory, children and adolescents were offered a measure of protection as was the rest of the community. Because those with the most in common are most likely to be in conflict, group membership was a kind of insurance against harm. Each street corner group developed a public reputation that acted as a warning to others. Moreover, the various street corner groups worked to spread the news about other groups' reputations. They acted as a communication channel for the neighborhood.[67]

It is only within this context of defense of territory and communication network that one can fully appreciate the morality of the street corner group. The morality is one of normality. Its two rules are: Be loyal to your friends and act consistently with your reputation. As Suttles emphasizes, these practical rules for success or survival actually constitute a kind of morality. The residents in this slum realize that many in the neighborhood do not adhere to a traditional morality. Consequently the next best thing is to demand that residents be normal, that is, that they remain true to their friends and their reputation.[68] Even if someone's reputation is that of car thief, demanding that the individual be consistent with that reputation allows one a forewarning. The norm of personal loyalty permits the street corner group to be *successful* in an amoral and hopeless situation; the norm of acting consistently with one's reputation increases others' chances for *survival.* The morality of the street corner group takes the form of the normal while its chief value is power (success and survival).

The peer group of corporate managers shares something in common with the street corner group – morality. Robert Jackall's study of the cultural world of corporate managers brilliantly sets forth its moral boundaries.[69] Based largely on a series of detailed interviews with executives at a variety of levels in four corporations, his study depicts a situational morality that parallels that of the most dangerous and disorganized slum.

The dangers of corporate life are many. There are the frequent shake-ups, often the result of a new CEO or division head taking command. The uncertainty of markets and the general volitility of the world capitalist economy create enormous instability within corporations. Success and failure are diffused through the organization and socially defined as such; hence there is little effort, especially at higher levels, to attempt to assign individual responsibility. When the time comes, however, to find an individual to blame for a failure, it becomes an act of scapegoating. Success, however, is perceived to be as capricious as failure; it amounts to being in the right place at the right time.[70]

When success and failure are viewed as beyond an individual's control, then "corporate gangs" offer a measure of protection. Jackall muses about whether to use the term *gang*, but opts for the term *circle*. For reasons that follow, we shall stick with *gang*. Loyalty to co-workers born out of common experiences, common enemies, similar work styles or the same patron (a higher level manager who acts as one's sponsor) provides the basis for these loosely organized alliances. The most important criterion for membership is that one is perceived as a team player. Only slightly less important are the prerequisites of style and flexibility. Style refers to one's demeanor and personality, and one is expected to be outgoing, sophisticated, well-organized, have a sense of humor, and appear shrewd. Flexibility means that one can adjust to new situations – new boss, new co-workers, new directives.[72]

These gangs (alliances, circles) are constantly in the state of flux because of promotions and reorganization. Moreover, there is no common patron for the entire gang. Competition within the gang for favorable recognition weakens the horizontal bonds among members. The vertical relationship to one's patron is ambiguous as well, for the same patron who pulls you up with his successes is the one who pulls you down with his failures. Furthermore, he may need to use you as a scapegoat. This leaves everyone in a state of moral and emotional anarchy. The one absolute rule of the corporate world, which explains the anarchy, is "to protect oneself, and, if possible, one's own."[73] Or, in other words, "the principal goal of each group is its own survival; of each person his own advancement."[74] Clearly the group goal and individual goal are often at odds with one another.

What do street gangs and corporate gangs share in common? Situational moralities whose paramount value is success/survival. The main differences center around loyalty and consistency. There is less personal loyalty in the corporate gang than in the street gang, just as there is less consistency in action (flexibility versus living up to one's reputation). Is it unfair to conclude, based on Jackall's splendid analysis, that there is less moral conviction and emotional attachment in the corporate gang than in the street gang?

The Other-Directed Mind

Just as technology and bureaucracy have given rise to the bureaucratic mind, so too have public opinion and the peer group given rise to the other-directed mind. I am using Riesman's term *other-directed* to refer to a state of mind (mind-set) rather than a character type,[75] but am still relying heavily on his insights.

The contrast between the inner-directed and other-directed character types is the key to his analysis. The inner-directed character occurs in a culture that forms an individual with a conscience, an internalized set of beliefs, that permits, actually requires, one to follow it when no one else is around or in the face of opposition from others. When the socialization process works according to its ideal, the individual comes to possess a certain measure of freedom, that is, the individual has some say in the selection of his own beliefs. Otherwise, the inner-directed individual will end up a conformist, at least in respect to the origin of his beliefs. Riesman understood that the concept of the individual was a rather late historical development, one initially peculiar to Western civilization.[76] Both the tradition-directed type and the inner-directed types were ethical types; but only the inner-directed type places the individual in charge of the application of morality. This is why only the inner-directed type experiences guilt; it is the negative judgment one renders upon oneself.[77]

The other-directed type is an aesthetical type in the sense that it is oriented around consumption, material pleasure, and fun. The context for these aesthetical pursuits is the peer group. As was previously indicated, the main goal is to be popular within the peer group; therefore, adjustment to the group's ever-changing standards is required. Riesman puts it baldly, "All the morality is the group's."[78] Of course, this is a morality that has been aestheticized.[79] Rather than an inner direction, there is now an other direction. There is no moral core to the self, no moral definition of the self; consequently, one becomes a moral chameleon, always adjusting one's viewpoint and beliefs to fit the expectations of others. If the inner-directed type experiences guilt about violating her internalized norms, the other-directed type feels anxiety in his relationships with others. Riesman refers to the peer group members as "antagonistic cooperators."[80] The striving to be popular is highly competitive as is the struggle to be minimally acceptable to a new peer group. The individualism of the other-directed type is shallow; it centers on consumption and leaves the individual no moral defenses against the tyranny of the group. Over forty years ago Riesman perceived that the other-directed character type was becoming the dominant character type in modern societies.

Karen Horney's superb analysis of the neurotic need for affection complements that of Riesman. In her still current *The Neurotic Personality of Our Time* (1937), she argues that the desire to be well-liked, even among those not neurotic, has become compulsive. The neurotic need for affection becomes one of several ways of reassuring one's self about others' perceived hostility. As previously discussed (in chapter 4), the basic anxiety is the "all-pervading feeling of being lonely and helpless in a hostile world."[81] If everyone likes me, no one will hurt me becomes our unconscious slogan. The hostility I feel toward my real and potential competitors prevents me from unselfishly loving the other, and the hostility I project onto others makes me need constant reassurance of affection from others.[82] Competitive and ambiguous relationships with others actually drive one into the arms of the peer group. I am led to embrace the perceived cause of my misery. The peer group, then, becomes an even stronger force in the individual's life.

J. H. van den Berg's exploration of the fragmented self's relations to others is especially helpful here. Vague and ambiguous relations with others result both in unconscious processes and a multiplicity of selves. Because my sense of self is largely dependent on the reactions of others to my actions and attitudes, when their reactions are vague, my sense of self becomes uncertain. There is little chance of achieving a unitary self. Moreover, in the absence of a moral community, each relationship becomes problematic. Consequently, I have as many selves as I have acquaintances.[83] Now each person is a peer group and a potentially nettlesome one at that.

The other-directed mind, in the face of enormous peer pressure and the great weight of public opinion, becomes overly dependent upon the attitudes and valuations of others. Not only one's peer group but each acquaintance is the other. My sense of self is weak, uncertain; the other appears strong, menacing. The other becomes, as it were, a powerful self that I fear but need and must please. The other is commissioned as captain of my fragile and ambiguous self.

To sum up, public opinion and peer group norms are two expressions of statistical normality – the majority viewpoint. Public opinion, based as it is upon desire, ultimately defines each issue in terms of material well-being (happiness and health). Public opinion represents the ephemeral side of a technological civilization in its openness to technological experimentation and its demand that consumer desires be fulfilled. Apart from the media, the peer group is the chief conveyor of public opinion. One of the primary functions of the peer group is schooling its members in the art of consumption; its other chief function is to act as a political interest group. One of technology's side effects is to exacerbate political tensions and create new political divisions.[84] As technology tends to destroy shared moral meaning, the competition for the spoils of technology – a higher standard of living – becomes more brutal. Success, if not survival, hinges upon the protection of the peer group. And yet the peer group proves to be as ephemeral as public opinion, for the loyalty of its members is weakened by their mutual fear of each other. Jackall's words about corporate life reverberate loudly: "The fundamental rule of corporate life is to protect oneself and, if possible, one's own."

In the following chapters, we turn our attention to the role visual images play in the formulation of the new morality. The images of the media also represent the ephemeral side of modern society, especially that which is most compensatory in regard to technology.

6

From the Moral to the Visual: the Compensatory

The proliferation of material visual images appears limitless; we are ensconced in a world of television, movies, music videos, photographs, camcorders, advertisements, billboards, computer games, and now virtual reality. Serious conversation and reading are on the wane.

Until the time of the mass production of visual images, nature and, to a secondary extent, art supplied people with visual images. In the fourteenth century, French historian Georges Duby has argued, the church sanctioned a plethora of images in the form of architecture, sculptures (especially statues), stained glass windows, frescoes, and other icons to create a greater participation of the laity (a project imagined centuries earlier) in its rites. What is unique here is the sheer quantity of images and their use to make concrete Christian mysteries a means of consolidating the church's hold over the laity.[1] Jacques Le Goff, for instance, has shown that the first iconography on purgatory occurs at the end of the fourteenth century, although the concept had existed since the late twelfth century.[2] By the sixteenth century, if not earlier, peddlers sold a religious counterpart to today's baseball cards – images of saints and religious dramas – to peasants. As befits the period, political heroes, such as members of the royal family, and even famous villains, became the subject of a secular iconography that was placed in the same bag of traveling images.[3]

All of this pales by comparison to the explosion of material visual images in the late nineteenth and twentieth centuries. The term *material visual images* refers to images that are artificially constructed and material, such as a photograph. The term *visual image* refers to the images of material objects that are formed in vision. We therefore have visual images of objects and material visual images. In this chapter our attention is directed toward images that are technically constructed. From this point on we shall refer to "material visual images" more simply as "visual images," implying, of course, that these images need to be seen. Most of this enormous increase in material visual images was not in the form of art; initially it was due to photography, advertising signs, newspapers, and magazines. Later the movies, television, the camcorder and the computer became more important in the proliferation of visual images.

The conjunction of advertising and photography assumes a major role initially in the ascendancy of visual images. Indeed, visual images play a larger role in advertising as time goes on.[4] As we have previously seen, advertising is a necessary outgrowth of the mass production of consumer goods. There is nothing voluntary about consumption in modern societies. Advertising provides the commands to consume under the guise of the freedom to achieve material well-being: Buy; Consume; Enjoy. There is freedom of choice about what to consume, but only within the larger demand that we approach life exclusively as consumers.[5]

Advertising, public relations, and political propaganda have contributed to the blurring of the distinction between the visual image and the word in the twentieth century in the forms of visual clichés and verbal images. Visual clichés are advertising images and scenes that reify commonplace sayings or clichés. Roland Marchand, in his study of American advertising between 1920 and 1940, identifies a number of visual clichés, such as "Master of All He Surveys." An ad for AT&T that materializes this expression depicts a business executive in his office looking out over the city with his telephone by his side. There is a similar ad for Gulf Oil, but this time the company scientist looks out a window to view the company's industrial plant. The point is to take a commonplace saying,[7] one that expresses a culture's most widely-held beliefs, and then find an appropriate visual scene to materialize the cliché. It becomes, as we will discover later, a means to objectify everyone's mental images.

The other side of the visual cliché is the verbal image (not to be confused with mental image). Instead of materializing a cliché, here one creates a kind of visual image through language. Daniel Boorstin calls the image a "means" that neither represents truth nor reality.[8] It is an attempt to manufacture a self-fulfilling prophecy, that is, a false definition that leads one to act as if it were true, thereby making it come true. The image is intended to make an impression, to have an emotional impact on its audience. To accomplish this it must be simple, vivid, and concrete.[9] The verbal image thus must be as much an object as the product it is intended to sell. At the same time, however, its meaning must be vague so that the product, organization, or person can be all things to all people.

The images of advertising and public relations have infiltrated American politics since the 1930s.[10] It is obvious that the image of the politician is all-important today. A party sells its candidate exactly the way Colgate sells its toothpaste. There is increasing evidence that images have overrun all of politics, not just political campaigns. Much of the news is a series of images – real events and pseudo events reduced and simplified to a formula – that can be transmitted through the mass media.[11]

Images are a major component of style – physical appearance and life-style – in a consumer-oriented society. Personal style is less an expression of character than of surface appearance.[12] Stuart Ewen even writes about some students who reveal a desire *"to be an image."*[13] The difference between self and appearance is obliterated. Clothes, hair-do, jewelry, tattoos, and messages on clothes create an image that is always subject to revision. Constant experimentation with personal appearance reflects the ephemeral nature of public opinion and peer group norms, on the one hand, and the psychological reality of multiple selves and role-playing, on the other hand.

Closely related to personal style is life-style. Based as much on the total ownership or access to goods and services as on the singular transformation of the self into a commodity, life-style is a collective phenomenon.[14] It is related to class, gender, and subculture. Advertisements provide images of life-style in the depiction of people using specific products, whereas the products and services that are consumed become an image of the life-style that has been assumed. The television show "Lifestyles of the Rich and Famous" is an apt example of modern lifestyle.

Style has always been an important dimension of status and class. Its importance as a form of *symbolic* differentiation and communication is rapidly diminishing, however.[15] Anticipating the subsequent argument, I shall briefly note that the visual image does not so much serve as a vehicle for symbolic meaning as for reified meaning – instinctual power. Style as a composite image still differentiates and communicates but primarily at an emotional level. Modern style, then, is different from traditional style in that it is superficial (external), ephemeral, and symbolically meaningless (in terms of cultural meaning).

The impact of visual images upon cultural forms is indeed pervasive. Television, for example, has affected both the form and the content of the modern novel. Characters discuss television programs and make reference to commercials. More than a mere backdrop, however, television and advertising provide a point of reference – no matter how tenuous and fleeting – for the protagonists. A character in a television series becomes an instantaneous model for emulation, just as a consumer product gives momentary psychological comfort within the "video novel."[16]

Some novelists, like Jerzy Kosinski (*Being There*) and Don DeLillo (*White Noise*), have moved television to the center of the novel's reality in a critical fashion; for others, like Bobbie Ann Mason and William Warner, television's hold on reality is to be at least implicitly celebrated.[17] Perhaps the most telling index of the author's own view is the form of the novel. As Cecelia Tichi puts it, in the video novel "the conventional chapter dissolves into a patchwork of loosely related scenes without causal sequence – parts of a perceptual environment."[18] Most noteworthy in the video novel and in recent fiction in general is a decline in narrative structure. An eternal present, loosely structured, viewed from multiple perspectives, without coherence, is characteristic of this "spatial form."[19] Technology, not just the visual images of the mass media, is responsible for the use of spatial form and the decline of narrative form in modern fiction. Yet, as we shall see later, technology's growth and increasing influence depend on visual images and image-dominated people.

Movies too have begun to make video images their subject. "Sex, Lies and Videotape" and "Speaking Parts" explore the ways in which taped images affect experience, knowledge, and communication. In "Speaking Parts," a video mausoleum permits the bereaved to watch tapes of their dead relatives and friends.[20] Such weird scenes act as a warning against the tendency to substitute image for reality or to hopelessly confuse the two.

Language itself reflects the onslaught of visual images. The primary meaning of image today is a material representation; moreover, the connotations invariably suggest the images of television, movies, and photographs. Image as mental image, idea, metaphor, and symbol has precipitously declined in everyday usage. Even in literary criticism the notion of image as live metaphor has given way to the idea of "something inert and single, like a painting or an idol or a reflection in a mirror."[21] Image, if not a material representation of an object, is at least a singular, literal concept. Image, then, has lost its earlier metaphorical or symbolic double-meaning.

Finally visual images as self-contained realities, triumphant spectacles, have invaded the world of visual art from set-design to architecture to special effects in movies. Paul Goldberger concludes that the "real star" of "Starlight Express" is the hideously expensive set. Certainly the set of "Phantom of the Opera" produced almost as much enthusiasm as the music. Operatic sets have become equally extravagant, as evidenced in Zeffirelli's "Turandot." Goldberger compares the work of architect Helmut John to that of movie director and producer George Lucas. For example, John's State of Illinois Center in Chicago is likened to a set for "Star Wars."[22] What is the equivalent of special effects in architecture? Buildings that only occupy the foreground, call attention to themselves, and seem designed to register a strong but exclusively emotional reaction. The new architecture cannot tolerate indifference. When special effects are used in movies they supplant plot and character development as a source of aesthetic pleasure. A heavy reliance on special effects insures that movies will be even more preoccupied with action scenes, including a heavy dose of violence. Earlier movies, it is well known, tended to emphasize dialogue to a much greater extent, thereby permitting plot and character development. In many contemporary films, the dialogue is a background, receding all the time, to the foreground of spectacular images as in action scenes. Goldberger concludes that "the notion that appearances are all seems characteristic of this age."[23]

The Symbol and the Visual Image: the Order of Truth and the Order of Reality

This section makes no pretense to resolve some of the thorniest issues in semantics, linguistics, and semiotics. I shall set forth as simply as possible a position on discourse in order to clarify the larger argument of the chapter, following the work of Ricoeur,[24] Todorov,[25] Bakhtin,[26] Lakoff and Johnson,[27] and Ellul[28] (without assuming that their views form a single position). In so doing we shall be distancing ourselves both from positivistic (objectivistic) and radical deconstructionist (subjectivistic) views. The above-mentioned authors share a set of assumptions: (1) discourse arises out of common but not identical human experiences that involve an interaction between self and other and self and world; (2) discourse is partly metaphorical and symbolic; (3) metaphor and symbol are the bases for the qualities that humans attribute to and infer from human interaction; (4) the meaning of key words and all discourse is set within a historical context; (5) cultural meaning is holistic so that a metaphor, symbol, or dialectical concept (concept about something at least partly qualitative) must be understood in relation to other linguistic expressions; (6) historical and cultural meanings are plural, that is, they emerge out of moral and political dialogue and conflicts that may or may not be eventually resolved.

With respect to visual images I shall follow the work of Ellul[29] and Gombrich.[30] The assumptions here include the following: (1) visual images are inherently ambiguous with regard to meaning; (2) the meaning of visual images flows indirectly from discourse as set within a cultural and historical context; (3) while ambiguous with regard to meaning, visual images can be more or less exact in relation to the world of objects; (4) the impact of images is first and foremost emotional.

There is increasing evidence that natural languages have a metaphorical basis in part because the human mind understands life in terms of comparisons and paradigms,[31] in part because life itself is experienced as tensive and mysterious.[32] George Lakoff and Mark Johnson have demonstrated that most concepts are derived from metaphorical insights. The reason, as Ricoeur[33] and Todorov[34] have indicated, is that metaphor and symbol cannot be understood and cannot remain vital without interpretation; the act of interpretation necessarily leads to conceptualization.

Metaphor and symbol are characterized by indirect meaning. Metaphor is a sign with a "double intentionality." The first meaning, the literal meaning, indirectly suggests the second meaning, the figurative meaning, because the literal meaning by itself is absurd. As Ricoeur indicates, the secondary signification of a metaphor is the meaning of a meaning (the primary or literal meaning).[35] Yet the two meanings of the metaphor are opposed to one another, they exist in a state of tension and, moreover, invite a comparison. Therefore a metaphor concomitantly states that something *is* and *is not* something else; in other words, it is *like* something else. The metaphor "love is a rose" suggests that in some but not all ways love is like a rose. Ultimately, then, the meaning of a metaphor flows from the tension between the two meanings, a tension that defies a final resolution. There is more in a metaphor that can be expressed in a single concept because a metaphor is more ambiguous and open-ended than a concept.

Ricoeur indicates at least three general uses of the term *symbol*; one of them is as a religious symbol. Whereas the symbol and the metaphor both contain indirect meanings, the religious symbol differs from the metaphor in two crucial ways – it has a non-semantic dimension and it is bound to a universe. The metaphor's two meanings are semantic, but the symbol's figurative meaning remains in part shrouded in mystery. A religious symbol refers in one way or another to that which is experienced as sacred. Yet the sacred is invariably elusive, beyond full human comprehension, because it only indirectly manifests itself. The figurative meaning of a symbol is only partly semantic, for it represents an effort to state the ineffable. The religious symbol, moreover, is bound to a universe, to a milieu; it is not a free creation. As Mircea Eliade has demonstrated, religious symbolism emerges from the interaction between humans and a universe (traditionally nature, but more recently society and even technology[36]) that appears all-powerful. It is as correct, for example, to say that the sky symbolizes itself as transcendence, as it is to say that humans symbolize the sky as such.[37] Ernst Cassirer has even gone so far as to suggest that myth and language originate in the shocking emotional experiences in relating to nature that stand behind traditional religious symbols (radical metaphors).[38] The bound nature of religious symbols is likewise indicated by their interrelatedness. Each symbol implies the entire system of symbols.[39] The reason is that what is being symbolized is not an autonomous, discrete phenomenon but a part of a sacred universe or milieu.

Religious and political symbols (and the myths that organize them) have provided societies with a sense of purpose and ultimate or final meaning. There are two kinds of meaning: ordinary meaning, the linguistic and conceptual definition of reality, and final meaning, the meaning of life, the meaning of history. The latter type of meaning is invariably expressed through symbols. Final meaning possesses two dimensions – significance and direction or orientation. Final meaning implies moral valuation in a temporal context. That is, the attribution of ultimate meaning involves a choice of ethical values and a narrative sense of their realization. Ultimate meaning is ethical in nature.

Ultimate meaning is related to the order of truth.[40] By this is meant the truth as a cultural form without specifying its content. We can thus speak about truth in a general way. The order of truth (until the ascendancy of radical immanentism) refers to the relationship between my actual words or actions and their ethical counterpart – what they should be. Moreover, it refers to the relationship between my words and my actions. Is my life true or false in regard to what I profess to believe? Truth and falsehood both belong to the order of truth. That is, as dialectical concepts, each term implies the other and is defined in relation to its opposite. The order of truth suggests an ethical ideal (even if not fully knowable) according to which words and actions can either be true or false. By contrast, the order of reality refers simply to whether something in the empirical world exists or not. Factual truth is a mixed case. On the one hand, it refers to whether what I say corresponds to what is; but, on the other hand, it refers to an ethical ideal that there should be a correspondence between words and reality. With the rise of radical immanentism, factual truth becomes dominant; ethical truth (in the full sense of the term) tends to disappear. With the increasing attack upon language's ability to reflect and create a commonly experienced reality, factual truth gives way to subjective truth: whatever I say is true; if nothing else, my words exist.

Just as the ethical is expressed through religious and political symbols, so too is truth. Thus Ricoeur refers to truth as metaphorical.[42] Similarly Todorov speaks of truth as wisdom, a wisdom, however, expressed metaphorically.[43] Cynthia Ozick writes about how a society retains its memory of the past through metaphors and narratives of good and evil events. For Jews, bondage in Egypt becomes a "metaphor of pity for the outsider; Egypt becomes the great metaphor of reciprocity."[44] Negative metaphors like those positive counterparts allow one to understand the ethical truth the event symbolizes, to retain the memory of the event, and thus become wise. Whether one is rooting truth in a sense of transcendence gleaned from literary or from historical narrative, the point is that truth can never be grasped directly enough to be reduced to a logical concept.

Only discourse allows us to express our experiences of the truth. Discourse can be used to describe reality, but its genius is to help us pursue the truth. By itself the visual image refers us to an empirical reality, actual or imaginary. Although the visual image and discourse can both be used to describe reality, the image is a more compelling source of empirical information.

Now what many have called reality, at least until recently, is actually a dialectic of the two orders of empirical reality and truth. Because societies more or less follow a common morality that places some limitations on power and retain some memory of the truth, reality is experienced as more than empirical reality. A sense of the mystery of life appears universal. What makes life mysterious, of course, is not just its incomprehensibility but the intimations of something transcendent. George Steiner suggests that the most mysterious part of our existence is the creation of art, music, and literature;[45] Jacques Ellul makes the same claim for language.[46]

A reality that is a union of the two orders of empirical reality and truth begins to wane with the triumph of science and technology. If modern science provides the intellectual superstructure for a thorough-going materialistic worldview, the visual images of the mass media supply its emotional infrastructure. Material visual images, especially those of the mass media, envelop us in a cozy atmosphere that is emotionally satisfying.

The Visual Images of the Mass Media: Reality without Truth

Television is the mass medium that most dominates our lives. The average American household has the television on 55 hours per week; the average individual, depending on age, watches television from just over three hours a day to over five hours a day.[47] For many it is the single most frequent and important leisure activity. The following discussion is mainly directed toward television although it applies at times to other visual media as well. I shall attempt to make a strong case that the visual images of the media, although invariably accompanied by the spoken or written word, dominate the form and content of what is communicated. The images of television in particular have come to constitute a kind of language.

The relationship between television and information is paradoxical. If television communicates information in bits and pieces,[48] "information in turn communicates television."[49] That is, information assumes the dramatic form of television; moreover, the emotional force of the information is more important to the viewer than its intellectual impact. Keep in mind that the visual image first and foremost affects the viewer emotionally. We have little memory, however, of televised images. Television creates an eternal present, but one that is ever new. To live in the moment alone is to live in the emotion. We will consider the emotional aspect of televised images later; first let us examine the information of the mass media in its intellectual aspect.

The information of television is decontextualized information. The temporal and spatial contexts of everyday life are eliminated on television, whose reality is anytime, anyplace. Space in the sense of place is meaningful to humans insofar as it is part of a cultural heritage. The places where key events have occurred acquire a symbolic meaning; they become metaphors for a group's identity and hooks upon which to hang memories of the past. Traditional societies often perform rituals at the real or imagined place where such events have occurred. Rites of renewal, for example, honor the time and place of the creation of the world or the birth of a society.[50] Historic sites abound in virtually every society; they are only meaningful, however, to the one who knows the history of the place. Otherwise they are only mildly interesting in a physical sense.

Television likewise creates chaos in social space. The distribution of social status on television bears little relationship to that in reality. Soap operas, for instance, have an inordinate number of the wealthy and glamorous and those in health-related professions.[51] But even more important is the juxtaposition of statuses and groups. The most unlikely set of relationships can occur as long as they are fascinating. Music videos take this to an extreme with the blurring of gender roles and the rapid transition from one image, status, and role to another.[52] In music videos there is no social order, but rather a constantly shifting set of relations. Madonna has made a career of frequently changing her image, status, and gender in the same video. Television turns all social positions and relationships into possibilities for everyone. Perhaps the blurring of the distinction between the private and public spheres of life is the most critical way in which television upsets all social arrangements.[53] The talk shows are only the logical conclusion of a medium that turns us into entertainer-exhibitionists, on the one hand, and spectator-voyeurists, on the other hand. The novel is the literary genre that delves most completely into psychological processes. On a purely emotional level television exceeds the novel in this regard. Everything previously considered personal or private is divulged on talk shows: the instant therapy of revealing traumatic event. The news and human interest programs allow ordinary people to do much the same. The same programs from the point of view of the audience – soap operas, human interest programs, and conventional dramas and comedies – permit us to become consumers of other peoples' experiences. To the extent that the lives of those on television are more interesting and spectacular than our own, we can live vicariously through their experiences. Hence what is private is revealed on television (the public) and what is on television becomes the private.

In creating an "eternal present" television eliminates the historical context of events. It places us exclusively in the present, but a random, incoherent present.[54] Existence has been typically experienced as a narrative – myth or history in the case of a society, and biography in the case of an individual. Narrative contains two main characteristics: temporal succession and transformation.[55] Temporal succession can either be continuous – duration time – or discontinuous – event time. While narrative includes duration time, its paramount concern is event time. Events mark the significant occurrences in the life of a group or an individual; moreover they take on a larger meaning in light of the story's denouement. Transformation refers to a critical change in the life of an individual or group. Reversal, as in a conversion, is the paradigm of narrative change. Transformation, even more so than the event, has great symbolic power in a narrative; it has the ability to signify the entire story. Denouement brings together significant events and transformations in a way that makes the narrative a totality of meaning.

Television in its overall impact is anti-narrative. Although it can be argued that individual programs have a narrative form (even here I shall argue that in the electronic media the visual images destroy the narrative structure of discourse), the entire spectrum of programs is random and incoherent. That is, there is no temporal and meaningful relationship among programs and commercials. One can go from the news of an earthquake in South Carolina, to a commercial for hemorrhoids, to a talk show about men who are looking for a mother figure in the women they date, to a game show, to a program that recreates "true" police encounters with criminals, to a rerun of *Gilligan's Island*, to *Studs*. All programs and commercials are equal; all visual images are equal. Therefore television in its total impact destroys the experience of event-time. One is left with duration time, the continuous time of description. Television describes reality for us but leaves us with no understanding of it. The more television one watches, the more life appears absurd, but interesting.

The main, if not exclusive, impact of the visual image is emotional. Emotional experiences are principally aesthetical, and as such leave us oriented to the moment of pleasure or pain. By itself emotion does not allow us to transcend the immediate present.[56] What is most distinctive about humans, Kierkegaard argues, is our imagination and anticipation of the future; without this, there is no sense of the past. Television's visual images permit no future and thus no past. As Ellul notes, television is anti-surrealistic; it subtracts meaning from life.[57]

Walter Benjamin has called attention to the destruction of meaning that occurs when a work of art is removed from its historical and cultural context and is technologically reproduced exclusively as a visual image for consumption.[58] This objectification is essentially what television does on a much larger scale. Joseph Frank notes that much of modern literature possesses a spatial form in which narrative as the common experience of past, present, and future gives way to a subjective present that can be viewed from multiple perspectives.[59] Television accomplishes this as well in its anti-narrative form and emotional impact on the viewer. Television concurrently makes reality fully objective through the visual image and makes it totally subjective in its anti-narrative structure. What is left out are intersubjective, symbolic experiences that are neither completely objective nor completely subjective.

Television not only weakens our sense of reality (as both the order of truth and order of reality) as narrative, it also eliminates our experience of reality as tensive or dialectical.[60] Life is traditionally experienced as replete with conflict, ambiguity, ambivalence, and contradiction. Some have argued that the tension between life and death is the origin of religious consciousness.[61] The dialectic of life and death includes the ideas that one's own life is sustained by the death of other living things and the idea that life and death co-exist in one's body. Television eliminates the sense of the unity of opposites and the notion that opposite forces act upon each other to change reality. Instead television presents visual images in a *logical* sequence.[62] Images replace one another in linear fashion. This allows for conflict, but a purely external conflict. Dialectical conflict is internal – within an individual, a society, a culture. External conflict is that between discrete, autonomous entities. The visual images of television present life, then, as a logical process involving autonomous objects in external conflict leading to an outcome – success or failure.

Television plays a large role in the representation of life as a spectacle. This idea is so important that we must consider the thoughts of its originator – Guy Debord.[63] All of life has been transformed into an image/object for immediate consumption. The spectacle includes both commodities as visual images and material visual images of commodities. The spectacle is the "language" of the commodity; it is the visualization of the commodity for spiritual consumption. Human beings become reified as commodities, and as such are equivalent to their visual image.

The spectacle idealizes reality by turning it into a speculative universe ruled by a kind of logical concept – the commodity form. Moreover, it strips existence of both experience and meaning and thus makes it abstract. Simultaneously, however, the spectacle reifies existence (in the visual image) and thus makes reality thoroughly materialistic.

The spectacle turns existence into "*appearing*, a project capitalism had already started by turning *being* into *having*." As the spectacle tends to eliminate the distinction between image and reality, there is less difference between living and vicariously living, between being a unified self and being a role–player, between truth and falsehood. Ultimately the image becomes even more important than lived reality itself. Life becomes a picture show, a screen on to which images are projected. Life as spectacle is a purely aesthetical existence; everything is judged as interesting or boring.[64]

Debord's concept of the spectacle applies most cogently to a reality mediated by television. Studies conducted on the impact of television on the human brain indicate that there is about as much activity in that side of the brain that assists in rational thinking when one is watching television as when one is asleep.[65] Television (and the movies), then, makes a fundamental appeal to our instincts and emotions. In short, television's images are pleasurable. Paul Goldberger maintains that "The rise in visual literacy has been accompanied by an almost desperate desire to be stimulated."[66] Our increased visual sophistication lowers our threshold for boredom; we require ever more spectacular spectacles.

Visual spectacle produces contradictory psychological effects: a feeling of unlimited power and a sense of apocalypse. Television places me at the center of the universe. All images come to me, and I control them by switching channels. Moreover, television fills me up with information that I can share with the less informed. Because reality is on television, by watching television I gain a certain control – if only at the level of information – over reality. Television in both advertisements and programs titillates our desires and creates new needs. With the abolition of time, television destroys expectancy and delayed gratification. It creates a sense of immediate fulfilment.[67] The motto is: if I watch television, these objects and images become mine.[67] The power of television becomes the extent of my own power.

At the same time, however, the visual spectacle of television conjures up a feeling of apocalypse, the end of the world. In studies of the effect of violence on television upon viewer attitudes, George Gerbner and Larry Gross demonstrate that heavy watchers (four or more hours a day) perceive the world to be a violent, scary place, and exaggerate their own risks, in part because the "world of television drama is, above all, a violent one in which more than half of all characters are involved in some violence."[68] Beyond the incidence of violence (an issue to which we will subsequently return), television produces on a purely emotional level a sense of catastrophe, of the end.[69] Every natural disaster, every war and political uprising, every spoilage of the environment, every personal tragedy in the world is compressed into a 30-minute news program. In traditional societies one had only to confront local tragedies, not those of the entire world simultaneously. Emotionally, then, one experiences the world of television as a place of ever-escalating disasters.

Television exacerbates the sense of disaster and doom in two other related ways. First, along with technology in general, it destroys the need for memory.[70] Visual images become a substitute for memory. Memory is tied to a remembrance of the past, of what is significant in the past. We remember those experiences that have been symbolically mediated or interpreted. Television requires us to live in an unstable present where memory only gets in the way of the pleasurable loss of self that comes from vicariously living through images. The decline of memory leaves us more anxious about life's problems because we do not have the benefit of learning how others have reacted to similar problems.

Second, at the level of visual images, television leaves us imprisoned in the order of reality. Without the infusion of the order of truth, of the attribution of meaning, reality becomes even more terrible, even more unbearable than it would be otherwise. Television and visual spectacle in general empty existence of meaning. This in itself is a major cause of the sense of apocalyptic doom, for hope derives solely from the order of truth.[71] The opposite of hope, of course, is despair.

In writing about the contemporary American novel, John Aldridge maintains that two frequent themes are those of "universal conspiracy" and "mass apocalypse."[72] Thomas Pynchon and Don DeLillo have dramatized both themes and the nexus between them in some of their novels. Universal conspiracy refers to the apparent interrelatedness of all human actions without the characters having the ability to understand and alter the situation. This leads, as Aldridge notes, to feelings of paranoia. The most improbable of events, e.g. an underground postal service in Pynchon's *The Crying of Lot 49*,[73] appears to be related to other bizarre phenomena. The reader, and usually one of the characters, has a sense of a "massive and mysterious" system that coordinates all human activity. At an emotional level, however, the characters seem to be falling apart; their lives exhibit maximum disorder. The reader is left with a sense that the human world at a sociological level is highly organized and at a psychological level highly disorganized. The simultaneous experience of order/disorder and the feeling that events are fully coordinated and yet beyond human intervention leads to a sense of apocalypse.

This theme will be taken up again in chapter 8, but for now let us simply relate the sense of apocalypse in television to that in the novel. I am not suggesting any simple cause and effect relationship. Television as a medium is a cause of the apocalyptic experience; the content of television is a reflection of that same experience. Novelists like other artists are sometimes sensitive to the unconscious experiences of a society. Therefore it is not surprising to discover that both television and the novel convey a sense of apocalypse.

Television, however, makes the apocalypse pleasurable. Television is the key factor in turning life into a series of spectacular images to be consumed and enjoyed. At the very least the encounter with the end of the world on television is interesting. In a related context, Benjamin speaks of humans so alienated that they can experience their own destruction in Futurist Art as an "aesthetic pleasure of the first order."[74] In *Mao II*, one of DeLillo's characters, a photographer, doubts the validity of her attempt to shock people about the squalor of the world: "No matter what I shot, how much horror, reality, misery, ruined bodies, bloody faces, it was all so fucking pretty in the end."[75]

If the society of the spectacle is dominated by the visual image, noise is its handmaiden. The proliferation of visual images in the modern world is matched by an increase in the kinds and level of noise.[76] Industrialization, of course, has added to the amount of ambient noise in human society. Like all other important words, *noise* has acquired a variety of meanings. Noise as unwanted sound dates back to the thirteenth century; noise as any loud sound is a more recent formulation.[77] The notion of unwanted sound is clearly subjective, just as that of loud sound is somewhat more objective. Taken together noise becomes any loud, unwanted sound. This I suggest is the main meaning of noise today, but it can readily be used in only one of the two senses – loud or unwanted.

The noise I am most interested in here is music, particularly rock music: wanted by some, unwanted by others, loud by anyone's standards. One's taste in music has become part of an image one projects. College students show off their CD collections the way another generation of college students put their book collections on display. More startling, however, is the way music has come to dominate life: from background as with Moozak to foreground as with the singles bar. Many bars and restaurants play music loud enough to drown out conversation. Never have so many spent so much time listening to music. Many young people appear to be addicted to music, especially rock; moreover, some feel the need to impose their choice of music on others. In large part this represents a means of communicating an image to others.

Rock music is above all vulgar, that is "common, noisy, crass, and untranscendent." "The vulgarian," according to Robert Pattison, "cannot transcend ordinary experience." "He goes wherever his passions take him."[78] Pattison's concept of vulgarity does not reflect class bias in the form of a critique of low culture, for he recognizes that a concern for the transcendent (the absence of which is the fundamental characteristic of vulgarity) is often present in folk art and folk culture in general. The languages of today's vulgarity are television and rock music. Mick Jagger put it succinctly: "It's noise we make that's all. You could be kind and call it music."[79]

The lyrics of rock music (with notable exceptions) are notoriously banal and repetitive, as well as being laden with sexual and violent images.[80] As everyone knows, the lyrics aren't the important part anyway. One critic even goes so far as to suggest that rock music represents at times a conscious attack upon language.[81] The music of rock is everything. It makes a fundamental appeal to the instincts. Some music, e.g. the fugues of Bach, is directed toward reason; some toward the emotions (Romantic music); rock toward the instincts – sexuality and aggression. Rock is erotically stimulating; it allows one to let go, to experience random sensations in the beat of the music.

The synthesis of television and rock music in the music video is an especially hypnotic spectacle. Some of my college students mention that they feel they could readily become addicted to the music videos on MTV and VH1. Music videos are anti-narratives, that is, the sequence of images is deliberately random, producing a dream-like state, the better to unleash fantasies.[82] A number of advertisements, e.g. Calvin Klein products and Levi's 501 jeans, use the video approach to visual images: rapidly changing, random images. Whereas music videos have less narrative structure than any other television program, concurrently they perfectly reflect television as a whole in its random mix of program, news, and advertisement. The music video, then, is a microcosm of television as a medium that represents life as meaningless and absurd.

Television and rock music both lead to a diminution of subjective reason. For reasons we shall examine later, the tempo and pressures of a technological civilization create an exaggerated need for humans to escape subjective reason and lose themselves in the sensation of the moment. Subjective reason requires silence, a time and a place free of the distractions of visual images and noise. Without such "positive silence," concentration, thought, and meditation become difficult. Only subjective reason allows us to ponder the question of the meaning of life. Without this life becomes as absurd as it is represented to be on television.

White noise, the use of one noise to blunt or diminish the impact of another noise, is prevalent in business and industry. Moozak is a kind of white noise designed to distract the shopper, for instance, from feelings of boredom and fatigue so that shopping purchases can be maximized.[83] Jeremy Murray-Brown refers to much of the information on television as "visual noise" that distracts the viewer from more serious reflection.[84] Along the same lines, DeLillo in *White Noise* uses television as one of the main protagonists. Television becomes for Jack and Babette white noise that allows them to escape the questions of death and the meaning of life.

The visual images of television and the other mass media represent reality as pleasurable, as a spectacle to be consumed. This is a purely aesthetical approach to life that leaves us prisoners of the moment. By contrast, reality in all other types of society is experienced as tragic:[85] life involves suffering only occasionally punctuated by periods of happiness, and eventually leads to death. The question all previous societies have faced, beyond that of survival, is the transcendent meaning of suffering and death, as the basis for the meaning of life. The experience that love makes suffering bearable, even overcomes it, becomes a commentary upon death. Milan Kundera's *The Unbearable Lightness of Being* is a profound meditation upon the relationship of love and freedom to suffering. He concludes that the meaning of life is to be found in ethical love. A life devoted exclusively to aesthetic pleasure suppresses the quest for ethical truth. Television turns life into a non-stop excursion boat in Adventureland.

Television appears to the viewer to be a description of reality; moreover reality is perceived to be on television. These two propositions – television is about reality, and reality is on television – are different but complementary ideas. There appears to be a one-to-one relationship between visual images and reality (actual or imagined). As has already been noted, the visual image is related to the order of reality. Sight is the sense that we most trust. Images are understood to be operational indicators of what they represent.[86] The image and reality create a unity that allows us certainty about the empirical world. The image provides us with the information necessary to manipulate and adjust to reality.

Television appears to be describing reality, particularly in news programs, documentaries, talk-shows and game shows. In effect, it is reconstructing reality by taking reality out of its temporal and cultural context. Reality as we live it still retains, no matter how small, some meaning (order of truth); but television expunges this meaning and recomposes reality as a logical sequence of image fragments. Reality appears in televised images as a series of objects that encounter one another in space.

There are many other programs on television, however, such as soap operas and prime-time dramas and comedies that appear cognitively to be unreal. But emotionally they are real, just as real as the programs that appear more congruous with empirical reality. At an emotional level all images are real: all images register an impact upon the emotions.

Jerry Mander, in reflecting on his own child's inability to distinguish television from reality, remarks that "*Seeing things on television as false and unreal is learned.*"[87] Just as with any other type of learning, this one may prove unsuccessful in certain cases. Gerbner and Gross's study of television viewing indicates that heavy watchers had a greatly distorted sense of reality. Among other things, heavy viewers "overestimated the percentage of the population who have professional jobs; and they drastically overestimated the number of police in the U.S. and the amount of violence." The errors in the heavy viewers' judgments were congruent with the distortions of television. It is hard to escape the conclusion that "the more television people watched, the more their view of the world matched television reality."[88]

Edmund Carpenter reports on an informal study of college students, who when told that television's report of an event was inaccurate, either accepted the inconsistency uncritically or doubted reality.[89] Television provides a more emotionally-satisfying reality. In DeLillo's *White Noise* Heinrich argues about whether it's raining outside or not, despite the fact that he can look for himself and see that it is raining, because he was told by the weatherman that it wouldn't rain. Carpenter suggests that some children "associate the ability to think with television."[90] Studies of television viewers indicate that while young people watch a lot of television, old people watch even more.[91] Perhaps the appropriate conclusion to be drawn is that the more isolated and lonely one is and the more television one watches, the more likely one is to experience reality through television.

We have now reached the turning point: not only is television about reality, but reality is on television. This assertion suggests that as spectators we live vicariously through and in visual images and that the medium of television is a principle epistemological authority that rivals the computer in terms of efficacy. When television momentarily focuses on an issue, it becomes a "real" issue; when television leaves it behind for a new issue, the old issue is eliminated from our immediate experiences and thus becomes a non-issue. A society of the spectacle turns life into a visual drama, a show, and the most real show, the most "objective" show, is that on television.[92] Television has become the most important authority of dramatized information among the various mass media. We are fascinated with the possibility of being on television or meeting someone who is on television (a celebrity) because it is only here – television – that my subjective experiences (which are experienced emotionally as real) can be objectified.

In chapter 4, I argued that technology tends to destroy symbolically-mediated experiences (organization-information) in the interest of technical information (service-information). Technology is the ultimate authority in modern societies and is equated with truth itself. Obviously television is a type of technology, but one serving a special purpose – compensation for the abstractness and impersonality of technology. That is, television provides *reverse* images of a technological civilization. It makes the abstract concrete and the impersonal personal by dramatizing information. We do not live emotionally in the computer except when we turn it too into a source of visual spectacle, as with animated computer games and virtual reality;[93] but we do live emotionally in television. The computer provides *direct* images[94] of a technological civilization in its visualized images – computer language.[95] Technology takes all the real drama out of life by reducing all action (including human interaction) to objective, logical procedures. Under these circumstances life would be unbearable, but along comes television (and the movies) to salvage the experience of human drama.

Therefore, we have two choices: to live in and through natural language with symbolically mediated experiences as our reality or to live in and through technology and material visual images with the computer and television as our reality. We have chosen the latter – a fragmented reality devoid of true symbolic quality. Television's images, compensation for the overall abstractness and impersonality of technology, are reified symbols.

The visual images of television (and the mass media) are only images of power and possessions. Leaving aside dialogue for the moment, autonomous visual images are about objects (possessions) and their relations (power), or, in other words, how some objects bring about the movement of other objects. Television makes all objects equal because all visual images are equal in their believability and their potential for emotional arousal;[96] moreover, in a consumption-oriented society all objects become equally consumable. The difference between human beings and products disappears: human beings are constantly being interrupted on television by advertised products and more importantly have themselves become reified products.

The relations between products are relations of power: possession, consumption, manipulation, control, and violence. A world devoid of symbolic meaning in the sense of ethical truth is a world of raw power. Because symbolic meaning flows directly or indirectly from discourse, autonomous visual images are only about relations of power. For example, on television a man and a woman embrace. Is this an instance of ethical love, sexual desire, or the desire to manipulate the other? The visual images by themselves make the first response impossible, for the visual image is about the order of empirical reality. We are left with a choice between or a combination of the second and third responses.

But even when we factor in discourse, the visual images of the mass media are still only images of possessions and power. The subversion of language by the visual images of the media, particularly television, is the result of the convergence of three phenomena: (1) the logical linking together of visual images to create a pseudo-language; (2) the visual images of the media as a more emotionally satisfying reality than the one we experience directly; (3) the impoverishment of natural language.

The visual images of television cut up and reconstruct reality according to a spatial logic of signifiers. The "meaning" of a television program is the final outcome – success or failure, survival or death, possession or nonpossession; in other words, power. The content of the various programs are about objects to be possessed and consumed, the power of which becomes that of the spectator/consumer; more exactly the content is about objects acting in relation to other objects – acts of possession, consumption, manipulation, control, or violence. These acts of power are spatially linked together in a television program or movie in a logical sequence that leads to an outcome – success or failure.[97]

Television provides us with a reality at once both spectacular and pleasurable; it is, however, a meaningless reality. At worst this reality is boring. Existence is, as we have seen, a symbolic reality (dialectic of the order of truth and order of reality). Reality, as we live it, involves suffering and is ultimately tragic. Only a sense of ultimate meaning, ethical truth, can allow one to face this reality honestly and begin to transcend it. Otherwise this reality is unbearable; experienced as such, one is driven to escape its hold. As our lived reality becomes less meaningful and thus more terrifying, television and the other media comfort us in the warm prison house of a spectacular reality.[98]

The decline of natural language is signaled by a number of related changes in discourse: (1) decline in the use of metaphor; (2) rapid change in meaning of symbols; (3) vagueness of meaning; (4) reification of symbols. The work of Kenneth Hudson,[99] John Holloway,[100] and Stanley Gerr[101] has called attention to the tendency for words to either become technical terms with one precise meaning or to lose much of their meaning and serve instead as a sign of emotional identification. The former tendency is a direct expression of technology; it takes the forms of a growing scientific and technical vocabulary where the fundamental concern is with functional relationships, operationalized terms, and quantified facts, and of a decline in metaphor in everyday speech. The tacit goal here is to create a completely rationalized language wherein each word has a single meaning. The latter tendency – using words in a vague way for the purpose of emotional identification – is an indirect consequence of technology. Jargon, whose superficial appearance is scientific, is actually the opposite of scientific and technical terminology, for it is not used to convey information and rational concepts but rather to sustain a feeling of collective identity, a sense of belonging. Jargon is intellectually sterile; its meaning is indeterminably vague. Jargon simultaneously protects the peer group from outside interference and is a kind of secret emotional code that fosters solidarity.[102] Both tendencies eschew the use of metaphor, the chief vehicle for expressing symbolic meaning. The two tendencies, a greater rationalization of discourse and a greater emphasis on emotion, perfectly reflect a technological civilization, which simultaneously enlarges the sphere of technical reason and that of instinctual emotion at the expense of subjective reason.

The decline of discourse is marked by the proliferation of symbols that are ephemeral. Baudrillard has called attention to how advertising turns every product into a symbol.[103] Cologne symbolizes sexual prowess, the sports car success, and so forth. But these symbols have no staying power, for advertising must constantly experiment with pseudo-meaning. The products come and go, and so do their symbolic meanings. These symbols are "sterilized symbols," for they (not the product but the symbolic meaning) no longer have a practical purpose in a technological civilization as an integral part of culture; rather they serve as a means of propaganda.[104] Political symbols suffer the same fate as advertising symbols. Politicians are sold like products.

A key issue in regard to modern discourse is its vagueness of meaning. By this I mean a loosening of the connection between sense and referent. The meaning of an utterance involves both sense (the *what* is said) and referent (the *about what*) of discourse. As Ricoeur notes, it is because we bring our experiences to light in discourse that discourse is about a world beyond discourse.[105] Vagueness in meaning can occur in two ways. First, the same word, sentence, or symbol can be used in relation to too many referents. The word *democracy* is used to refer to virtually every extant government, no matter how totalitarian it is, by one party or another. Second, the word or symbol may come to possess *no* referents. This what Henri Lefebvre calls "the decline of referentials."[106] Qualitative concepts like love and freedom may increasingly have nothing to refer to in lived reality. As has been argued, a technological civilization makes ethical meaning superfluous.

Finally, the meaning of many key concepts has been reified: visual images become the operational indicators of qualitative concepts. At the same time that symbolic meaning becomes vague, and thus subjective, it likewise becomes objectified in visual images. Language is becoming subordinate to visual images. This is perhaps less serious with regard to positive concepts, that is, concepts that refer to objects, but in respect to dialectic concepts, that is, concepts that refer to qualities, it is devastating. The turning of language into an accessory to the visual image suggests that every concept expressed in discourse refers to an "object." The result is a thoroughgoing quantitative reality. When the protagonist says, "I love you," to the object of his affection on the soap opera, the "meaning" of love is the passionate embrace that accompanies the dialogue. There is evidence, moreover, that an increasing number of people, especially the heaviest television viewers, are losing their ability to think abstractly in and through language. Some now think, Ellul argues, in largely emotional terms, that is, they think from image to image (or emotion to emotion).[107] This is accompanied by a shrinking vocabulary.[108]

The subjectivization (sterilization) of symbols and their reification in visual images effectively reduces meaning to instinctual power. Visual images hit us at an emotional level. When visual images are subordinate to language and symbolic meaning, as in traditional art, then the emotions unleashed are integrated by subjective reason and made meaningful. When, on the other hand, visual images become autonomous, reified symbols, they leave the emotions under the control of the instincts: survival, aggression, sexuality, and so forth. For the individual, then, (a spectacular reality creates a radical individualism) reality is emotional and meaning is instinctual. The implications of this are astounding. Technology is first and foremost an efficient or powerful means of acting; the visual images are images of power and possessions; and the "meaning" of autonomous visual images is instinctual power. The circle is now complete: a reality of power, a reality without meaning.

The Visual Image as Norm: Reality as Truth

The autonomous visual image blurs the distinction between truth and reality. Truth becomes the perceived correspondence between image and reality.[109] The order of truth and order of reality are unified in a culture of radical immanentism. Empirical reality is self-contained in this view; there is no sense of transcendent purpose. Reality by itself presents us with two possibilities: adjustment and manipulation. The latter is more advantageous to one's interests than the former, for it is an expression of power *over* reality, the power to create reality. Truth becomes, then, in its pseudo-ethical form, "success relative to reality."[110] Success is a stronger form of power than survival as an accommodation to reality.

The implications of this are that both technology and the visual images of the media allow us to simulate reality and to create reality. There is evidence, as both Baudrillard[111] and Ellul[112] have indicated, that some people today perceive that the visual images of television and other media are only signifiers with no referent, a self-contained visual reality. This is especially the case with regard to certain absurd comedies and dramas on television. The realization, whether conscious or tacit, that reality can be created leads to cynicism.

When the distinction between reality and truth disappears and when reality can be manipulated into and out of existence through visual images, a cynical, mocking attitude toward life becomes efflorescent. Over twenty years ago Jacob Brackman, in the unfairly neglected book, *The Put-On*, called attention to this attitude. From art to role-playing to propaganda, he uncovers the widespread view that "what passes for 'truth' and 'reality' is often cruelly deceptive."[113] At the same time, however, he notes that our "fascination with the possibly fraudulent" is a form of sociability.[114] A profound contradiction no doubt: we become spectators to our own deception. Brackman's insight that a "mocking style" denies content is echoed by Mark Crispin Miller in his analysis of the cynicism of television.[115] Television, in its advertisements and programs that often ape the ads, takes an ironic stance: it mocks the very thing it advocates. This ironic mocking is disarming. Hulk Hogan, the professional wrestler, makes fun of his own image and the product in commercials. A recent ad for Weight Watchers has an attractive young woman warning the audience about the risk you assume by joining Weight Watchers of becoming a living advertisement for them. After telling the audience how the organization will use them, she says something to the effect, "Isn't it worth it?" Such television commercials are making audience members insiders to their manipulative tactics. The audience is receiving a trade-off: let us con you, but we will admit to it so that you can demonstrate your superiority at the same moment you become the spectator-consumer. Television programs, especially the comedies, demonstrate the same mocking attitude – nothing the characters do is to be taken seriously. For example, the popular television series *Cheers* will have the bartender Woody express a sentimental attitude toward something, only to overlay the sentimentality with cynicism a few moments later.

It is evident that when reality masquerades as truth in the visual image, then a morality of conformity to reality is a consequence. This conformity can be either an adjustment to or a manipulation of reality in the interest of survival or success – power. Visual images serve both as models and imperatives for action.

Don DeLillo's *White Noise* catches this idea perfectly. Throughout the novel there are descriptions of people and their actions in the context of commercials and other television programs. Jack Gladney muses: "A woman in a yellow slicker held up traffic to let some children cross. I pictured her in a soup commercial taking off her vil-skin hat as she entered the cheerful kitchen where her husband stood over a pot of smoky lobster bisque, a smallish man with six weeks to live." John Frow points out that DeLillo is making a comment about the level of reality at which visual images serve as norms.[116] That is, typical moral norms which formulated as logical or dialectical concepts are general and abstract enough to require thoughtful application to actual life. By contrast, television commercials and programs provide extremely detailed, particular actions as normative models – visual norms. It cannot be otherwise when reality becomes truth. Celebrities become models for identification and emulation. We live vicariously through our idols. We join fan clubs, discover every intimate detail about our idols, perhaps dress like them, and adopt their speech and behavior patterns. Fans often fantasize about being with the celebrity or even being the celebrity. Television, we noted earlier, tends to make all visual images equal. The celebrity is just one image in a sea of images. Commodities are advertised as powerful and pleasurable objects. The power of the product becomes my power. Humans are reified as image-objects for consumption along with all other products. Therefore we not only identify with celebrities but with other products as well. The visual image is an implicit norm of consumption: enjoy the life-style of this attractive and powerful product.

More than just models for emulation, the visual images of the media are *imperatives* for action.[117] The visual image is a source of information about reality allowing us to manipulate or adjust to it. Previously I argued that visual images are images of possessions and power. The images of power include those of possession, consumption, control, coercion, and violence. These acts of power, when directed toward a human, have often been considered unethical. Ethical meaning arises from a limitation of power.

Even when one allows for the discourse accompanying the visual images of television and the movies to provide meaning for the action, the primary mode of human interaction is domination/submission. In commenting on several media, Andrew Tudor argues: "Violent actions themselves are only the logical extension of this basically coercive image of human relations."[118] Television as a medium favors the more spectacular, peak events such as catastrophes, war, violence, death, sexuality, and conflict of any kind. This is the bias of the medium whose sole purpose is to entertain us.[119] The more subtle forms of human interaction such as compassion, ethical love, trust, and patience cannot be transmitted through autonomous visual images; and even if they could be, they are not as interesting. Power is more spectacular than the limitation of power.

Visual images make a fundamental appeal to our emotions. Visual reality is an emotional reality. At this level, the intellectual credibility of the visual image is less important than how spectacular it is, the emotional response it can produce. Studies indicate that the most believable (emotionally speaking) of realistic depictions on television are violent scenes.[120] Violent images are the *most real* images because they provoke the strongest emotional response: they simultaneously give us a sense of being alive and of having control over our relations with others. In an existence increasingly made abstract, impersonal, and meaningless by technology, unusual, spectacular, and frightening images allow us vicariously to experience a crisis, a turning-point in our lives. We are placed time and again in a crucible. This is undoubtedly behind the popularity of horror films.

The violence on television and in movies often functions as a kind of magic.[121] Violence solves human problems; it can even put an end to violence. From the martial arts films to those of Clint Eastwood and Arnold Schwarzenegger, the good guy is the one who is ultimately most violent. Power and virtue are equivalent; moreover, the more powerful the action, the more virtuous it is. Violence as magic is the mirror image of technology. We look to technology as the solution to all problems. *Violence in the media is a reverse image of technology.* Technology is abstract and rational, violence is concrete and irrational; both are expressions of ultimate power.[122]

The compelling nature of images of power (coercion and violence) is a result of the conjunction of three factors: a technological reality, which is itself coercive and manipulative; the mass media, which over-represent the amount of physical violence;[123] autonomous visual images, which are exclusively images of power. Both the form and content of television reduce reality to a struggle for power. And the reality beyond television has come to reflect its own image.

To make a stronger case for visual images acting as moral norms, we need to examine how effective television is as a motivator. How has it influenced our relationships with others? We know that television and the movies are replete with acts of coercion and violence, television videos[124] and soap operas[125] being only the most obvious examples. Yet it would be absurd to argue that there is a one-to-one relationship between the images on these programs and our actions.

Unquestionably television exerts a profound influence on our lives. A French study involved twenty families who were asked to give up television for a month. For even such a brief period the results were striking. A few families found the experience intolerable, but the majority underwent a metamorphosis. Initially they were lost with so much free time; they experienced an "inner void." Their own lives seemed routine and dull, and they had little to talk about. As Ellul notes, "The experience of empty time which we have to fill on our own by conversation, by relations with other people, by reflection or by reading, has become a traumatic one for our generation."[126] At some point within the month, however, the majority had the feeling of being liberated. They understood that television is both an addiction and an authoritarian force. They now found more time to spend with spouse, children, and friends and more time for reading and reflection. When their television sets were returned to them after a month, some families accepted them reluctantly and put them away. When these families were asked whether they would be willing to do without television for six months, only one family out of twenty said no. At the same time, the vast majority, willing to do without television for themselves, were unwilling to let go of it for their children. This is, of course, an enormous paradox: we can do without this bittersweet sedative, but our children must not be deprived of it. No study of television with which I am familiar better poses the main issue – that television invades the inner life and replaces our lived reality with its spectacular reality.

The extent to which television motivates one to act (consumption not included), rather than merely live vicariously, is another matter. Natural experiments in the social sciences are vastly superior to laboratory experiments for most issues because artificial experiments take what one is studying out of context. In the 1970s a team of Canadian psychologists made a study of three communities in Western Canada, one of which was without television (because of its geographical location) but due to receive it within a year. The communities were studied both before television was introduced to the one community without it and two years afterwards. The study's main purpose was to ascertain the impact of television upon the attitudes, thought processes, and behavior of the residents of Notel (a pseudonym). Most of the attention was devoted to children, but adults were studied as well. The following conclusions are only a partial list of what they discovered.

Television watching in Notel slowed down children's "acquisition of fluent reading skills;" moreover, children who watched a lot of television were poorer readers than those who watched but little (correcting for intelligence). The introduction of television to Notel reduced the level of creativity among its children to what it was in the other two towns. Children's sex-role attitudes became markedly stereotyped after the introduction of television in Notel.[127]

Most important, for our purposes, are their findings about television's impact upon the aggressive behavior of children. The researchers classified aggression according to physical and verbal behavior. The physical behaviors included, among others, hit, slap, punch, bite, spit, snatching property, damage property, threaten with a held object, and so forth. The verbal behaviors numbered humiliation, disparagement, condemnation, rejection, and threat. Their conclusions, because they are so crucial, are worth quoting:

> The aggressive behavior of Notel children increased significantly following the introduction of television. This conclusion that TV viewing and aggression are linked has been reached by most other researchers, but several aspects of our results are new. They are based on observations of actual behavior rather than self-reports or ratings. Effects occurred for both girls and boys and for both physical and verbal aggression. Increases occurred for children initially low in aggression, not just a small subsample of highly aggressive children. The effects were substantial enough to be observable 2 years after the introduction of television to Notel.[128]

Another study, a laboratory experiment of more limited intent, compared American college students whose primary mode of thought involved words and numbers (abstract) and those whose approach was through images and sounds (concrete) to discover which group was more influenced by violent images. The latter group exhibited a much higher emotional response to visual violence.[129] The researchers offer several speculative interpretations. The one consistent with my argument in this chapter is that heavy television and movie viewers, who think concretely through images, tend to live more fully in their visual environment.

So far we have been examining the ability of visual images to induce physical and verbal aggression. The other side of the issue is to what extent does visual aggression increase one's fear of the world and heightened sense of the need for adjustment or conformity. As previously mentioned, heavy viewers of television overestimate the amount of violence in the world, the number of police, and the chances of being a victim. The researchers conclude that those who experience the world as such are very likely to become obedient to and dependent upon authority of all kinds.[130] They will have an exaggerated sense of the need to adjust or conform to reality. My speculative conclusion is that television simultaneously leads to both an increase in manipulative, coercive, and aggressive action and an increase in the subservient, fawning behavior of abject adjustment even in the same individual. Both are an expression of a tacit understanding that there are few, if any, limitations of power.

Considering the aforementioned studies together, the conclusion seems inescapable that television has a differential impact upon viewers. Those most adversely affected include: (1) heavy viewers; (2) lonely and isolated viewers; (3) viewers with limited ability to experience life in and through language. For such viewers the visual images of coercion and violence will tend to have a much stronger normative influence. Yet the issue is not simply images of coercion causing behavioral aggression; rather it is television and the movies exercising influence as part of an entire social environment. Technology, public opinion, peer group norms, and the images of the media all make normative contributions to create a morality of power.

The Image-Directed Mind

We have previously seen that the modern self tends to be multiple, to be unstable, and to be readily subject to the external controls of technical rules and the peer group. The modern mind is bureaucratic, therapeutic, other-directed, and likewise image-directed. Mander argues that we have become "image shells" with nothing of our own inside.[131] Our subjectivity has been objectified in visual images. One of my former graduate students has spoken about when a popular song that once evoked memories of his actual girl friend and their life together had become part of a music video, the song then triggered memories of the woman in the music video and the scenes in which she appeared.

The emptying out of the subjectivity (based on lived experiences) of the self and its replacement with objective images involves a reversal of the impersonal and the personal. There appears to be a marked increase in recent years in the willingness of people to reveal intimate details of their personal lives to total strangers. The model for this is, of course, the talk show where ordinary people along with celebrities proclaim to a national audience that they once were drug addicts, victims of child abuse, or suffered from illiteracy. Even apart from television people seem ready to tell their personal problems to those with whom they have at best a casual relationship. We have explored in our discussion of the therapeutic mind some of the motivation for this occurrence, but the point here is that what is personal becomes impersonal when it is shared with strangers and casual acquaintances. Our discourse comes to resemble the *anonymous* discourse of the mass media. It is no longer important to whom I address my remarks.

At the same time, however, we divest ourselves of what is truly personal, we try to make ourselves personal by identifying with celebrities and products on television. The reason is that reality is on television, and the celebrities and other products have lives infinitely more interesting than our own boring lives. We become interesting and alive by living through these celebrities and products. Under the psychological domination of a visual reality on television, humans become reified as image–objects.

What prevents everyone from becoming the same image-object is the myriad of ways one can "assemble" one's total image. The fragmented self is a collection of images that have no meaningful unity; yet the various fragments with which one experiments give the impression of a total self because visually each image is a totality. This totality is ever changing because the images we live in and live out can readily be substituted for others. Life as represented on television is an experimental life. Georg Simmel's remarkable essay, "The Metropolis and Mental Life," indirectly speaks to this issue.[132] He argues that as the logic of capitalism and bureaucracy imposes a standardized objective existence on us, our dwindling subjectivity retreats into the accidental differences that distinguish us from each other, such as our physical appearance. He maintains that we exaggerate these less important differences to preserve a sense of our own individuality. Life becomes a search for new and better images that communicate to others our pseudo-individuality.

Perhaps the most disturbing aspect of the image-directed mind is its almost schizophrenic desire to live in a world of fantasy. A life vicariously experienced through visual images is a life of fantasy in which our wishes and desires are satisfied. When meaning becomes instinctual power, then the place where instinctual desire is always satisfied – fantasy – becomes reality. The disjunction between fantasy and reality (we still have to live in a reality beyond the media) causes us to demand our desires be satisfied immediately.

I have argued earlier that technology stimulates desire, and public opinion demands its fulfilment. The chief way technology does this is through spectacular visual images that arouse desire. The visual images of the computer supply a technological society with abstract information necessary for the coordination of technology. These are *direct* images of a technological civilization. The visual images of the media are *reverse* images of a technological civilization that compensate for its abstractness and impersonality by providing a spectacular, emotionally-satisfying reality.

Visual images in the media are images of possessions and images of power. The former set of images makes a fundamental appeal to the mythical value of material well-being (happiness and health as consumption). The media present to us attractive and powerful objects to be consumed. The latter set of images are about the values of success and survival. The principle impetus of the mass media is less to make us act (apart from consumption) than to make us live vicariously in the spectacle. In this sense the visual images in the media turn both possessions (objects of consumption) and power into objects of visual consumption. The mythical value of material well-being reigns supreme in the visual image.

In summary, technology is the necessary side of modern society; it is the chief guarantee of collective success and survival. It concurrently demands the individual's strict obedience (happiness and health as the emotional well-being of adjustment). Public opinion and peer group norms and the universe of visual images in the media are its ephemeral side. Peer group norms which revolve around the values of success and survival provide protection for the individual in those aspects of life in which technology exacerbates competition. Visual images vicariously provide as compensation for technology the very life that public opinion demands – a life devoted to material well-being (happiness and health as consumption).

7

A Morality of Power, a Morality
Without Meaning

It is time to pull the threads of the argument together. I have suggested that modern American morality is organized about a series of dialectics involving both its content (mythological symbols) and its form (technical rules, statistical normality, and the material visual image). Moreover, I have attempted to show how the mythological symbols of success, survival, happiness, and health in various ways are implicit in the norms of technology, public opinion, the peer group, and visual images. Ultimately this morality is a mirror of technology's ambivalent relationship to human society: it simultaneously creates efficient order in the form of technical rules and organization and permits a plethora of ephemeral consumer opinions and choices and a series of compensations for its corrosive effect upon cultural meaning and the human psyche.

The starting point for this reconstruction of American morality has been Ellul's interpretation of technology as both milieu[1] and system.[2] A milieu is an environment, at once both material and symbolic, in relation to which humans face their most formidable problems and from which they derive the means of survival and some hope for the future. A milieu has three basic characteristics: immediacy, sustenance and peril, and mediation. We are in immediate and direct relationship with our milieu; it forces us to adapt, to conform, just as surely as we manipulate it. From the milieu we derive all that we need to live – sustenance for the body and the spirit: food, clothing, shelter, order, and meaning. Concurrently, however, the milieu is the greatest threat to human existence as in pestilence, famine, poisons, wild animals, political strife, war, and pollution. The milieu, then, is ambiguous in value and produces an ambivalent reaction on our part – attraction and revulsion, desire and fear.

In Ellul's theory there are three milieus humans have lived in – nature, society, and technology. Humans begin the slow transition from the milieu of nature to the milieu of society nine to eleven thousand years ago depending upon the specific geographical location. The milieu of society becomes complete with the emergence of the city and the rise of civilizations. The movement to the milieu of technology occurs in the nineteenth century and becomes more fully established with the widespread use of the computer in the twentieth century. Ellul's theory is no finalist theory in which the last stage represents the culmination of history; moreover, there is no deterministic principle underlying the process.

Each subsequent milieu, e.g. society in relation to nature, *mediates* the preceding one, rendering it an indirect force. The preceding milieu becomes an ideological model for the subsequent milieu, thereby providing an illusion of where power resides. In dialectical fashion, however, it is actually the subsequent milieu that is used to interpret the preceding. In the milieu of society, for example, nature is actually read through society, that is, it is anthropomorphized. Therefore, nature as a model for society is to a great extent a nature that is already a reflection of society. Similarly society serves as a model in the milieu of technology but it is a society interpreted through a technological logic and increasingly rendered technological. Each preceding milieu continues to exert an influence on the subsequent one, but the threat it represents tends to be less important overall. In the milieu of nature, the major problems are wild animals, poisons, and so forth; in the milieu of society the greatest threats are political and military conflicts; in the milieu of technology, the principal obstacles to survival are posed by technology as with pollution and psychological stress. Not only does the subsequent milieu mediate the previous milieu, but also it sometimes exacerbates the tensions and conflicts of the preceding one. For example, in the milieu of technology, political and economic problems are aggravated, as witnessed by increasing ethnic, racial, and nationalistic strife.

The most telling characteristic of technology as a milieu is that it actually (and not just theoretically) functions as a kind of open system. Technology is an open system in that it interacts with its two environments – nature and human society – but it is *not* open in that it does not possess genuine feedback. Technology could only begin to approximate a system by first establishing itself as the most important factor in human progress. The nineteenth century witnessed an incredible efflorescence of technical inventions made possible by centuries of innovation and patient experimentation. As these various technologies emerged, there was a conscious intention to find new and different uses for them, eventually leading to a search for their interrelationships. More and more technology began to dominate every domain of human existence. Along with technology's material domination, however, came its spiritual domination. It assumed the form of an absolute value, a sacred;[3] western societies looked upon it as the engine of progress, the solution to all problems.

What finally allows technology to become an open system is the widespread use of the computer. The computer allows each technique to become a source of information for the coordination of the various technologies. Technology is a system, then, at the level of information. This means, however, that each subsystem loses some of its flexibility, for its courses of action have to be adjusted to the needs of the other subsystems. The mutual interaction and mutual dependency of subsystems made possible by the computer is the technological system. In large urban areas, for example, the various technological subsystems such as communication, transportation, law enforcement, and commerce become more dependent upon one another for the smooth operation of the overall urban system.

Although the technological system is an open system it is more or less autonomous (as a system) in relation to its human environment. That is, the only way humans could intervene decisively in the "self-augmentation" of technology would be to destroy it as a system (not the technology itself). But because of our supreme faith in technology and the illusion that as creators of it we are its masters, we do not perceive the dilemma. The problem is that the technological system allows for no effective feedback, that is, self-regulation. Feedback means that a system, e.g., an ecological system, has the ability to correct the problem at its source. For instance, if the technological system possessed feedback, then the use of the automobile, a major cause of air pollution, would be eliminated or severely curtailed. Instead we attempt to discover a way of countering the negative effects of the automobile on the environment.

Even if we attempt to use the computer as a feedback mechanism, it can only handle quantitative data. The computer rules out the possibility of evaluating the impact of technology upon the qualitative side of life. How does technology affect culture and the human psyche? As I have suggested in chapter 4, the cumulative impact of technology results in an erosion of shared (cultural) meaning and a fragmentation of the self. The ability of technology to create an efficient order at the level of social structure is offset by its disordering impact upon culture and personality. The computer, however, is constitutionally unable to make such an historical and cultural interpretation; moreover, the various psychological techniques and therapies are interested in bringing about a better adjustment to the cause of the stress, rather than helping us modify the cause. We cannot resist attempting to repair the damage after the fact; but without genuine feedback, the technological system is a system out of control.

The most ominous feature of the technological milieu is that it makes symbolically mediated experiences irrelevant. Technique as an objective, logical procedure supplants human experience; the material visual image (technology's discourse) subordinates symbolic discourse to itself. The intersubjective based on human experience and expressed in discourse is replaced by the objective in the form of technology and visual images. Under these circumstances meaning becomes purely subjective and assumes the form of instinctual power and pleasure. Technology as the embodiment of instrumental rationality actually enlarges the domain and importance of the irrational (instinctual). Modern American morality is formed within a technological milieu, or at least a milieu that is rapidly moving in that direction.

Two of the dialectics of modern American morality – the necessary and the ephemeral and the necessary and the compensatory – reflect perfectly the internal conflicts of a technological civilization. These conflicts, set in dialectical tension, make it difficult to comprehend this morality as a totality. Often the tendency is to emphasize the ephemeral nature of modern morality, readily apparent in a shifting public opinion and transitory peer group norms. Often overlooked as a kind of morality are technical rules (the necessary) and the images of the media as reverse images (the compensatory) of a technological civilization. It is the rapid change in the content of public opinion and peer group norms that provides us with a sense of freedom. Today freedom is largely an aesthetic freedom, the freedom of the consumer. The visual images of the mass media, especially television, keep us within the realm of the ephemeral, but they provide us with a compensation for the abstract, impersonal, and authoritarian nature of technological imperatives – a vicarious and spectacular life subject to our own passive experimentation. The more totalitarian a technological civilization becomes, the more necessary it is to present a series of consumer choices expressed in public opinion and materialized in visual images that leave us with the impression of maximum freedom.

The content of contemporary American morality centers on the mythological symbols of success, survival, happiness, and health. These symbols are related in various ways to the forms of this morality: technical rules, public opinion, peer group norms, and the visual images of the media. As part of the myth of technological utopianism, all four symbols are interrelated; moreover, each one implies the rest. The value of success was gradually transformed from an individual to a collective phenomenon. Success became by the late nineteenth century the success of the organization, but especially the success of the nation-state. The equation of the American nation with technology meant that national progress was insured by technological growth. Technological utopianism grew especially strong in the United States.

The value of success is related to that of survival: both are expressions of collective power turned into a value. Survival is minimalist success. If success today is most epitomized in technological growth, then survival is related to the destructive aspects of that same growth. The value of survival grows increasingly important as we become acutely aware of problems such as pollution, overpopulation, and potential nuclear catastrophe that require repair. Success (as technological growth) stands in a contradictory relationship to survival (as technological repair).

As success is collectivized in the nation-state and technology, it is redefined for the individual in terms of well-being (happiness and health). Happiness and health possess two distinct meanings. Happiness refers to the consumption of goods and services and to adjustment; health refers to the perfection of the body and to adjustment (mental health). Therefore, happiness and health have a common meaning in adjustment; concurrently happiness as consumption and health as the perfection of the body share the common meaning of physical well-being. Happiness and health (taken together) have two overall meanings: physical well-being and emotional well-being (adjustment). The overall meanings, moreover, are related because a consumption-oriented life-style is a major part of adjustment and because physical well-being and emotional well-being are seen to be mutually dependent. Just as success can threaten survival, happiness as consumption can impair one's physical health. In the mythological world of technological utopianism the symbols are compatible; in the real world they are often at odds.

Technological utopianism not only unites the four symbols but merges the collective and individual levels of social life. This myth suggests that technology solves all our problems (problem to solution) and that it provides us with total pleasure through consumption (discontent to content). Success and survival are mythological symbols that are related to technique as a collective means of efficient action; happiness and health are expressions of technology's ability to provide for consumption and to bring about the adjustment of the individual.

Technology is one of the forms that modern morality assumes; its greatest moral influence is exerted through organizational and psychological technique. Although the two kinds of technique are typically used together, they embody different symbolic values. Organizational technique's goal is efficiency; it is therefore linked to the value of success (and survival). Psychological technique, whose chief purpose is to facilitate the emotional adjustment of the individual, is related more to the value of happiness and health as adjustment or emotional well-being. Organizational technique and psychological technique illustrate the first dialectic: manipulation and adjustment. As users of technique we manipulate reality; as recipients of technique we adjust to reality. Technology as a system suggests that the human use of technology is organized and programmed, so that the individual's main function is to adjust. The power of technique is in the organization, not the individual.

Public opinion and peer group norms are both a kind of statistical morality in which the majority viewpoint or statistically average behavior becomes the norm. Although technology is the chief determining factor (the necessary) in modern societies, it shows itself everywhere in a state of rapid change. That is, technology can only continue to grow through constant experimentation. Technology through the images of the media manipulates and creates desire.

Public opinion is part of the ephemeral side of a technological civilization open to technological experimentation in its demand that consumer desires be fulfilled. Based as it is upon desire, public opinion defines each issue in terms of material well-being (happiness and health). Public opinion revolves around the possibility of technology.

Apart from the media, the peer group is the primary carrier of public opinion. The peer group socializes its members in the art of consumption; in addition, it acts as a political interest group. One of technology's unintended consequences is to intensify extant political tensions and create new political divisions. As technology attentuates a common morality, the competition for the fruits of technology – increased consumption – becomes more brutal. Success and survival depend upon the protection of the peer group. The peer group attempts to fill the void in those areas of life not fully subject to technology. In its orientation to success, the peer group mimics technology. The peer group and its norms, however, prove to be as ephemeral as public opinion (dialectic of the necessary and the ephemeral).

The visual images of the mass media (especially television) are part of the ephemeral side of a technological civilization, the part that provides greatest compensation for the rigors of technology. The mass media serve up reverse images of a technological civilization, whereas the computer generates direct images. The visual images of the media are in harmony with public opinion in that they appear variously as an accurate representation of *what is* and as an imaginative alternative of what is *possible*. Technology's psychological hold over us is at the level of possibility. Visual images in the media present us with objects and experience that are spectacular and public opinion demands their realization. This morality replaces the dualism of the real and the ideal with that of the real and the possible. Reality and possibility exist in the space that technology, public opinion, and visual images create.

The visual images of the media are images of possessions and power. Insofar as the images provide us with attractive and powerful objects to be consumed, they are oriented to the value of material well-being (happiness and health); insofar as they focus on relations of power (coercion, manipulation, possession, control, and violence) between objects, they are oriented to the values of success and survival. Yet because the media represent life as spectacle, they turn all images into objects of consumption (happiness and health). The more life shrinks to an abstract, logical format, the more the images of the media provide an alternative – a vicarious, pleasurable life (dialectic of the necessary and the compensatory).

Modern American morality in its totality (content and form) is an expression of the marriage between technological utopianism (mental structure) and technological power (material structure). The moral forms (technique, public opinion, peer group norms, and visual images) give expression in various ways to the symbolic values of technological utopianism. At this level technology has the ability to provide maximum success and happiness with no side effects. In the real world, however, technology's impact upon human society gives rise to a series of contradictions, which form the basis for the three main dialectics of this morality: (1) manipulation and adjustment; (2) the necessary and the ephemeral; and (3) the necessary and the compensatory. These three dialectics are related to the symbolic values of technological utopianism in the following ways: (1) the dialectic of manipulation and adjustment is reflected in the tension between collective success and individual happiness and health (as emotional well-being); (2) the dialectic of the necessary and the ephemeral is reflected in the tension between success and happiness and health (as material well-being), on the one hand, and between success (as technological efficiency) and success or survival (as determined by the political interest group), on the other hand; (3) the dialectic of the necessary and the compensatory is reflected in the tension between success and survival and happiness and health (as material well-being).

The myth of technological utopianism smoothes over and eliminates all these tensions. It transports us into an imaginary world where technology satisfies all our desires and solves all our problems. In actuality, however, these four mythological values are in conflict because technology itself is in conflict with its two environments – nature and society. To recognize the contradictory nature of modern morality is to understand technology's ambiguous and contradictory effect upon nature, culture, and the human psyche. Modern American morality is not simply a technological morality, but a morality that attempts to deal with the negative impact of technology as evidenced by problems of repair, adjustment, and compensation.

The question remains: but how does this morality work? The various forms of this morality exert a differential influence upon us. In general, technical rules (organizational and psychological rules) are experienced as mandatory, as evidenced by the phenomenon of the bureaucratic mind. Public opinion, when it is crystallized, and peer group norms are only somewhat less efficacious in their impact. The more the individual has a fragmented, uncertain self, the more susceptible he is to the influence of the group and public opinion. There are always those capable of resistance if they understand the dilemma. The visual images of the media exercise the greatest influence as a reinforcement for public opinion and peer group norms. That is, to the extent that visual images are seen to accurately reflect reality, they provide norms congruous with public opinion as the attitudes and behavior of the majority. When the images of the media, television in particular, become mere signs or create a reality obviously only imaginary, their impact upon specific behaviors is less dramatic. As I argued previously, the visual images of violence are most effective in regard to the lonely and isolated and heavy television viewers (image-directed minds). Even with visual images that are clearly only signs, however, there is an indirect effect of enormous import. All visual images of the media are ultimately only images of power and (powerful) possessions. Whether the visual image seems realistic or fantastic (even here images are experienced emotionally as real), the effect is the same – to turn reality into truth by creating norms of consumption and power. Thus, fantastic images reinforce "realistic" images.

Technical rules, public opinion, peer group norms, and visual images, therefore, converge to create a morality of power, a morality without meaning. This morality of power, morality without meaning, is, of course, an anti-morality from the perspective of traditional morality, for it destroys symbolically-mediated experiences. Technology and the visual images of the media tend to destroy meaning, without which all norms become exclusively norms of power.

Even if this morality is not fully established, it is the dominant morality today. Humanistic and Christian moralities at the level of lived reality are in rapid retreat. My discussion so far has taken the form of an interpretation of what is. What started out as an intellectual puzzle to be solved has become a profound existential problem that demands some kind of response. The following chapter explores one such course of action.

8

Against the New Morality

World domination, as everyone knows, is divided between demons and angels. But the good of the world does not require the latter to gain precedence over the former (as I thought when I was young); all it needs is a certain equilibrium of power. If there is too much uncontested meaning on earth (the reign of the angels), man collapses under the burden; if the world loses all its meaning (the reign of the demons), life is every bit as impossible.

Milan Kundera, *The Book of Laughter and Forgetting*

This new morality is both cynical and nihilistic – cynical in its total advocacy of power and nihilistic in its destruction of meaning. Although this morality is not fully in place, this is hardly consoling given that it is the *dominant* social morality.

To oppose this morality one should do so from one or both of two convictions: (1) that the new morality actually creates enormous unhappiness and stress in the lives of individuals and in their relations with each other; (2) that the new morality is destructive of traditional meaning. My analysis so far has suggested both of these. We need now to discuss these issues in greater detail.

The myth of technological utopianism is everywhere betrayed by our experiences. It should be clear that while technology solves some material problems, it exacerbates others and creates still new problems. Its effect upon culture, personality, and human relationships is devastating. In a word, technology does not make us happy. At best it brings momentary pleasure that in its aftermath leaves the individual empty.

Boredom and Unhappiness

Work, school, and leisure today appear to produce widespread feelings of boredom and even alienation. Studs Terkel's *Working* sheds light on the extent to which Americans find their work mortifying. In an interview shortly after the publication of the book, Terkel remarked that he was surprised to discover how widespread the alienation from work was; he said that he expected to find alienation among those with jobs that are both repetitive and require little skill but not among skilled and professional laborers. Instead the alienation was omnipresent. In general the alienation assumed the form of a "lack of personal worth" in the work people perform.[1] For those who reveled in their work, Terkel mused that this may be more revealing about the person than the job.[2] Terkel, I surmise, is talking here about the ability of some individuals to rise above the lack of aesthetical pleasure in their work and find *meaning* in it. This suggests a limitation to a purely aesthetical view of labor, such as Marx's. For Marx, labor in the sense of self-creation is what makes us uniquely human. Marx's communist utopia purported to be an aesthetical paradise in which one would be free to be creative in ways commensurate with one's skills and interests.

No matter how unpalatable the work may be it can become meaningful when set within a moral context. Work that is an expression of reciprocal trust and respect within a moral community acquires an ethical meaning that transcends its aesthetical value. Without this, the work, no matter how satisfying, is meaningless. Perhaps the complaint against work today has less to do with its aesthetic value than with its bureaucratic and technological context, which militates against moral relationships between worker and co-worker and between worker and client.

Students tend to experience school the way adults often experience work: as at best a necessary evil. Ralph Larkin's study of a suburban high school documents the widespread estrangement of students from school.[3] Above all else the students are bored; this is the common denominator that cuts across all social divisions within the high school. Most students perceive the various ways in which they are being manipulated. When cultural authority declines, the only possibilities for control are coercion and manipulation.[4] The faculty do not fare much better in this bleak environment. Demoralized and apathetic teachers no longer perceive themselves as transmitters of a community's morality but as enforcers of bureaucratic rules.[5] In thinking that they are on safer ground with the latter, they unconsciously recognize that the bureaucratic rules are the effective morality of American society.

The school has become an organization rather than an institution and as such is unable to persuade its participants – student and teacher alike – to believe in it.

More surprising perhaps than the boredom the students experience in school is the lack of joy they experience in sex and drugs. Experimentation with sex and drugs, as initiation rites into adulthood, appear to be compulsory – at least in the sense of having tried them. These activities, however, are entered into in the spirit of work rather than that of genuine leisure. Their compulsive pleasure is devoid of meaning and joy; it is almost as boring as the school they openly eschew.[6]

In a study of the English working class, a class Studs Terkel claims is quite similar to the American working class in aspiration, Jeremy Seabrook discovered that a higher level of consumption left people even more unhappy.[7] Consumption cannot offset the loss of tradition, the loss of function at work, and more competitive and violent human relationships. Technology, as we have seen, makes human relationships abstract and impersonal and destroys the efficacy of symbolically-mediated experiences. This leads to an unhappiness that cannot in actuality be compensated for by consumption and visual spectacle. And yet because technological utopianism promises us happiness, for us to admit we are not happy is tantamount to saying there is something wrong with us. Unless one challenges the myth, then the problem is with humans and their practices. We expect and are expected to be happy.

There is evidence that, apart from the fatuous promise of consumption, the lack of time in general and specifically the attempt to cram as many leisure activities into as short a period of time as possible creates unhappiness. We wish to be as productive in leisure as we are in work; consequently, we don't take the time to enjoy a single activity in a leisurely manner.[8] Instead we perform many activities simultaneously, e.g. listening to the radio, watching television, and talking. An obvious example of the latter is travel become tourism: travel for the purpose of education becomes travel for the purpose of maximum spectacle – tourism.

Steffan Linder has demonstrated that technology does not provide us with more leisure time but rather with less. Time becomes the chief scarcity in a technological civilization.[9] Technology increases both the number and complexity of rules and the number of objects for consumption. Becoming informed about these rules and objects, shopping for the goods and services, and keeping them in good working order are a full time job. As Linder indicates,[10] there is no hierarchy of purpose in respect to consumption: art, literature, and education in general are turned into consumable objects; they possess no more cultural importance than the ownership and use of an automobile or a snowblower.

More important even than the loss of quantitative time is the sterilization of time. When time loses its meaning – the memory of significant events and transformations within a narrative framework – it becomes the space within which we produce and consume as much as possible. When time becomes meaningless, it becomes mere repetition. The disappearance of qualitative time is soporific; it produces boredom. The loss of quantitative and qualitative time results concomitantly in psychological stress and boredom.

The signs of stress are everywhere: anxiety, depression, alcohol and drug addiction, susceptibility to religious cults and bizarre psychological therapies, widespread divorce, and other damaged or broken relationships. Herbert Hendin's study of college students at Columbia University indicates that "[w]hat distinguishes this generation is its active pursuit of disengagement, detachment, fragmentation, and emotional numbness."[11] The discovery of an intense hostility between the sexes came as a surprise. Women in the study were preoccupied with emotional vulnerability; they perceived men as not just sexual but emotional predators. Becoming involved with a man was a threat to grades and career. These women, moreover, had invariably been involved in destructive relations with parents. More often than not they had faced weak and ineffectual fathers and domineering mothers.[12]

The young men had similar experiences with their parents. Their fathers were alternately distant and aloof and jealous competitors; their mothers were either domineering or passive. The main difference between the sexes was that young men were frightened of their own destructive tendencies. Passion was thought to result in someone becoming a victim. Their attitude toward women was either that of fear and dependency or that of disdain.[13]

Both sexes discovered two principal ways of avoiding strong emotional commitment to others: (1) a total "machine-like" control of one's emotions; (2) a giving in to random sensations (the absence of control), such as drugs, alcohol, and sex. Although many individuals used both approaches, female students were more included to total control and male students to the absence of control. Human relationships have apparently become so transitory, ambiguous, and combative that it is best to protect oneself against serious involvement in the life of the other. We sometimes have many superficial friendships as a hedge against having a few genuine friendships.

The lives of protagonists in recent American fiction bear a striking resemblance to the lives of the college students at Columbia University.

The underlying theme of this literature is that the most the individual with no shared sense of the past in a disintegrating culture can hope for is psychological survival, that is, for a "shock-resistant" life without passion. Josephine Hendin identifies two kinds of fiction that address this issue – holistic and anarchic.[14] In the former case the characters seem to be attempting to achieve a "mechanical efficiency" in all activities, including their relations to others. A well-managed self becomes the way to survive in a world of ambiguous values and ambivalent relationships. Hendin points to John Barth as an example of an author of holistic fiction.

Anarchic fiction features characters who are in various stages of disintegration. Their lives are fragmented into a series of random mystical or ecstatic experiences. This response to the pain of serious commitment is in part a more passive response than self-management: one is enveloped in the pleasure of the moment. Kurt Vonnegut and Thomas Pynchon provide examples of anarchic fiction. The parallels between literature and life are remarkable here. The characters in holistic fiction closely resemble the students who have chosen the path of total control, just as those in anarchic fiction are similar to the students who have given themselves over to the pursuit of random sensations. No wonder we are preoccupied with relationships in our conversations and on talk shows: they have become a phantom.

Boredom and unhappiness punctuate the lives of everyone from time to time; they are universal experiences. What is unusual is the extent to which boredom and unhappiness today can be attributed to the decline of common meaning.

Meaning and Power

Hyperboredom[15] and *existential nihilism*[16] are the terms sometimes used to refer to the experience of meaninglessness. As was indicated earlier, meaning in the sense of the meaning of life and the meaning of history is ethical meaning. If life is typically (historically speaking) experienced as overflowing with meaning, how does a society reach the point in which the experience of meaninglessness is widespread and longstanding?

I want to advance two propositions: life has no meaning, and life has meaning. At the level of empirical evidence it is impossible to determine whether life has an objective or transcendent meaning. The evidence is inherently ambiguous. The attribution of meaning to existence is always a matter of belief. But then there is no knowledge that is not indirectly based upon belief. The belief that history is directed toward a denouement is the major source for the belief that life has objective meaning.

At the same time, however, humans create meaning in their attempt to make sense of the tension, conflicts, and problems of life, namely, suffering. The questions of suffering and death have to be answered with the direction and orientation of our lives. Not to respond is to give in to these very forces and thereby increase the intensity of psychological suffering. In the attempt to transcend suffering, subjective meaning is discovered – ethical love that allows for a moral community set within a tradition. J. H. van den Berg, for instance, has demonstrated that the experience of physical pain in the case of injury or disease is moderated when one is well integrated into a community and aggravated to the extent one is isolated and lonely.[18] Now whether this subjective attribution of meaning – ethical love – to the misery of life is itself a sign of transcendent meaning is, of course, a matter of belief. One thing is certain: meaning has to be shared with others (intersubjective) for it to be effective. Moreover, meaning must be more than merely theoretical; it must be lived out in concert with others.

Traumatic events such as natural disasters, military defeat, and the loss of religious or political leadership can make a society begin to doubt its answer to the question of meaning. Apart from traumatic events, the problem of meaning arises when one or more of the following situations is present: (1) human relationships become abstract and impersonal; (2) human actions become trivial in regard to what is essential to life – survival and meaning; (3) human action becomes subject to multiple and conflicting interpretations, in other words, it becomes almost fully ambiguous.[19]

In American society today and, for that matter, all modern societies, all three factors are present. To the extent that technology mediates human relationships, it transforms them into objective relationships that deny the subjective individuality of both parties. A technical relationship is concerned with efficacy and efficiency; meaning has no place in it. Technology has taken over responsibility for the production of subsistence; moreover, we have all become specialists who at best make a small contribution to our own survival. Our actions, based on subjective experiences, count for little in an objectified world of production. But even more importantly, we make no contribution to the creation and sustenance of common meaning. What meaning there is, is reified in consumption. Edward Sapir says it well:

> Here lies the grimmest joke of our present American civilization. The vast majority of us, deprived of any but insignificant and culturally abortive share in the satisfaction of the immediate wants of mankind, are

further deprived of both opportunity and stimulation to share in the production of non-utilitarian values. Part of the time we are dray horses; the rest of the time we are listless consumers of goods which have received no least impress of our personality. In other words, our spiritual selves go hungry, for the most part, pretty much all of the time.[20]

Finally, as has been indicated in chapter 6, the decline in the ability of discourse to refer to the qualitative side of life has resulted simultaneously in the subjectivization of symbolic meaning and its reification in visual images. From the standpoint of symbolic meaning, human action has indeed become intensely ambiguous. Unlike previous societies, where the question of ultimate meaning arose only in relation to a specific event, modern societies have institutionalized meaninglessness.

The reason for this has to do with the relationship between power and ethical meaning. Ethical meaning arises in the limitations placed on power. The values of freedom, justice, love, and equality all place limits on acting out of individual or collective self-interest. Freedom involves the idea that the other does not have the right to unduly interfere with my life; justice, that no one has the right to take more than one deserves; love involves the idea of self-sacrifice for the other; equality, the notion that no one is entitled to more advantages than someone else. Even a virtue such as courage does not imply that there are no limits to one's response while under attack. The various virtues or ethical values form a cultural totality and as such cannot be appropriately understood as autonomous. As many have observed in different periods and cultures, there exists an inverse relationship between power and values. The more power increases, the more values decline at the level of practice. The values may still exist at the level of discourse and can thereby work to conceal the fact of their disappearance as *effective* limitations on power.

The unprecedented nature of modern technological power has two consequences: (1) symbolic meaning is destroyed; (2) power has itself become a value.[21] In the past, when societies experienced nihilism, it was not just because of a traumatic event but also because power in the form of authority had begun to disintegrate.[22] Today power and existential nihilism co-exist, for technology has supplanted cultural authority. That power and nihilism go hand in hand suggests that power, which up to now has been quantitative, has become qualitative (a value). This is perhaps best evidenced by the decline of ideologies today. Nationalism and racism have proved stronger: the power of the nation-state, the race, the ethnic group. Furthermore, within a society the equality of power in a purely materialistic sense has become the exclusive goal of groups that have been discriminated against. The "value" of power is a jealous value; it permits no others.

The question remains, however, why are we acquiescent in the face of meaninglessness? Action requires knowledge and the will to change things. We are only dimly aware of this meaninglessness; we experience it without being fully aware of it. But as Kierkegaard always maintained,[23] will is more decisive than knowledge. Even were we to face this meaninglessness head on, our will to act has been co-opted. That is, in a technological civilization every possibility is a technological one.

Kierkegaard's profound insights into the nature of freedom are apt.[24] He uses three terms – necessity, possibility, and actuality – to frame the question. Actuality (lived reality that embodies freedom) is a dialectic of necessity and possibility. What one is at the moment is necessity; what I aspire to be in the future is possibility. Freedom involves the struggle to make actuality more than necessity, to bring possibility into existence. Without possibility, everything is necessary, that is, completely determined. But possibility without necessity exists only in imagination. Kierkegaard offers the example of an infant making nonsensical sounds. The necessity to make these sounds comes from discomfort or pleasure. Only the possibility that language provides can turn the sounds into words.[25] Freedom is the endless struggle to turn possibility into necessity and to make necessity yield new possibilities.

Ellul has applied these thoughts about possibility and necessity to technology. The computer and television give us visual evidence of the infinite possibilities of technology as information, means, and object. Technology seems to make everything possible; like an almighty being there is nothing it cannot accomplish. Yet technology's possibility is not my possibility, for technology does not depend upon my subjective experience. Nor can I control its growth and consequences in any decisive way. I am merely along for the ride. Most importantly, technology has become the *universal* means of acting. There is no domain of life not mediated by technique. Every effective possibility is technical. An exclusive possibility is a necessity. When possibility becomes necessity, freedom disappears.[26]

Every individual, every society, according to Kierkegaard, must have the experience that human possibility can be realized. Freedom is essential to the hope that meaning can be realized in the struggle against adversity. Without the anticipation of human possibility, hopelessness ensues. Hopelessness, then, is intimately linked to meaninglessness. In a sense, hopelessness is the experience that suffering is both without meaning and without end. Hopelessness is an intensification of meaninglessness. The signs of hopelessness, which will be discussed subsequently, include the derision of others and self-destructive behavior.

In establishing a link between meaninglessness and hopelessness, we have tied love (as a primary source of meaning) to freedom (the possibility of meaning's realization). But love and freedom are related in other ways. To love the other one has to be free to some extent, both from the tyranny of others and from self-tyranny. Concurrently freedom that does not involve the love of the other becomes self-indulgence and even slavery to instinct. This is the central message of Milan Kundera's *The Unbearable Lightness of Being*.

Tomas, the main character in Kundera's novel, devotes himself to a life of aesthetical freedom. His philandering goes beyond sexual indulgence, for in his various encounters he seeks out that aspect of each woman, no matter how small, that differentiates her from the others. He has become a connoisseur of women, their personalities as well as their bodies. Tomas believes this to be his freedom, his lightness of being, an escape from the demands of medicine and the dreary world of eastern European politics.

In his eventual commitment to Tereza, the woman he had lived with but could never be faithful to, Tomas discovers that real love is ethical love freely given to another. He then sees his previous affairs as a heaviness of being, an enslavement to eros. Ethical love is freedom, he concludes. Because sex and love are so inexorably linked together and because the sexual instinct is so strong, freedom resides in the ability to place limits on that instinct for the sake of another whom one loves as a complete human being, not merely a sexual being.

The morality of power, morality without meaning, destroys the possibility of love and therefore destroys freedom itself. Because this morality is devoid of symbolic meaning, the freedom to interpret it, use it creatively, and even resist it is absent. It is a morality wherein freedom is purely aesthetical – the "freedom" of the consumer to demand that desires be realized and to choose among the plethora of products and images. This morality ultimately has nothing in common with traditional morality, for it places no ethical limitations on power. For that reason alone, love and freedom are incompatible with this morality of power, morality without meaning.

In this morality's most demanding form – technical rules – we are left with two options: manipulation and adjustment. These are precisely the choices when one confronts reality as truth. The manipulation of others is the opposite of love. It is a form of psychological violence in which the other is treated as an object. The establishment of moral norms, at least when they are not applied in an authoritarian manner, allows one the freedom to resist because the expectations are communicated rationally. By contrast, manipulation makes a fundamental appeal to irrational desires and fears. In the face of overwhelming and widespread manipulative techniques, one's only choice is adjustment. Even when we are the manipulators, the power of manipulation resides in technique, not in us. Objectified manipulation in the form of technique means that most of us, most of the time, simply adjust to technology. Manipulation rules out the possibility of love, just as adjustment denies the possibility of freedom. This morality thus destroys both meaning and hope.

A Self-Destructive Ethic Versus a Life-Affirming Ethic

This new morality, at once both cynical and nihilistic, gives rise to self-destructive behavior. It is sign of societal decline and a vital contributor to that decline. Hopelessness is an extension of and intensification of meaninglessness. The despair of meaninglessness is in part a conscious despair; the despair of hopelessness is deeply unconscious. With a partial consciousness of despair, one retains the possibility of doing something about it; with hopelessness, one loses all will to resist. One begins to give in to the maelstrom of self-destruction. That is, even if one does not fully participate in it, e.g., drug and alcohol addiction, one escapes its more dramatic forms only through less intense expressions, e.g., addiction to consumption and the visual spectacle. Compensatory mechanisms exist in all societies; but when they become more important to most people than the perennial issues of survival and meaning, collective hopelessness has taken hold.

Colin Turnbull's ethnography *The Mountain People* is instructive here.[28] At the time he lived with the Ik tribe (1964-1967), they had been starving to death for several decades. This once successful and proud group of hunters had been forced by the Ugandan government to abandon hunting in land by then a National Park and to become farmers on poor soil. Turnbull depicts the life of a people whose culture had all but been abandoned. Only a few adults kept alive memories of their traditions and ritualistic practices. The extreme competition for food resulted in the dissolution of the extended family. Children were pushed out at the age of three to form bands (gangs) that searched for food. What is good came to be identified with the individual possession of food.

Turnbull calls the IK the loveless people. With the exception of one old married couple, there was no evidence of any acts of compassion and kindness. Their attitudes ranged from indifference to the plight of others, to "smoldering anger," to mocking contempt. They lost their sense of humor except for tragedy: they delighted in death, disease, and accident. They took no joy in life, but expressed contemptuous humor toward the misfortune of others. One of their few maxims was "Do not love anyone." There were even cases of someone snatching food out of the hands of a dying person. Their only belief was in self-survival.

Toward the end of his book, Turnbull (a British anthropologist) compares the Ik to people in modern societies.[29] The extreme individualism that advertising and the media promote – the universe of consumer goods and visual images exist for my benefit – is exactly the same as that of the Ik. An affluent society, however, can more readily conceal its selfishness than can a starving society. We give to charities, for example, out of our surplus; but concurrently we ruthlessly compete with one another to get ahead, to have more. We participate in the manipulation of others and we preach adjustment to those who should be resisting the enslavement to technology and capitalism.

It is our modern humor that perhaps best demonstrates how similar we are to the Ik. So much of American and British humor is psychologically violent; it involves a contempt for and derision of others. The more gentle humor of a Garrison Keillor has given way to the mocking humor of *Saturday Night Live*, *Married with Children*, Eddy Murphy, and Roseanne Barr. Instead of a laughing with (in which I identify with the other) we have a laughing at (in which I am superior to the pathetic other). The routine of Mr. Bill on *Saturday Night Live* is most illustrative of this tendency. Mr. Bill is a puppet but he represents every man. Terrible things, in the form of physical violence, happen to Mr. Bill, but invariably in the context of verbal assurances to the contrary. What a cynical, hopeless view of life: no matter what anyone says, one will invariably be hurt. Not far behind is the program *Married with Children*. If ever there were a completely cynical view of family life, this is it. It possesses no redeeming qualities. The only time this family shows any semblance of being human is in their opposition to a common enemy – a scapegoat. Other comedy programs, less obviously cynical, exhibit the same view of life. *Cheers*, for example, overrides every sentimental attitude with a cynical attitude expressed by Carla, Norm, or Fraser. The inescapable conclusion *Cheers* arrives at is that in the crucible of existence minimum consolation is the most a group of pathetic losers can provide one another.

Two other signs of hopelessness are universal suspicion and the attack upon language. Many have analyzed the suspicion that the work of Marx, Nietzsche, and Freud has engendered. In short, it is the suggestion that everything is done out of individual or collective self-interest. Consequently, there is no morality that does not represent the will to power of some special interests. The impact of this is to create suspicion of each and every political and moral pronouncement. Once again, we return to the cynicism that a view that reality is exclusively a struggle for power engenders. Perhaps this modern cynicism is but a variation of idealism, one that refuses to place modern cynicism into historical perspective.[30]

The attack upon language today goes well beyond a skepticism about the ability of discourse to reveal an objective reality.[31] Radical deconstructivism represents an extreme subjectivistic reaction to objectivism. That is, discourse tells us nothing about the world but only about our subjective experiences. Hence we are forever encapsulated in our subjectivity. This facile view of discourse, at once anti-historical and cynical, overlooks the obvious fact that our understanding of a world beyond language is born out of our interaction with a world that simultaneously influences us. We may never know things as they are in themselves, but we can begin to know them as they affect us and we influence them. Discourse, as we have seen, represents the potential to explore the order to truth. Cynicism about language closes off this possibility, and encapsulates us in a reality transformed into truth. Rather than being only an expression of the will to power (which it can be at times), language represents our only opportunity to place limitations on power.

Cynicism and nihilism imprison us in the moment of power. There is no definitive intellectual answer to these twin diseases of the will and the intellect. There are only existential responses. When hopelessness is not confronted head-on, but indirectly responded to through compensations, then our ability to act is deflected into a kind of adjustment. Compensation and adjustment merely reinforce the self-destructive movement of the morality of power, morality without meaning. Not only must we become conscious of this new morality, but also we must muster the will to resist it.

What is required, then, is a life-affirming ethic instead of a self-destructive ethic. This ethic, however, must be as unrelenting as the civilization it opposes. A life-affirming ethic today must be an ethic of non-power and freedom.[32] Most importantly we must resist all pressures to manipulate others. Psychological violence is the opposite of love. Just by living in a technological civilization, many of our actions will contribute to the collective manipulation of others. Bureaucracy and psychological technique are everywhere. Each one of us must speak out against them and decide when and how to resist using these techniques. We must find ways of saying no, of violating organizational rules. Only in total opposition to this civilization can we begin to regain some semblance of freedom.

The opposition is not to technology as such but to technology as milieu and as a system out of control. Only by relativizing technology, the chief sacred of the modern world, can we regain a critical perspective toward it. Because technology is first and foremost a system of powerful means without effective ends, we must not pretend that an abstract code of ethics, premised on the assumption that technology is neutral and the only problem is the human use of it, will accomplish anything. A new ethics will only begin to emerge in the course of radical opposition. Anything else will simply be ideology.

Assuredly the idea of an ethic of non-power seems preposterous. Why does it have to be so extreme in practice? Have not all traditional moralities contained a dimension of power in the authority that transmits and enforces it? The reason is the unprecedented nature of technological power. The means for the control and exploitation of nature and human beings grows ever more powerful. Only action that is diametrically opposed in every way has any chance (no matter how slim) of succeeding. Therefore, this ethic must be one of non-power, not just non-violence. If we can choose not to manipulate others, not to compete (except in the spirit of play), not to be conformed to the peer group and public opinion, not to become powerful through the consumption of objects and images, then we will make a beginning, no doubt a stammering, faltering beginning.

A genuine revolution against a technological civilization must be first a cultural one and it must start with the individual.[33] Despite the facade of individualism, a technological civilization is at base thoroughly collectivistic. Politics is so heavily laden with technique that it cannot possibly be the place to start. The rediscovery of meaning will not come by resurrecting traditional values. It will come from the attempt to live out as nearly as possible an ethic of non-power. A sense of history is indispensable and in this context, so is a knowledge of traditional values. Because the meaning of all values comes from the context of their application, the knowledge of past values can only be a rough guide to the future.

Such an ethic of non-power and freedom must be negative, exist in opposition to the morality of power, morality without meaning. It is not an ethic being applied to a neutral situation. It is an ethic that must find some tiny crack in a structure of near total power. Were it ever to attempt to become a morality, rather than an ethic of individual love and freedom, it would be swallowed up by the very civilization it had chosen to oppose.

Can an ethic of love and freedom, as weak and fragile as it would appear, restore some measure of meaning and hope? Only if someone chooses to live it out will we discover the answer.

Notes

Preface

1 This idea is present implicitly or explicitly in all of Kierkegaard's writings. One may wish to consult *Concluding Unscientific Postscript,* trans. Howard and Edna Hong (Princeton: Princeton University Press, 1992), for a detailed discussion of it.
2 Jacques Ellul, *The Ethics of Freedom,* trans. Geoffrey Bromiley (Grand Rapids: Eerdmans, 1976), pp. 335 – 36.

1 The Absence of Morality, or Morality Assumes New Forms

1 Daniel Patrick Moynihan, "Defining Deviancy Down," *The American Scholar,* 62 (Winter 1993), pp. 17 – 30.
2 Maria Ossowska, *Social Determinants of Moral Ideas* (Philadelphia: University of Pennsylvania Press, 1970), p. 26.
3 Alvin Gouldner, *The Coming Crisis of Western Sociology* (New York: Basic Books, 1970), pp. 140 – 41.
4 Robert Jackall, *Moral Mazes* (New York: Oxford University Press, 1988).
5 P.M. Baumgartner, *The Moral Order of a Suburb* (New York: Oxford University Press, 1988).
6 I am excluding surveys on American beliefs and values, which, for reasons that will become clear later, never get us beyond individual opinion. One cannot perform a serious study of social morality primarily by the use of survey data.
7 David Riesman, *The Lonely Crowd* (New Haven: Yale University Press, 1950).
8 Robert Bellah et al., *Habits of the Heart* (Berkeley: University of California Press, 1985).
9 James Davison Hunter, *Culture Wars: the Struggle to Define America* (New York: Basic Books, 1991).
10 Louis Dumont, "On Value, Modern and Nonmodern," in *Essays on Individualism* (Chicago: University of Chicago Press, 1986), p. 260.

11 Alasdair MacIntyre, *After Virtue* (Notre Dame: University of Notre Dame Press, 1981), p. 33.

12 The difference between practical knowledge and theoretical knowledge is discussed in chapter 4. Practical knowledge is tacit knowledge based upon experience paradigms, the interrelationships among which always remain partly unconscious. Theoretical knowledge is conscious knowledge expressed in the form of concepts.

13 Hunter, *Culture Wars*, pp. 44 – 5.

14 C. Wright Mills, *The Sociological Imagination* (New York: Oxford University Press, 1959), chs. 2 and 3.

15 John Rawls, *A Theory of Justice* (Cambridge: Harvard University Press, 1971).

16 Among the better works of this type see Daniel Yankelovich, *New Rules* (New York: Random House, 1981); Ronald Inglehart, *Culture Shift in Advanced Industrial Society* (Princeton: Princeton University Press, 1990).

17 I have described this method in Richard Stivers, "The "Determining Relationship" Method: How to Understand and Explain an Irish Folksaying," *Studies in Symbolic Interaction*, ed. by Norman Denzin, 10 (1989), pp. 503 – 29.

18 On the theory of the sacred see especially Roger Caillois, *Man and the Sacred*, trans. Meyer Barash (New York: The Free Press, 1959); and Mircea Eliade, *Patterns in Comparative Religion*, trans. Rosemary Sheed (New York: New American Library, 1974).

19 Essential reading on the relationship of the sacred to practical knowledge is Willem Vanderburg, *The Growth of Minds and Cultures* (Toronto: University of Toronto Press, 1985), ch. 7.

20 Jacques Ellul, *To Will and to Do*, trans. C. Edward Hopkin (Philadelphia: Pilgram Press, 1969), pp. 112 – 98.

21 Ossowaska, *Social Determinants of Moral Ideas*, pp. 5 – 26.

22 Ellul, *To Will and to Do*, pp. 127 – 8.

23 Karl Mannheim, *Ideology and Utopia*, trans. Louis Worth and Edward Shils (New York: Harcourt, Brace, and World, 1936).

24 Ellul, *To Will and to Do*, pp. 133 – 4.

25 Jacques Ellul, *The Ethics of Freedom*, trans. Geoffrey Bromiley (Grand Rapids: Eerdmans, 1976).

26 Jurgen Moltmann, *The Trinity and the Kingdom*, trans. Margaret Kohl (San Francisco: Harper and Row, 1981), pp. 151 – 2.

27 Jacques Ellul, *The Subversion of Christianity*, trans. Geoffrey Bromiley (Grand Rapids: Eerdmans, 1986), ch. II; see also the works of Søren Kierkegaard, for a devastating critique of Christendom.

28 Ellul, *To Will and to Do*, ch. 11. My book starts with Ellul's insights but goes beyond them in directions suggested by Ellul's work on a technological civilization.

29 Jacques Ellul, *The New Demons*, trans. C. Edward Hopkin (New York: Seabury, 1975), ch. 3; see also Richard Stivers, *Evil in Modern Myth and Ritual* (Athens: University of Georgia Press, 1982), ch. 2.

30 MacIntyre, *After Virtue*, pp. 6 – 21.

31 Ibid., p. 12.

32 Ibid., pp. 19 – 20, 227 – 37.

33 J.H. van den Berg, *Medical Power and Medical Ethics* (New York: Norton, 1978).

34 Christina Sommers, "Ethics Without Virtue," *The American Scholar*, 53 (Summer 1984), pp. 381 – 9.

35 Ibid., pp. 383 – 8.

2 Success Morality: From Economic to Political Ideology

1 Robert Bellah et al., *Habits of the Heart* (New York: Harper and Row, 1986).
2 Reinhold Niebuhr, *The Nature and Destiny of Man*, vol. I: *Human Nature* (New York: Scribner's, 1964), ch. 3.
3 Georges Duby, *The Age of the Cathedrals*, trans. Eleanor Levieux and Barbara Thompson (Chicago: University of Chicago Press, 1981); see also Johan Heizinga, *The Waning of the Middle Ages* (Garden City: Anchor Books, 1954).
4 Erich Auerbach, *Mimesis*, trans. Willard Trask (Princeton: Princeton University Press, 1953).
5 Georges Duby, *The Three Orders*, trans. Arthur Goldhammer (Chicago: University of Chicago Press, 1978), pp. 322 – 7.
6 Ibid., ch. 10.
7 Jacques Ellul, *The New Demons*, trans. C. Edward Hopkin (New York: Seabury, 1975), ch. 1.
8 Duby, *The Age of the Cathedrals*, pp. 251 – 2.
9 Werner Sombart, *Luxury and Capitalism* (Ann Arbor: University of Michigan Press, 1967).
10 Albert Hirschman, *The Passions and the Interests* (Princeton: Princeton University Press, 1977).
11 Louis Dumont, *From Mandeville to Marx* (Chicago: University of Chicago Press, 1977), Part I.
12 Ibid., p. 79.
13 Ibid., p. 5.
14 R.H. Tawney, *The Acquisitive Society* (New York: Harcourt, Brace and World, 1920), p. 17.
15 Carl Becker, *The Heavenly City of the Eighteenth Century Philosophers* (New Haven: Yale University Press, 1932), ch. II.
16 R.H. Tawney, *Religion and the Rise of Capitalism* (New York: Harcourt, Brace and World, 1926), pp. 72 – 91.
17 Jacques Ellul, *The Ethics of Freedom*, trans. Geoffrey Bromiley (Grand Rapids: Eerdmans, 1976), pp. 498 – 9.
18 Tawney, *Religion and the Rise of Capitalism*, p. 92.
19 Ibid., p. 93.
20 Ibid., pp. 167 – 89.
21 Ibid., pp. 189 – 210.
22 Ibid., p. 204.
23 Max Weber, *The Protestant Ethic and the Spirit of Capitalism*, trans. Talcott Parsons (New York: Scribner's, 1958).
24 David Zaret, *The Heavenly Contract* (Chicago: University of Chicago Press, 1985), chs. 5 and 6.
25 Ibid., p. 201.
26 Bernard Groethuysen, *The Bourgeois*, trans. Mary Ilford (New York: Holt, Rinehart and Winston, 1968), pp. 175 – 90.
27 Elinor Barber, *The Bourgeoisie in 18th Century France* (Princeton: Princeton University Press, 1955), p. 85ff.
28 Ibid., pp. 78 – 81.
29 H. Richard Niebuhr, *The Social Sources of Denominationalism* (New York: New American Library, 1929), pp. 86 – 7.
30 Groethuysen, *The Bourgeois*, p. 231.

31 Weber, *The Protestant Ethic*, p. 53.
32 Tawney, *Religion and the Rise of Capitalism*, p. 111.
33 Kai Erikson, *Wayward Puritans* (New York: John Wiley, 1966), pp. 189 – 92.
34 Tawney, *Religion and the Rise of Capitalism*, pp. 112 – 15.
35 Niebuhr, *The Social Sources*, p. 104.
36 Benjamin Franklin, *The Works of Benjamin Franklin*, vol. II (Boston: Hilliard, Gray, and Co., 1840), pp. 87 – 9 and pp. 94 – 103.
37 Rex Burns, *Success in America* (Amherst: University of Massachusetts Press, 1976), p. 12.
38 Ibid., p. 1.
39 Ibid., p. 167.
40 Kenneth Lynn, *The Dream of Success* (Boston: Little, Brown, 1955), p. 3.
41 Richard Huber, *The American Idea of Success* (New York: McGraw-Hill, 1971), p. 95.
42 Ibid., p. 97.
43 See Irvin Wyllie, *The Self-Made Man in America* (New Brunswick: Rutgers University Press, 1954); John Cawelti, *Apostles of the Self-Made Man* (Chicago: University of Chicago Press, 1965).
44 Richard Weiss, *The American Myth of Success* (New York: Basic Books, 1969), pp. 35 – 60; Huber, *The American Idea of Success*, pp. 42 – 61.
45 Weiss, *The American Myth of Success*, pp. 59 – 60.
46 Lynn, *The Dream of Success*, p. 251.
47 Richard Hofstadter, *Social Darwinism in American Thought* (Boston: Beacon Press, 1955), ch. 2.
48 Huber, *The American Idea of Success*, pp. 124 – 85.
49 Donald Meyer, *The Positive Thinkers* (New York: Pantheon Books, 1980), ch. 2.
50 Huber, *American Idea of Success*, pp. 155 – 6.
51 Quoted in Meyer, *The Positive Thinkers*, p. 165.
52 Ibid., pp. 164 – 67.
53 Huber, *American Idea of Success*, p. 231.
54 Quoted in *Ibid.*, pp. 239 – 41.
55 Quoted in Ibid., p. 244.
56 On this issue see J.H. van den Berg, *Divided Existence and Complex Society* (Pittsburgh: Duquesne University Press, 1974).
57 Meyer, *The Positive Thinkers*, p. 188.
58 Quoted in Wyllie, *The Self-Made Man in America*, p. 4.
59 Burns, *Success in America*, p. 167.
60 On the issue of the interiorization of human existence see J.H. van den Berg, *The Changing Nature of Man*, trans. H.F. Croes (New York: Norton, 1961).
61 Frederick Taylor, *The Principles of Scientific Man* (New York: Harper, 1911).
62 Huber, *American Idea of Success*, p. 219.
63 Weiss, *American Myth of Success*, pp. 183 – 6.
64 Theodore Greene, *America's Heroes* (New York: Oxford University Press, 1970), p. 319.
65 Joseph Schumpeter, *Capitalism, Socialism, and Democracy* (New York: Harper and Row, 1962), p. 132ff.
66 Ibid., p. 133.
67 Weiss, *American Myth of Success*, pp. 184 – 5.
68 Meyer, *The Positive Thinkers*, pp. 181 – 3.
69 Greene, *America's Heroes*, ch. 8; C. Wright Mills, *White Collar* (New York: Oxford University Press, 1951), ch. 12.

70 Quoted in Weiss, *American Myth of Success*, p. 9.
71 Henry Jacoby, *The Bureaucratization of the World*, trans. Eveline Kanes (Berkeley: University of California Press, 1973).
72 Meyer, *The Positive Thinkers*, p. 195.
73 William Whyte, *The Organization Man* (Garden City: Anchor Books, 1956), ch. 20.
74 Greene, *America's Heroes*, p. 337.
75 Weiss, *American Myth of Success*, p. 15.
76 Cawelti, *Apostles of the Self-Made Man*, p. 202.
77 Ibid., pp. 217 – 18.
78 Lawrence Chenoweth, *The American Dream of Success* (North Scituate: Duxbury Press, 1974).
79 Dale Tarnowieski, *The Changing Success Ethic* (New York: American Management Associations, 1973), p. 43.
80 Leo Lowenthal, "The Triumph of Mass Idols," in *Literature and Mass Culture* (New Brunswick: Transaction Books, 1984), pp. 203 – 35.
81 David Riesman, *The Lonely Crowd* (New Haven: Yale University Press, 1969), p. 81.
82 Paul Nagel, *This Sacred Trust* (New York: Oxford University Press, 1971).
83 Perry Miller, "Shaping of the American Character," *The New England Quarterly*, 28 (December, 1955), pp. 435 – 54.
84 Erikson, *Wayward Puritans*, p. 188ff.
85 Ernest Tuveson, *Redeemer Nation* (Chicago: University of Chicago Press, 1968), pp. vii – viii.
86 Ibid., p. viii.
87 Miller, "Shaping of American Character," p. 437.
88 Tuveson, *Redeemer Nation*, pp. 96 – 7.
89 Quoted in Ibid., p. 127.
90 Quoted in Ibid., p. 157.
91 Quoted in Hofstadter, *Social Darwinism*, p. 179.
92 Arthur Schlesinger Jr., "Introduction" to Herbert Croly, *The Promise of American Life* (Cambridge: Belknap Press, 1965), p. xix.
93 Croly, *The Promise of American Life*, p. 1.
94 Tuveson, *Redeemer Nation*, p. x.
95 Quoted in Will Herberg, *Protestant, Catholic, Jew* (Chicago: University of Chicago Press, 1983), p. 258.
96 Leo Marx, *The Machine in the Garden* (New York: Oxford University Press, 1964), p. 206.
97 Ibid., p. 208.
98 Ibid., pp. 209 – 26.
99 Hugo Meier, "Technology and Democracy, 1800 – 1860," *The Mississippi Valley Historical Review*, 43 (March, 1957), p. 622.
100 Ibid., p. 624.
101 John Kasson, *Civilizing the Machine* (New York: Grossman, 1976), ch. 2.
102 John Higham, "Hanging Together: Divergent Unities in American History," *The Journal of American History*, 61 (June, 1974), p. 19.
103 Ibid., p. 24.
104 Robert Wiebe, *The Search for Order 1877 – 1920* (New York: Hill and Wang, 1967) pp. 161 – 63.
105 William Graebner, *The Engineering of Consent* (Madison: University of Wisconsin Press, 1987).

106 Howard Segal, *Technological Utopianism in American Culture* (Chicago: University of Chicago Press, 1985), chs. 4 – 6.
107 Ibid., p. 21.
108 Ibid., pp. 27 – 8.
109 Ibid., p. 124.
110 Charles Sanford, "Technology and Culture at the End of the Nineteenth Century: the Will to Power," in *Technology in Western Civilization*, vol. I, ed. Melvin Krazberg and Carroll Pursell (New York: Oxford University Press, 1967), p. 730.
111 Bertrand de Jouvenel, *On Power*, trans. J.F. Huntington (Boston: Beacon Press, 1962), p. 123.
112 Sanford, "Technology and Culture," p. 730.
113 Ernest Gellner, *Nations and Nationalism* (Ithaca: Cornell University Press, 1983).
114 Ibid., p. 127.
115 The sacred is that which is experienced as ultimately powerful and the greatest value. Myth and ritual develop in relation to that which is experienced as sacred. For a fuller discussion of the sacred, see Roger Caillois, *Man and the Sacred*, trans. Meyer Barash (New York: The Free Press, 1959). On the specific issue of the nation-state as sacred see Ellul, *The New Demons*, ch. 3.
116 John Kouwenhoven, *Made in America* (New York: Doubleday, 1948), p. 15.
117 See chapter 6 for a discussion of the role the visual images in the mass media play in establishing a common sense of reality.
118 Robert Cialdini et al., "Basking in Reflected Glory," *Journal of Personality and Social Psychology*, 34 (1976), pp. 366 – 75.
119 Wilbert Leonard II, *A Sociological Perspective of Sport* (New York: Macmillan, 1988), p. 67.
120 Gary Gumpert, "The Telltale Tape, or the Video Replay and Sportsmanship," in *Talking Tombstones* (New York: Oxford University Press, 1987), pp. 54 – 75.
121 Janet Lever, *Soccer Madness* (Chicago: University of Chicago Press, 1983), ch. 5.
122 Charles Perrow, *Normal Accidents* (New York: Basic Books, 1984).
123 Jacques Ellul, *The Technological System*, trans. Joachim Neugroschel (New York: Continuum, 1980).
124 Elias Canetti, *Crowds and Power*, trans. Carol Stewart (New York: Seabury, 1978), p. 227.

3 A Morality of Happiness and Health: Advertising as Mythology

1 Georges Duby, *The Age of the Cathedrals*, trans. Eleanor Levieux and Barbara Thompson (Chicago: University of Chicago Press, 1981), pp. 251 – 2ff.
2 Werner Sombart, *The Quintessence of Capitalism*, trans. M. Epstein (New York: Howard Fertig, 1967), pp. 103 – 4.
3 Erich Auerbach, *Mimesis*, trans. Willard Trask (Princeton: Princeton University Press, 1953), p. 202.
4 Although most of my references are about the French bourgeoisie, the discussion is applicable to much of Western Europe and North America.
5 Jacques Ellul, *Metamorphose du Bourgeois* (Paris: Calmann-Levy, 1967); Elinor Barber, *The Bourgeoisie in 18th Century France* (Princeton: Princeton University Press, 1955), 34 – 54, 78 – 81.
6 Bernard Groethuysen, *The Bourgeois*, trans. Mary Ilford (New York: Holt, Rinehart and Winston, 1968).

7   Ibid., p. 127.
8   Barber, *The Bourgeoisie*, p. 39.
9   Søren Kierkegaard, *For Self-Examination, Judge for Yourself*, trans. Howard and Edna Hong (Princeton: Princeton University Press, 1990), pp. 99 – 105.
10 Groethuysen, *The Bourgeois*, pp. 180 – 1.
11 Nicholas Berdyaev, "The Bourgois Mind" in *The Bourgeois Mind and other Essays* (Freeport: Books for Libraries Press, 1934), p. 18.
12 Barber, *The Bourgeoisie*, pp. 39 – 46.
13 Groethuysen, *The Bourgeois*, pp. 233 – 9.
14 Kierkegaard, *For Self-Examination, Judge for Yourself*, pp. 202 – 3.
15 Sombart, *The Quintessence*, p. 187.
16 In *Democracy in America*, Tocqueville argued that the tendency in a commercial civilization was for individuals to withdraw into a private circle of family and friends at the same time they lost interest in civic affairs.
17 In *At Odds: Women and the Family in America from the Revolution to the Present* (New York: Oxford University Press, 1980), Carl Degler maintains that the American family becomes by the twentieth century a "sentimental institution."
18 Barber, *The Bourgeoisie*, pp. 79 – 81.
19 Ibid., p. 37.
20 Quoted in Groethuysen, *The Bourgeois*, p. 127.
21 Norbert Elias, *The Court Society*, trans. Edmund Jephcott (New York: Pantheon, 1983).
22 Rosalind Williams, *Dream Worlds* (Berkeley: University of California Press, 1982), pp. 34 – 5.
23 Barber, *The Bourgeoisie*, pp. 85 – 98.
24 Williams, *Dream Worlds*, p. 36.
25 Groethuysen, *The Bourgeois*, pp. 127 – 8; Barber, *The Bourgeoisie*, p. 38.
26 Berdyaev, "The Bourgeois Mind," p. 25.
27 Jacques Ellul, *A Critique of the New Commonplaces*, trans. by Helen Weaver (New York: Knopf, 1968), pp. 3 – 27.
28 At the level of ideology the differences between classes are relatively unimportant. Therefore this integration is more than the "fusion of the bourgeois ethos and nobility ethos" that Maria Ossowska talks of in her *Social Determinants of Moral Ideas* (Philadelphia: University of Pennsylvania Press, 1970), pp. 168 – 173; for it includes the working class as well (the "embourgeoisement" of the working class).
29 Barber, *The Bourgeoisie*, p. 38.
30 Neil McKendrick, John Brewer and J.H. Plumb, *The Birth of a Consumer Society* (Bloomington: Indiana University Press, 1982), p. 13.
31 Ibid., p. 9.
32 A full-blown consumer society is one in which increased consumption is both the paramount social goal and the source of identity for the individual. Ultimately it turns everything, including people, into objects of consumption.
33 McKendrick, *The Birth of a Consumer Society*, pp. 21 – 5.
34 Neil Haris, "The Drama of Consumer Desire," in *Yankee Enterprise*, ed. Otto Mayr and Robert Post (Washington, D.C.: Smithsonian Institution Press, 1981), pp. 192 – 3.
35 McKendrick, *The Birth of a Consumer Society*, p. 1.
36 Michael Miller, *The Bon Marché: Bourgeois Culture and the Department Store, 1869 – 1920* (Princeton: Princeton University Press, 1981), p. 167.
37 Grant McCracken, *Culture and Consumption* (Bloomington: Indiana University Press, 1988), p. 132.

38 Daniel Boorstin, *The Americans: the Democratic Experience* (New York: Vintage, 1974), pp. 128 – 9.
39 Rosalind Williams, *Dream Worlds* (Berkeley: University of California Press, 1982), p. 59.
40 Ibid., pp. 59 – 60.
41 Cited in ibid., p. 61.
42 Miller, *The Bon Marché*, p. 167.
43 Ibid., p. 46.
44 Ibid., pp. 168 – 75.
45 Ibid., p. 169.
46 Ibid., p. 180.
47 Ibid., p. 183.
48 Boorstin, *The Americans*, p. 104.
49 Ibid., p. 128.
50 Ibid., p. 129.
51 Williams, *Dream Worlds*, p. 53.
52 Ibid., p. 53.
53 Harris, "The Drama of Consumer Desire," p. 209.
54 Cited in ibid.
55 Ibid.
56 Don DeLillo, *White Noise* (New York: Penguin, 1985), pp. 83 – 4.
57 Harris, "The Drama of Consumer Desire," p. 212.
58 Colin Campbell, "Romanticism and the Consumer Ethic: Intimations of a Weber-style Thesis," *Sociological Analysis*, 44 (1983), p. 287.
59 Ibid., p. 288.
60 Miller, *The Bon Marché*, p. 184.
61 David Riesman, *The Lonely Crowd* (Abridged edition; New Haven: Yale University Press, 1969), pp. 81 – 2.
62 Guy Debord, *Society of the Spectacle* (Detroit: Black and Red, 1983), para. 42.
63 Ibid., para. 67.
64 Ibid., para. 69.
65 Boorstin, *The Americans*, p. 137.
66 Ibid., pp. 142 – 3.
67 William Leiss, Stephen Kline, and Sut Ihally, *Social Communication in Advertising* (New York: Metheun, 1986), pp. 74 – 5.
69 Leiss et al., *Social Communication*, p. 76.
70 Frank Presbrey, *The History and Development of Advertising* (New York: Greenwood Press, 1968), pp. 455 – 6.
71 Ibid., pp. 479 – 481.
72 Ibid., p. 482.
73 Christopher Wilson, "The Rhetoric of Consumption," in *The Culture of Consumption*, ed. Richard Fox and T.J. Jackson Lears (New York: Pantheon, 1983), p. 49 – 53.
74 Leiss et al., *Social Communication*, pp. 83 – 4.
75 Ibid., p. 113.
76 Ibid., p. 89.
77 Pat Aufderheide, "Music Videos: the Look of the Sound," *Journal of Communication*, 36 (1986), pp. 57 – 78.
78 Leiss et al., *Social Communication*, p. 93.
79 Ibid., p. 98.

80 Michael Schudson, *Advertising, the Uneasy Persuasion* (New York: Basic Books, 1984), p. 171.
81 Leiss et al., *Social Communication*, p. 101.
82 Ibid., p. 180.
83 Roland Marchand, *Advertising the American Dream* (Berkeley: University of California Press, 1985), p. 234.
84 Leiss et al. *Social Communication*, pp. 244 – 6.
85 Jules Henry, *Culture Against Man* (New York: Vintage, 1965), ch. 3.
86 Daniel Boorstin, "The Rhetoric of Democracy," in *Democracy and Its Discontents* (New York: Random House, 1974), pp. 26 – 42.
87 Ibid., pp. 39 – 42.
88 The disintegrative effect of technology upon culture is the subject of chapters 4 and 6.
89 Richard Stivers, "The Deconstruction of the University," *The Centennial Review*, XXXV (Winter, 1991), pp. 115 – 36.
90 On the difference between the past and history see J.H. Plumb, *The Death of the Past* (Boston: Houghton Miflin, 1970).
91 Leiss et al., *Social Communication*, p. 233.
92 Ibid., p. 246.
93 Gunnar Andren et al. *Rhetoric and Ideology in Advertising* (Stockholm: Liber Foilag, 1978), pp. 137, 151.
94 Ibid., p. 140.
95 Jonathan Price, *The Best Thing on TV* (New York: Viking Press, 1978) pp. 44, 53.
96 Marchand, *Advertising the American Dream*, p. 264.
97 Ibid., p. 363.
98 Andren et al., *Rhetoric and Ideology in Advertising*, p. 137.
99 Stuart Ewen, *Captains of Consciousness* (New York: McGraw-Hill, 1976), p. 143.
100 Andren et al., *Rhetoric and Ideology*, p. 121.
101 Ewen, *Captains of Consciousness*, p. 47.
102 Leiss et al., *Social Communication*, pp. 210 – 15.
103 Andren et al., *Rhetoric and Ideology*, p. 139.
104 Leiss et al., *Social Communication*, pp. 221 – 2.
105 Jerry Mander, *Four Arguments for the Elimination of Television* (New York: Quill, 1978), pp. 323 – 8.
106 Ewen, *Captains of Consciousness*, pp. 191, 213.
107 Andren et al., *Rhetoric and Ideology*, p. 151.
108 Richard Stivers, *Evil in Modern Myth and Ritual* (Athens: University of Georgia Press, 1982), pp. 92 – 100.
109 See chapter 6 for a full discussion of the material visual image's corrosive effect on symbolism and narrative.
110 Neil Postman, "The Parable of the Ring Around the Collar," in *Conscientious Objections* (New York: Knopf, 1988), pp. 66 – 71.
111 Leiss et al., *Social Communication*, pp. 189 – 90.
112 Ibid., p. 232.
113 Ibid., p. 231.
114 Andren et al., p. 152.
115 Howard Mumford Jones, *The Pursuit of Happiness* (Cambridge: Harvard University Press, 1953).
116 Ibid., pp. 113 – 30.
117 Donald Meyer, *The Positive Thinkers* (New York: Pantheon, 1980), chs 1 and 2.
118 Ibid., ch.3.

119 Louis Schneider and Sanford Dornbusch, *Popular Religion* (Chicago: University of Chicago Press, 1958), pp. 27 – 9.
120 Ibid., p. 27.
121 Meyer, *The Positive Thinkers*, p. 263.
122 Ibid., pp. 175 – 80.
123 Schneider and Dornbusch, pp. 28 – 42.
124 Barbara Wootton, *Social Science and Social Pathology* (London: George Allen & Unwin, 1959), p. 218.
125 Quoted in ibid., p. 211.
126 Ibid., p. 214.
127 Joseph Veroff, Richard Kulka, and Elizabeth Douvan, *Mental Health in America* (New York: Basic Books, 1981), p. 5.
128 Maurice North, *Secular Priests* (London: George Allen & Unwin, 1972), p. 132.
129 Paul Halmos, *The Personal Service Society* (New York: Schocken Books, 1970).
130 Jones, *The Pursuit of Happiness*, ch. 5.
131 Philip Rieff, *The Triumph of the Therapeutic* (New York: Harper and Row, 1966), p. 261.
132 See, for instance, T.J. Jackson Lears, "From Salvation to Self-Realization: Advertising and the Therapeutic Roots of the Consumer Culture, 1880 – 1930," in *The Culture of Consumption*, pp. 3 – 38; and Marchand, *Advertising the American Dream.*
133 Jones, *The Pursuit of Happiness*, pp. 146 – 7.
134 Both Meyer, (*Positive Thinkers*) and Schneider and Dornbusch (*Popular Religion*) explicitly refer to many of these psychological techniques as forms of magic. There is a sizeable body of literature that compares modern psychotherapy with the magical and ritualistic healing practices of primitive peoples. On this see Stivers, *Evil in Modern Myth and Ritual*, ch. 5.
135 *Symbol* is here defined as a sign with a double intentionality. The two meanings, literal and figurative, involve a metaphorical comparison. Paul Ricoeur, *Interpretation Theory: Discourse and the Surplus of Meaning* (Fort Worth: Texas Christian University Press, 1976), pp. 53 – 69, argues that religious symbols have a non-semantic dimension to their figurative meaning. That is, a religious symbol transports us at least in part into the realm of the mysterious. While religious symbols communicate meaning they leave part of the figural meaning unexplained. Religious symbols, moreover, as spontaneous and collective creations, are bound to a universe, our most immediate life-milieu. In this instance the life-milieu is technology as reflected in the dominant myth of technological utopianism.
136 Mircea Eliade, *Patterns in Comparative Religion*, trans. Rosemary Sheed (New York: New American Library, 1974), ch. 13.
137 Jones, *The Pursuit of Happiness*, p. 163.
138 Jacques Ellul, *The New Demons*, trans. C. Edward Hopkin (New York: Seabury, 1975), ch. 3; and Stivers, *Evil in Modern Myth and Ritual*, ch. 2.
139 Cited in Jacques Ellul, *The Technological System*, trans. Joachim Neugroschel (New York: Continuum, 1980), pp. 308 – 9.

4 From the Moral to the Technical: the Necessary

1 On the point of a technological civilization see Jacques Ellul, *The Technological Society*, trans. John Wilkinson (New York: Vintage, 1964), ch. 1; see also Jacques

Ellul, *What I Believe*, trans. Geoffrey Bromiley (Grand Rapids: Eerdmans, 1989), ch. 11.

2 Ellul, *The Technological Society*, p. xxv.

3 Ibid., ch. 1.

4 Jacques Ellul, *The Technological System*, trans. Joachim Neugroschel (New York: Continuum, 1980).

5 Ellul, *The Technological Society*, ch. 5.

6 Lewis Mumford, *The Pentagon of Power* (New York: Harcourt Brace Jovanovich, 1970).

7 MacIntyre's idea of virtue as a set of practices in which the means are consistent with the ends and which comes to constitute the narrative of a human life within a living tradition, is closer to this notion than is the idea of morality as a closed system of logical rules. See Alasdair MacIntyre, *After Virtue* (Notre Dame: University of Notre Dame Press, 1981).

8 The hostile reaction to human technique, especially bureaucracy, is well known. This will be dealt with later in the chapter. For now I simply point out that except for a few dissidents, most negative reaction to technique is either irrational or based on the assumption that the problem was not technique itself but inferior technique. The solution is even more efficient technique!

9 See chapter 6 for a detailed discussion of the decline of meaning in modern symbols.

10 Joseph Weizenbaum, *Computer Power and Human Reason* (San Francisco: W. H. Freeman, 1976) pp. 45 – 6.

11 Max Weber regarded abstract rules as a paramount characteristic of bureaucracy; see Max Weber, *Economy and Society*, vol. 2 (Berkeley: University of California Press, 1978), ch. XI.

12 Henry Jacoby, *The Bureaucratization of the World*, trans. Eveline Kanes (Berkeley: University of California Press, 1976).

13 James Q. Wilson, *Bureaucracy* (New York: Basic Books, 1989), p. 342.

14 Ellul, *The Technological Society*.

15 Herbert Kaufman, *Red Tape* (Washington, D.C.: The Brookings Institution, 1977), pp. 7, 98.

16 Jacoby, *The Bureaucratization of the World*, ch. 6.

17 Robert Heilbroner, *Business Civilization in Decline* (New York: Norton, 1976).

18 Elinor Langer, "Inside the New York Telephone Company," *The New York Review of Books*, XIV (March 12, 1970), p. 19.

19 Ibid., p. 22.

20 James William Gibson, *The Perfect War: Technowar in Vietnam* (Boston: Atlantic Monthly Press, 1986).

21 Ida Hoos, *Systems Analysis in Public Policy* (Berkeley: University of California Press, 1983), ch. 2.

22 Gibson, *Perfect War*, pp. 15 – 16.

23 Ibid., p. 129.

24 Ibid., pp. 130 – 1.

25 Ibid., pp. 112 – 13ff.

26 Ibid., p. 125.

27 Ibid., p. 141.

28 Ibid., p. 121.

29 Thomas Scheff, "The Societal Reaction to Deviance: Ascriptive Elements in the Psychiatric Screening of Mental Patients in a Midwestern State," *Social Problems*, 11 (Spring, 1964), pp. 401 – 13.

30 Ibid., pp. 402 – 3.
31 Ibid., p. 408.
32 Ibid., p. 411.
33 Abraham Blumberg, *Criminal Justice* (Chicago: Quadrangle Books, 1970).
34 Ibid., ch. 5.
35 Erving Goffman, *Asylums* (Garden City: Anchor Books, 1961).
36 Ibid., p. 384.
37 Erving Goffman, "The Insanity of Place," in *The Collective Definition of Deviance*, ed. F. James Davis and Richard Stivers (New York: The Free Press, 1975), pp. 325 – 33.
38 Jacques Ellul, *The Technological Society*, trans. John Wilkinson (New York: Vintage, 1964).
39 Langer, "Inside the New York Telephone Company," pp. 23 – 4.
40 Charles Perrow, "The Bureaucratic Paradox: the Efficient Organization Centralizes in Order to Decentralize," *Organizational Dynamics*, 5 (Spring, 1977), pp. 3 – 14.
41 Shoshana Zuboff, *In the Age of the Smart Machine* (New York: Basic Books, 1988).
42 Perrow, "The Bureaucratic Paradox," pp. 5 – 6.
43 Hoos, *Systems Analysis in Public Policy*.
44 Richard Edwards, *Contested Terrain: The Transformation of the Workplace in the Twentieth Century* (New York: Basic Books, 1979), pp. 149 – 50.
45 Perrow, "The Bureaucratic Paradox," p. 6.
46 Ellul, *The Technological System*, ch. 8.
47 Edwards, *Contested Terrain*, p. 33.
48 Charles Perrow, *Normal Accidents* (New York: Basic Books, 1984), pp. 93 – 4.
49 Ibid., pp. 72 – 100.
50 Zuboff, *In the Age of the Smart Machine*, chs. 6 – 8.
51 Ibid., p. 180f.
52 Ibid., pp. 387 – 414.
53 Zuboff's forecast is based on the assumption that a certain number of jobs will be automated (in the mechanical sense) so that the remaining jobs are more similar in terms of the skills and the knowledge about the product or service that are demanded. Otherwise, the informated workplace will have almost as rigid a hierarchy as the automated workplace.
54 Ibid., p. 346.
55 Ibid., ch. 7.
56 Barbara Garson, *The Electronic Sweatshop* (New York: Simon and Schuster, 1988).
57 Ibid., p. 150.
58 Ibid., p. 169.
59 Hoos, *Systems Analysis in Public Policy*, ch. 7.
60 Jacques Ellul, *The Technological Bluff*, trans. Geoffrey Bromiley (Grand Rapids: Eerdmans, 1990), pp. 327 – 8.
61 Jacques Ellul, *The Humiliation of the Word*, trans. Joyce Hanks (Grand Rapids: Eerdmans, 1985), p. 31.
62 Perrow, "The Bureaucratic Paradox," pp. 10 – 13.
63 Guillermo Grenier, *Inhuman Relations: Quality Circles and Anti-Unionism in American Industry* (Philadelphia: Temple University Press, 1988), p. 4.
64 Ibid., pp. 46 – 9.
65 Ibid., p. 131.
66 Ibid., p. 135.
67 Jacoby, *The Bureaucratization of the World*, p. 154.

68 C. Wright Mills, *The Sociological Imagination* (New York: Oxford University Press, 1959), p. 117.
69 Owen Barfield, *Saving the Appearances* (New York: Harcourt Brace Jovanovich, 1959), ch. 8.
70 Jacoby, *The Bureaucratization of the World*, pp. 155 – 6.
71 Stanley Milgram, *Obedience to Authority* (New York: Harper & Row, 1974), ch. 1.
72 Hanna Arendt, *Eichmann in Jerusalem* (New York: Viking Press, 1963), pp. 253 – 6; see also Harold Rosenberg, "The Trial and Eichmann," *Commentary*, 32 (November, 1961), pp. 378 – 80, for similar reflections.
73 Milgran, *Obedience to Authority*, p. 7.
74 Ibid., pp. 113 – 15.
75 Zuboff, *In the Age of the Smart Machine*, pp. 296 – 7, 352 – 3, 401.
76 Ibid., pp. 346 – 51.
77 Ibid., pp. 356, 349.
78 Ibid., pp. 403 – 5.
79 Reinhold Niebuhr, *Moral Man and Immoral Society* (New York: Charles Scribners, 1960).
80 Mark Crispin Miller, *Boxed In: The Culture of TV* (Evanston: Northwestern University Press, 1988).
81 Jeffrey Goldfarb, *The Cynical Society* (Chicago: University of Chicago Press, 1991).
82 Erich Kahler, *The Disintegration of Form in the Arts* (New York: Braziler, 1967).
83 Jacob Brackman, *The Put-On* (Chicago: Henry Regnery, 1971).
84 A life milieu is the symbolic environment that is both the primary source of life and the major threat to it. The life milieu is thus fundamentally ambiguous. For instance, nature provides the means of subsistence and presents a clear danger, as with wild animals, natural disasters, and poisons; Jacques Ellul, *What I Believe*, trans. Geoffrey Bromiley (Grand Rapids: Eerdmans, 1989), pp. 104 – 40, identifies three milieus: nature, society, and technology.
85 Hans Kelsen, *Society and Nature* (New York: Arno Press, 1974), p. 259.
86 Arnold Gehlen, *Man in the Age of Technology*, trans. Patricia Lipscomb (New York: Columbia University Press, 1980).
87 See Perrow, *Normal Accidents*; Hoos, *Systems Analysis and Public Policy*, ch. 8; Ellul, *The Technological Bluff*, ch. 2.
88 See *The Changing Nature of Man*, trans. H. F. Croes (New York: Norton, 1961); *Divided Existence and Complex Society* (Pittsburgh: Duquesne University Press, 1974).
89 *The Tower and the Abyss* (New York: George Braziller, 1957).
90 Gehlen, *Man in the Age of Technology*.
91 Van den Berg, *The Changing Nature of Man*.
92 Van den Berg, *Divided Existence and Complex Society*.
93 Karl Marx, "The Power of Money in Bourgeois Society" in *The Economic and Philosophic Manuscripts of 1844*, ed. Dirk Struik (New York: International Publishers, 1964), p. 167.
94 Jacques Ellul, *The Ethics of Freedom*, trans. Geoffrey Bromiley (Grand Rapids: Eerdmans, 1976), p. 309.
95 Josephine Hendin, *Vulnerable People* (New York: Oxford University Press, 1978), pp. 8 – 27.
96 Arlie Hochschild, *The Managed Heart* (Berkeley: University of California Press, 1983), pp. 33 – 42.
97 Ibid., p. 105.

98 Ibid., pp. 18 –23.

99 John Molloy, *Dress for Success* (New York: Peter Wyden, 1975), pp. 147 – 8.

100 Guy Oakes, *The Soul of the Salesman* (Atlantic Highlands, N.J.: Humanities Press, 1990), p. 96.

101 Ibid., p. 20.

102 Ibid., p. 18.

103 Ibid., p. 29.

104 Ibid., pp. 34, 91 – 9.

105 Steven Tipton, *Getting Saved from the Sixties* (Berkeley: University of California Press, 1982), p. 176.

106 Andrew Malcolm, *The Tyranny of the Group* (Totowa: Littlefield, Adams, 1975).

107 Tipton, *Getting Saved from the Sixties*, p. 188.

108 Milton Maxwell, "Alcoholics Anonymous: An Interpretation," in *Society, Culture and Drinking Patterns*, ed. David Pittman and Charles Snyder (New York: Wiley, 1962), p. 580.

109 J. David Brown, "Cultural Isomorphism: A Reinterpretation of the Institutionalization and Proliferation of Substance Abuse Treatment," paper presented at the Midwest Sociological Society Meetings, April 3, 1992.

110 Richard Stivers, *Evil in Modern Myth and Ritual* (Athens: University of Georgia Press, 1982), pp. 123 – 31.

111 Claude Levi-Strauss, "The Sorcerer and His Magic," in *Structural Anthropology*, trans. Claire Jacobson and Brooke Schoepf (Garden City: Anchor Books, 1967), pp. 161 – 80.

112 Jerome Frank, *Persuasion and Healing* (New York: Schocken Books, 1974), p. 164.

113 Victor Turner, *The Forest of Symbols* (Ithaca: Cornell University Press, 1967), pp. 359 – 93.

114 Stivers, *Evil in Modern Myth and Ritual*, p. 126.

115 Perry London, *Behavior Control* (New York: Harper & Row, 1969), chs. 3 – 5.

116 Jovel Kovel, *A Complete Guide to Therapy* (New York: Pantheon, 1976), p. 69.

117 William Arney and Bernard Bergen, *Medicine and the Management of Living* (Chicago: University of Chicago Press, 1984), p. 133.

118 Alexis de Tocqueville, *Democracy in America*, trans. George Lawrence (Garden City: Anchor Books, 1969), p. 692, discusses dependency in terms of the increased power of the state to regulate the lives of the citizens to the point that it "relieve[s] them from the trouble of thinking and all the cares of living." Later in the nineteenth century the coming together of the political state and technology became the basis for the "therapeutic state."

119 John McKnight, "Professionalized Service and Disabling Help," in Ivan Illich et al., *Disabling Professions* (Boston: Marion Boyars, 1978), pp. 69 – 91.

120 Don Delillo, *White Noise* (New York: Penguin, 1985).

121 Philip Rieff, *The Triumph of the Therapeutic* (New York: Harper and Row, 1966).

122 Van den Berg, *The Changing Nature of Man*, ch. 5.

123 Karen Horney, *The Neurotic Personality of Our Time* (New York: Norton, 1937), ch. 15.

124 Ibid., p. 89.

125 Ibid., p. 286.

126 Ibid., p. 97.

5 From the Moral to the Normal: the Ephemeral

1 For a detailed discussion of how modern science affected discourse and conceptualization see Owen Barfield, *Saving the Appearances* (New York: Harcourt Brace Jovanovich, 1957).

2 Jeffrey Bergner, *The Origin of Formalism in Social Science* (Chicago: University of Chicago Press, 1981), ch. 1.

3 Jacques Ellul, *The Technological Bluff*, trans. Geoffrey Bromiley (Grand Rapids: Eerdmans, 1990), pp. 327 – 32.

4 Hans Kelsen, *Society and Nature* (New York: Arno Press, 1974), p. 266.

5 For a discussion of radical immanentism see Gabriel Vahanian, *The Death of God* (New York: George Braziller, 1961).

6 For a fuller discussion of this see Richard Stivers, *Evil in Modern Myth and Ritual* (Athens: University of Georgia Press, 1982), pp. 82 – 5.

7 William Arney and Bernard Bergen, *Medicine and the Management of Living* (Chicago: University of Chicago Press, 1984), ch. 7.

8 Ibid., pp. 169 – 70.

9 Elisabeth Noelle-Neumann, "Toward a Theory of Public Opinion," in *Surveying Social Life*, ed. Hubert O'Gorman (Middletown: Wesleyan University Press, 1988), pp. 289 – 300.

10 Michel Foucault, *The Birth of the Clinic*, trans. A.M. Smith (New York: Vintage Books, 1975), pp. 22 – 38.

11 Dag Osterberg, *Metasociology* (Oslo: Norwegian University Press, 1988), pp. 18 – 19.

12 Elisabeth Noelle-Neumann, *The Spiral of Silence* (Chicago: University of Chicago Press, 1984), pp. 74 – 8.

13 Ibid., p. 77.

14 Carl Becker, *The Heavenly City of the Eighteenth-Century Philosophers* (New Haven: Yale University Press, 1932).

15 Ibid., p. 436.

16 Alexis de Tocqueville, *Democracy in America*, trans. George Lawrence (Garden City: Anchor Books, 1969), p. 256.

17 Elisabeth Noelle-Neumann (*The Spiral of Silence*) has developed a theory of public opinion as a form of control that uses the fear of isolation to keep dissent from being expressed once opinion is settled. She notes that the kernel of the theory is present in Tocqueville.

18 Søren Kierkegaard, *The Present Age*, trans. Alexander Dru (New York: Harper and Row, 1962), p. 64.

19 Kierkegaard''s great insight anticipates one of Debord's about life as the "seemingly lived" in the society of the spectacle.

20 Kierkegaard, *The Present Age*, p. 47.

21 Ibid., p. 52.

22 Søren Kierkegaard, *Concluding Unscientific Postscript*, trans. David Swenson and Walter Lowrie (Princeton: Princeton University Press, 1968), p. 288.

23 Daniel Boorstin, *Democracy and Its Discontents* (New York: Random House, 1974), pp. 12 – 15.

24 Jacques Ellul, *Propaganda*, trans. Konrad Kellen (New York: Knopf, 1969), pp. 95 – 102.

25 Boorstin, *Democracy and Its Discontents*, p. 20.

26 Ibid., p. 19.

27 Neil Postman, "The News," in *Conscientious Objections* (New Knopf, 1988), pp. 72 – 81; see also Mark Crispen Miller, *Boxed In: the Culture of TV* (Evanston: Northwestern University Press, 1988), pp. 3 – 27.

28 Ellul, *Propaganda*, pp. 205 – 06.

29 Henry Jacoby, *The Bureaucratization of the World*, trans. Eveline Kanes (Berkeley: University of California Press, 1976), ch. 6.

30 Ellul, *Propaganda*, pp. 206 – 7.

31 Boorstin, *Democracy and Its Discontents*, p. 19.

32 Ellul, *Propaganda*, p. 101.

33 Jacques Ellul, *The New Demons*, trans. C. Edward Hopkin (New York: The Seabury Press, 1975), p. 113.

34 Ibid., ch. IV.

35 Jacques Ellul, *The Political Illusion*, trans. Konrad Kellen (New York: Knopf, 1967), pp. 49 – 67.

36 Jacques Ellul, *The Technological System*, trans. Joachim Neugroschel (New York: Continuum, 1980), p. 37.

37 Ronald Troyer, *Cigarettes, the Battle over Smoking* (New Brunswick: Rutgers University Press, 1983), chs 4 – 5.

38 Ibid., pp. 60 – 1.

39 Tocqueville, *Democracy in America*, pp. 503 – 6.

40 Francois Furet, "The Conceptual System of 'Democracy in America,' " *In the Workshop of History*, trans. Jonathan Mandelbaum (Chicago: University of Chicago Press, 1984), p. 190.

41 Tocqueville, *Democracy in America*, p. 673.

42 Tzvetan Todorov, *"Notes from the Underground,"* in *Genres in Discourse* (New York: Cambridge University Press, 1990), p. 84, attributes Nietzsche"s views on the psychology of the master-slave relation to Dostoevsky.

43 Ibid., pp. 82 – 6.

44 Ibid., p. 86.

45 Ellul, *The Technological System*, p. 71.

46 John Kenneth Galbraith, *The Culture of Contentment* (Boston: Houghton Mifflin, 1992).

47 Stephen Cole and Robert Fiorentine, "The Formation of Public Opinion on Complex Issues: the Case of Nuclear Power," in *Surveying Social Life*, ed. Hubert O'Gorman (Middletown: Wesleyan University Press, 1988), p. 323.

48 Ibid., p. 311.

49 Ibid., pp. 313 – 14.

50 Ann Douglas, *The Feminization of American Culture* (New York: Anchor Books, 1988).

51 Viviana Zelizer, *Pricing the Priceless Child* (New York: Basic Books, 1985).

52 Christopher Lasch, *Haven in a Heartless World* (New York: Basic Books, 1977).

53 Daniel Yankelovich, *New Rules* (New York: Random House, 1981), p. 3.

54 M.P. Baumgartner, *The Moral Order of a Suburb* (New York: Oxford University Press, 1988), pp. 10 – 13, 55 – 71.

55 Louis Dumont, *Homo Hierarchicus*, trans. Mark Sainsbury, Louis Dumont, and Basea Gudate (Chicago: University of Chicago Press, 1980).

56 Louis Dumont, "The Anthropoligical Community and Ideology" in *Essays in Individualism* (Chicago: University of Chicago Press, 1986), p. 229.

57 John Gillis, *Youth and History* (New York: Academic Press, 1981), ch. 1.

58 J.H. van den Berg, *The Changing Nature of Man*, trans. H.F. Croes (New York: Norton, 1961), pp. 71 – 2.

59 Gillis, *Youth and History*, pp. 18 – 35.
60 Ibid., pp. 61 – 6.
61 David Riesman, *The Lonely Crowd* (New Haven: Yale University Press, 1969), chs. 2 and 3.
62 Daniel Boorstin, *The Americans: the Democratic Experience* (New York: Vintage, 1974), pp. 89 – 164.
63 Peter Blau and Marshall Meyer, *Bureaucracy in Modern Society* (New York: Random House, 1971), pp. 46 – 50; for a study of an organization that effectively denies informal work groups see Michel Crozier, *The Bureaucratic Phenomenon* (Chicago: University of Chicago Press, 1964), ch. 2.
64 Alvin Gouldner, *Patterns of Industrial Bureaucracy* (New York: The Free Press, 1954), pp. 174 – 6.
65 Gerald Suttles, *The Social Order of the Slum* Chicago: University of (Chicago Press, 1968), ch. 9.
66 Ibid., ch. 10.
67 Ibid., ch. 5.
68 Ibid., ch. 12.
69 Robert Jackall, *Moral Mazes* (New York: Oxford University Press, 1988).
70 Robert Jackall, "Moral Mazes: Bureaucracy and Managerial Work," *Harvard Business Review*, 61 (September-October, 1983), pp. 121 – 7.
71 Jackall, *Moral Mazes*, pp. 39, 213 – 14.
72 Robert Jackall, "The Moral Ethos of Bureaucracy," *State, Culture and Society* 1 (Fall, 1984), pp. 185 – 91.
73 Jackall, *Moral Mazes*, p. 90.
74 Jackall, "The Moral Ethos of Bureaucracy," p. 191.
75 Riesman, *The Lonely Crowd*, pp. 3 – 4, distinguishes between personality on the individual level and character on the cultural level. Each individual"s personality is formed within the boundaries of her culture"s main character type.
76 Jacques Ellul, *The Betrayal of the West*, trans. Matthew O'Connell (New York: Seabury Press, 1978), ch. 1.
77 Riesman, *The Lonely Crowd*, pp. 24 – 5.
78 Ibid., p. 73.
79 Kierkegaard, *Concluding Unscientific Postscript*, p. 288.
80 Riesman, *The Lonely Crowd*, pp. 81 – 2.
81 Karen Horney, *The Neurotic Personality of Our Time* (New York: Norton, 1937), p. 89.
82 Ibid., p. 107.
83 J.H. van den Berg, *Divided Existence and Complex Society* (Pittsburgh: Duquesne University Press, 1974), ch. 8.
84 Ellul, *The Technological Bluff*.

6 From the Moral to the Visual: the Compensatory

1 Georges Duby, *The Age of the Cathedrals*, trans. Eleanor Levieux and Barbara Thompson (Chicago: University of Chicago Press, 1981).
2 Jacques LeGoff, *The Birth of Purgatory*, trans. Arthur Goldhammer (Chicago: University of Chicago Press, 1981), pp. 367 – 8.
3 Michael Miller, *The Bon Marché* (Princeton: Princeton University Press, 1981), p. 175.

4 Roland Marchand, *Advertising the American Dream* (Berkeley: University of California Press, 1985), p. 235.
5 *Jean Baudrillard: Selected Writings*, ed. Mark Poster (Stanford: Stanford University Press, 1988), pp. 29 – 56.
6 Marchand, *Advertising the American Dream*, pp. 238 – 47.
7 On commonplace sayings as evidence of cultural belief see Jacques Ellul, *A Critique of the New Commonplaces*, trans. Helen Weaver (New York: Knopf, 1968), pp. 3 – 27.
8 Daniel Boorstin, *The Image* (New York: Harper Colophon, 1964), p. 198.
9 Ibid., pp. 185 – 94.
10 Dan Nimmo, *The Political Persuaders* (Englewood Cliffs: Prentice-Hall, 1970), pp. 35 – 6.
11 Jacques Ellul, *The Political Illusion*, trans. Konrad Kellen (New York: Vintage, 1967), ch. 3.
12 Stuart Ewen, *All Consuming Images* (New York: Basic Books, 1988), pp. 20 – 3.
13 Ibid., p. 6.
14 Arnold Mitchell, in *Nine American Life Styles* (New York: Macmillan, 1983), attempts to categorize the various American life-styles.
15 Kenneth Hudson, *The Language of the Teenage Revolution* (London: Macmillan, 1983), especially chs. 2 and 3; for a different point of view see Dick Hebdige, *Subculture: the Meaning of Style* (New York: Methuen, 1979).
16 Cecelia Tichi, "Video Novels," *Boston Review* XII (June 1987), pp. 12 – 14.
17 On the issue of celebratory and critical post modernism see Gerald Graff, *Literature Against Itself* (Chicago: University of Chicago Press, 1979), pp. 55 – 9.
18 Tichi, "Video Novels," p. 13.
19 Joseph Frank, "Spatial Form in Modern Literature," in *The Idea of Spatial Form* (New Brunswick: Rutgers University Press, 1991), pp. 5 – 66; see also Erich Auerbach, *Mimesis*, trans. Willard Trask (Princeton: Princeton University Press, 1953), ch. 20.
20 Caryn James, "A New Role for Movies: Video-Age Peeping Tom," *New York Times* (March 21, 1990).
21 P.N. Furbank, *Reflections on the Word "Image"* (London: Secker and Warburg, 1970), p. 81.
22 Paul Goldberger, "Design: The Risks of Razzle-Dazzle," *New York Times* (April 12, 1987), pp. 1, 34.
23 Ibid., p. 34.
24 Paul Ricoeur, *Interpretation Theory: Discourse and the Surplus of Meaning* (Forth Worth: Texas Christian University Press, 1976); Paul Ricoeur, *The Rule of Metaphor*, trans. Robert Czerny (Toronto: University of Toronto Press, 1977).
25 Tzvetan Todorov, *Symbolism and Interpretation*, trans. Catherine Porter (Ithaca: Cornell University Press, 1982).
26 Tzvetan Todorov, *Mikhail Bakhtin: the Dialogical Principle*, trans. Wlad Godzich (Minneapolis: University of Minnesota Press, 1984).
27 George Lakoff and Mark Johnson, *Metaphors We Live By* (Chicago: University of Chicago Press, 1980).
28 Jacques Ellul, *The Humiliation of the Word*, trans. Joyce Hanks (Grand Rapids: Eerdmans, 1985).
29 Ibid.
30 E.H. Gombrich, "The Visual Image," *Scientific American*, 227 (September, 1972), pp. 82 – 96.

31 Lakoff and Johnson, *Metaphors We Live By*; George Lakoff, *Women, Fire, and Dangerous Things* (Chicago: University of Chicago Press, 1987).
32 Philip Wheelwright, *Metaphor and Reality* (Bloomington: Indiana University Press, 1962), ch. 8.
33 Ricoeur, *Interpretation Theory*, p. 57.
34 Todorov, *Symbolism and Interpretation*, pp. 19 – 20.
35 Ricoeur, *Interpretation Theory*, p. 55.
36 See Jacques Ellul, *The New Demons*, trans. C. Edward Hopkin (New York: Seabury, 1975), pp. 64 – 8; Richard Stivers, "The Festival in Light of the Theory of the Three Milieus: a Critique of Girard's Theory of Ritual Scapegoating," *Journal of the American Academy of Religion* 61 (1993), pp. 501 – 34.
37 Mircea Eliade, *Patterns in Comparative Religion*, trans. Rosemary Sheed (New York: Sheed and Ward, 1958), pp. 38 – 41.
38 Ernst Cassirer, *Language and Myth*, trans. Susanne Langer (New York: Dover, 1946), pp. 83 – 99.
39 Eliade, *Patterns in Comparative Religion*, pp. 448 – 53.
40 Ellul, *The Humiliation of the Word*, pp. 22 – 34.
41 Friedrich Nietzsche attempted to define truth in aesthetical terms but in so doing he actually turned the aesthetical into the ethical, as Kierkegaard had foreseen.
42 Ricoeur, *The Rule of Metaphor*, pp. 247 – 56.
43 Tzvetan Todorov, *Literature and Its Theorists*, trans. Catherine Porter (Ithaca: Cornell University Press, 1987).
44 Cynthia Ozick, "The Moral Necessity of Metaphor," *Harpers*, 272 (May, 1986), p. 67.
45 George Steiner, *Real Presences* (Chicago: University of Chicago Press, 1989).
46 Ellul, *The Humiliation of the Word*.
47 George Comstock, *Television and the American Child* (New York: Academic Press, 1991), p. 57.
48 Neil Postman, "The News," in *Conscientious Objections* (New York: Knopf, 1988), pp. 72 – 81; see also Neil Postman, *Amusing Ourselves to Death* (New York: Viking, 1985), ch. 5.
49 Jacques Ellul, *The Technological Bluff*, trans. Geoffrey Bromiley (Grand Rapids: Eerdmans, 1990), pp. 333 – 4.
50 Jonathan Smith, *To Take Place* (Chicago: University of Chicago Press, 1987).
51 Mary Cassata, Thomas Skill, and Samuel Boadu, "Life and Death in the Daytime Television Serial: A Content Analysis," in *Life on Daytime Television*, ed. Mary Cassata and Thomas Skill (Norwood: Ablex, 1983), p. 52.
52 Pat Aufderheide, "Music Videos: the Look of the Sound," *Journal of Communication* 36 (1986), pp. 69 – 71.
53 Joshua Meyrowitz, *No Sense of Place* (New York: Oxford University Press, 1985), ch. 6.
54 Postman, *Amusing Ourselves to Death*, pp. 136 – 7.
55 Tzvetan Todorov, "The Two Principles of Narrative," in *Genres in Discourse*, trans. Catherine Porter (New York: Cambridge University Press, 1990), pp. 27 – 38.
56 On the concept of the aesthetical I am following Kierkegaard, who distinguishes between the aesthetical and the ethical in a number of works including *Either/Or*, *Stages on Life's Way*, and *Concluding Unscientific Postscript*.
57 Ellul, *The Humiliation of the Word*, p. 140.

58 Walter Benjamin, "The Work of Art in the Age of Mechanical Reproduction," in *Illuminations*, trans. Harry Zohn (New York: Schocken Books, 1969), pp. 217 – 51.

59 Frank, "Spatial Form in Modern Literature," pp. 5 – 66; see also Auerbach, *Mimesis*, ch. 20.

60 Wheelwright, *Metaphor and Reality*, ch. 8.

61 Adolf Jensen, *Myth and Cult Among Primitive People*, trans. Marianna Cholden and Wolfgang Weissleder (Chicago: University of Chicago Press, 1963), p. 190ff.

62 Ellul, *The Humiliation of the Word*, pp. 140 – 41.

63 Guy Debord, *Society of the Spectacle* (Detroit: Black and Red, 1977).

64 Kierkegaard anticipated Debord with his category of the interesting and his concept of the intellectual aesthete (see f.n. 57).

65 Jerry Mander, *Four Arguments for the Elimination of Television* (New York: Quill, 1978), pp. 205 – 11.

66 Goldberger, "Design: the Risks of Razzle-Dazzle," p. 1.

67 Ellul, *Humiliation of the Word*, p. 208.

68 George Gerbner and Larry Gross, "Living with Television: the Violence Profile," *Journal of Communication*, 26 (Spring, 1976), p. 192; see also George Gerbner and Larry Grass, "The Scary World of TV's Heavy Viewer," *Psychology Today* (April, 1976), pp. 41 – 5, 89.

69 Ellul, *Humiliation of the Word*, p. 209.

70 Ibid., pp. 121 – 8.

71 The loss of hope is a major factor in many psychological maladies. See, for example, Erich Fromm, *The Revolution of Hope* (New York: Harper and Row, 1968). For what a total loss of hope can do to a society, see Colin Turnbull, *The Mountain People* (New York: Simon and Schuster, 1972).

72 John Aldridge, *The American Novel and the Way We Live Now* (New York: Oxford University Press, 1983), pp. 9 – 16.

73 Thomas Pynchon, *The Crying of Lot 49* (New York: Bantam, 1967).

74 Benjamin, "The Work of Art in the Age of Mechanical Reproduction," p. 242.

75 Don Delillo, *Mao II* (New York: Viking, 1991), p. 24.

76 R. Murray Schafer, *The Tuning of the World* (New York: Knopf, 1977), pp. 185 – 9.

77 Ibid., pp. 182 – 3.

78 Robert Pattison, *The Triumph of Vulgarity* (New York: Oxford University Press, 1987), pp. 6 – 7.

79 Cited in ibid., p. 10.

80 Bernice Martin, "The Sacralization of Disorder: Symbolism in Rock Music," *Sociological Analysis*, 40 (1979), pp. 87 – 124.

81 Kenneth Hudson, *The Language of the Teenage Revolution* (London: Macmillan, 1983).

82 Aufderheide, "Music Videos," pp. 65 – 6.

83 Schafer, *The Tuning of the World*, p. 96.

84 Jeremy Murray-Brown, "Video Ergo Sum," in *Video Icons and Values*, ed. Alan Olson, Christopher Parr, and Debra Parr (Albany: State University of New York Press, 1991), p. 25.

85 Miguel de Unamuno, *The Tragic Sense of Life in Men and Nations*, trans. J.E. Flitch (New York: Dover, 1954).

86 Ellul, *Humiliation of the Word*, p. 134.

87 Mander, *Four Arguments for the Elimination of Television*, p. 252.

88 Cited in ibid., p. 255.

89 Edmund Carpenter, *Oh, What a Blow That Phantom Gave Me!* (New York: Holt, Rinehart & Winston, 1973), pp. 61 – 6.

90 Ibid., p. 47.

91 Comstock, *Television and the American Child*, pp. 66 – 7.

92 Ellul, *The Technological Bluff*, pp. 332 – 6.

93 "Virtual reality" refers to a system of computer programs that generate what appears to be three-dimensional space through images projected by special headgear and goggles. It allows one to become encapsulated in an artificial three-dimensional space that feels real.

94 Jean Baudrillard, "The Ecstasy of Communication," *The Anti-Aesthetic*, (Seattle: Bay Press, 1983), pp. 126 – 33; and Jonathan Crary, "Eclipse of the Spectacle," *Art After Modernism*, ed. David Godine (Boston: David Godine, 1984), pp. 283 – 94, argue that Debord's concept of the spectacle is less applicable the more the abstract information of the computer dominates modern communication. They miss the point, I think, that both kinds of images are required in a technological civilization - the direct, abstract images of computer-based communication and the reverse, concrete images of the mass media. They are two sides of the same phenomenon. We live simultaneously in a society of abstract information and of the spectacle.

95 Computer languages are radically different from natural languages in being non-dialectical. The former operate according to a strict formal logic, whereas the latter is based upon metaphorical comparison.

96 Mander, *Four Arguments for the Elimination of Television*, pp. 286 – 7.

97 Richard Stivers, "The Deconstruction of the University," *The Centennial Review*, XXXV (Winter 1991), pp. 119 – 22.

98 One can argue that pleasure pursued for its own sake, as in a spectacular society, ultimately makes one unhappy. A life vicariously lived is no substitute for a life of suffering and joy. This point will be elaborated in chapter 8.

99 See especially Kenneth Hudson, *The Jargon of the Professions* (London: Macmillan, 1978); Hudson, *The Language of the Teenage Revolution*; Kenneth Hudson, *The Language of Modern Politics* (London: Macmillan, 1978).

100 John Holloway, *The Slumber of Apollo* (Cambridge: Cambridge University Press, 1983), ch. 4.

101 Stanley Gerr, "Language and Science," *Philosophy of Science* 9 (April 1942), pp. 146 – 61.

102 Hudson, *The Jargon of the Professions*.

103 Jean Baudrillard, "The System of Objects" in *Jean Baudrillard*, ed. Mark Poster (Stanford: Stanford University Press, 1988), pp. 10 – 28.

104 Jacques Ellul, "Symbolic Function, Technology and Society." *Journal of Social and Biological Structure*, 1 (1978), pp. 214 – 16.

105 Ricoeur, *Interpretation Theory*, pp. 19 – 22.

106 Henri Lefebvre, *Everyday Life in the Modern World*, trans. Sacha Rabinovitch (New Brunswick: Transaction, 1990), pp. 110 – 27.

107 Ellul, *Humiliation of the Word*, pp. 210 – 21.

108 Hudson, *The Language of the Teenage Revolution*.

109 Postman, *Amusing Ourselves to Death*, pp. 16 – 29.

110 Ellul, *Humiliation of the Word*, p. 31.

111 Jean Baudrillard, *Simulations*, trans. Paul Foss, Paul Patton and Philip Bertchman (New York: Semiotext(e), Inc., 1983).

112 Ellul, *Humiliation of the Word*, p. 145.

113 Jacob Brackman, *The Put-On: Modern Fooling and Modern Mistrust* (Chicago: Henry Regnery, 1971), p. 129.
114 Ibid., p. 60.
115 Mark Crispin Miller, "The Hipness Unto Death," in *Boxed In: the Culture of Television* (Evanston: Northwestern University Press, 1988) pp. 3 – 27.
116 John Frow, "The Last Things Before the Last: Notes on White Noise," *South Atlantic Quarterly*, 89 (Spring 1990), pp. 413 – 29.
117 Ellul, *Humiliation of the Word*, pp. 7 – 10.
118 Andrew Tudor, *Image and Influence* (New York: St. Martin's Press, 1975), p. 215.
119 Mander, *Four Arguments for the Elimination of Television*, pp. 313 – 22.
120 U.S. Department of Health and Human Services, *Television and Behavior*, vol. 2 (1982), p. 57, cited in Murray-Brown, "Video Ergo Sum," p. 25.
121 Tudor, *Image and Influence*, p. 213.
122 Richard Stivers, *Evil in Modern Myth and Ritual* (Athens: University of Georgia Press, 1982), pp. 37 – 40, 162 – 6.
123 Gerbner and Gross, "Living with Television," p. 183.
124 Barry Sherman and Joseph Dominick, "Violence and Sex in Music Videos: TV and Rock 'n' Roll," *Journal of Communication*, 36 (Winter 1986), pp. 79 – 93.
125 Cassata, Skill, and Boadu, "Life and Death in the Daytime Television Serial."
126 Ellul, *The Technological Bluff*, p. 338.
127 Tannis Williams, *The Impact of Television* (Orlando: Academic Press, 1986), pp. 395 – 401.
128 Ibid., p. 401.
129 Herb Karl, D.H. Van Dercar, and Charles Weingartner, "The Word Processor and Image Processors: a Comparson of Their Emotional Responses to Violence in Film," *Et cetera*, 37 (Spring 1980), pp. 77 – 83.
130 Gerbner and Gross, "Living with Television: the Violence Profile," pp. 193 – 4.
131 Mander, *Four Arguments for the Elimination of Television*, p. 287.
132 Georg Simmel, "The Metropolis and Mental Life," in *The Sociology of Georg Simmel*, trans. Kurt Wolff (New York: Free Press, 1950), pp. 409 – 24.

7 A Morality of Power, a Morality Without Meaning

1 Jacques Ellul, *What I Believe*, trans. Geoffrey Bromiley (Grand Rapids: Eerdmans, 1989), chs. 8 – 11.
2 Jacques Ellul, *The Technological System*, trans. Joachim Neugroschel (New York: Continuum, 1980).
3 Jacques Ellul, *The New Demons*, trans. C. Edward Hopkin (New York: Seabury, 1975), ch. 3; see also Richard Stivers, *Evil in Modern Myth and Ritual* (Athens: University of Georgia Press, 1982), ch. 2.

8 Against the New Morality

1 Studs Terkel, *Working* (New York: Avon Books, 1975), pp. xxix – xxx.
2 Ibid., p. xiv.
3 Ralph Larkin, *Suburban Youth in Cultural Crisis* (New York: Oxford University Press, 1979).

4 See Edgar Friedenberg, *The Vanishing Adolescent* (New York: Dell, 1959), for a discussion of how freedom and authority are intimately connected. Manipulation greatly diminishes the possibility of freedom.
5 Larkin, *Suburban Youth in Cultural Crisis*, pp. 150 – 1.
6 Ibid., ch. 4.
7 Jeremy Seabrook, *What Went Wrong* (New York: Pantheon, 1978).
8 Walter Kerr, *The Decline of Pleasure* (New York: Simon and Schuster, 1965), p. 39f.
9 Steffan Linder, *The Harried Leisure Class* (New York: Columbia University Press, 1970), ch. 1.
10 Ibid., ch. 8.
11 Herbert Hendin, *The Age of Sensation* (New York: Norton, 1975, p. 6.
12 Ibid., ch. 2.
13 Ibid., ch. 3.
14 Josephine Hendin, *Vulnerable People* (New York: Oxford University Press, 1978), chs. 1, 10.
15 Sean Healy, *Boredom, Self, and Culture* (Rutherford: Fairleigh Dickinson University Press, 1984), ch. 3.
16 The various works of Kierkegaard and Nietzsche are indispensable here; for an excellent discussion of the topic see Helmut Thielicke, *Nihilism* (New York: Harper and Row, 1961); for a recent overview of the work on nihilism see Donald Crosby, *The Specter of the Absurd* (Albany: State University of New York Press, 1988).
17 Jacques Ellul, *What I Believe*, trans. Geoffrey Bromiley (Grand Rapids: Eerdman, 1989), pp. 13 – 18.
18 J. H. van den Berg, *Divided Existence and Complex Society* (Pittsburgh: Duquesne University Press, 1974), ch. 10.
19 Jacques Ellul, *The Ethics of Freedom*, trans. Geoffrey Bromiley (Grand Rapids: Eerdmans, 1976), p. 463.
20 Edward Sapir, "Culture, Genuine and Spurious," in *Culture, Language and Personality*, ed. David Mandelbaum (Berkeley: University of California Press, 1970), p. 101.
21 Jacques Ellul, *The Technological Bluff*, trans. Geoffrey Bromiley (Grand Rapids: Eerdmans, 1990), p. 94.
22 Jacques Ellul, *The Betrayal of the West*, trans. Matthew O'Connell (New York: Seabury, 1978), ch. 1.
23 Søren Kierkegaard, *The Sickness Onto Death*, trans. Alastair Hannay (London: Penguin, 1989), pp. 120 – 8.
24 Ibid., pp. 65 – 72.
25 Cited in Ellul, *The Technological Bluff*, p. 217.
26 Ibid., pp. 217 – 20.
27 Jacques Ellul, *Hope in Time of Abandonment*, trans. C. Edward Hopkin (New York: Seabury, 1973), pp. 69 – 70.
28 Colin Turnbull, *The Mountain People* (New York: Simon and Schuster, 1972).
29 Ibid., pp. 287 – 95.
30 Ellul, *Hope in Time of Abandonment*, pp. 48 – 54.
31 Ibid., pp. 29 – 35; see also Jacques Ellul, *The Humiliation of the Word*, trans. Joyce Hanks (Grand Rapids: Eerdmans, 1985), ch. 4.
32 Jacques Ellul, "The Power of Technique and the Ethics of Non-Power" in *The Myths of Information*, ed. Kathleen Woodward (Madison: Coda Press, 1980), pp. 242 – 7.

33 The reader may conclude that my argument about individual love and freedom reveals the same shortcomings as the kind of analytical moral philosophy that attempts to establish rational principles as the basis for a common morality. I am not, however, grounding my argument in logic but in history and literature. Neither do I believe that morality is created through a social contract. I am simply urging an existential response to meaninglessness and hopelessness, whether or not, that response succeeds or convinces others to do likewise.

Index